**Kiplinger's**

# Financial Solutions for the Sandwich Generation

## ENSURING YOU HAVE ENOUGH FOR YOU, YOUR CHILDREN, AND YOUR PARENTS

From the Editors of
*Kiplinger's Personal Finance*

**KAPLAN** PUBLISHING

This publication is designed to provide accurate and authoritative information in regard to the subject matter covered. It is sold with the understanding that the publisher is not engaged in rendering legal, accounting, or other professional service. If legal advice or other expert assistance is required, the services of a competent professional should be sought.

President, Kaplan Publishing: Roy Lipner
Vice President and Publisher: Maureen McMahon
Acquisitions Editor: Michael Cunningham
Development Editor: Trey Thoelcke
Production Editor: Karen Goodfriend
Typesetter: the dotted i
Cover Designer: Michael Warrell, Design Solutions

Printed in the United States of America

06 07 08   10 9 8 7 6 5 4 3 2 1

**Library of Congress Cataloging-in-Publication Data**

Kiplinger's financial solutions for the sandwich generation / the editors of Kiplinger's personal finance magazine.
     p.    cm.
   Includes index.
   ISBN-13: 978-1-4195-9055-9
   ISBN-10: 1-4195-9055-3
   1.  Sandwich generation—Finance, Personal   2.  Middle-aged persons—Finance, Personal.
3.  Sandwich generation—Life skills guides.   4.  Middle-aged persons—Life skills guides.
I.  Kiplinger's personal finance magazine.
HG179. K5573 2006
332.0240084'4—dc22

2006020976

# Contents

Contents

**M**idlife crisis takes on new meaning these days. No longer does it refer only to middle-age men or women stressing over the aging process. For many, the crisis also includes the financial, emotional, and physical strain of dealing with aging parents or grandparents on one hand, their own children on the other, and planning for retirement all at the same time.

Welcome to the Sandwich Generation, where the big squeeze is on. That's especially true for many of the nation's 76 million baby boomers—those born from 1946 to 1964. As the first of this generation turns 60 this year, retirement and its complicated financial needs loom—as do the often-overshadowing financial responsibilities to kids and elderly parents.

The Sandwich Generation is hardly shirking those responsibilities. Thirteen percent of boomers provide financial support to an elderly parent or parent-in-law at the same time they're raising a minor child or supporting an adult one. Two in ten provide financial support for an aging parent or parent-in-law. Two-thirds consider it a parental responsibility to provide for their child's college education, and more than half believe it's their responsibility to allow an elderly parent to live in their home if he so desires. That's according to a December 2005 Pew Research Center report, *Baby Boomers: From the Age of Aquarius to the Age of Responsibility.* If those aren't enough responsibilities, boomers must save for their own futures, too.

Thanks to better medical care, those futures keep extending. Americans are living longer today than ever before. The average life expectancy for a man is more than 74 years, and for a woman, almost 80 years. That compares with more than 65 and just over 71, respectively, little more than a half-century ago, according to government data from the National Center for Health Statistics. Although that's great news medically, it also means that retirement nest eggs—healthy or not—must stretch further. Combine increased longevity with the uncertainty of no-longer-guaranteed-for-life pensions, underfunded retirement plans, and soaring costs for housing, health care, college, insurance, long-term care, and more, and the result is that many boomers struggle simply to get by. Some succeed, others don't, and some thrive in a multigenerational environment while enjoying their caregiving roles.

Across the board, though, the sandwich is exacting its toll. From a psychological and emotional viewpoint, many adult children and their own children stress over providing care and support to aging family members, sometimes at the expense of their own comfort and security. Meanwhile, aging parents resist burdening their adult children or grandchildren with their own problems. Compounding the stress is the fact that nearly half of the boomers worry about their own financial future. According to Pew numbers, 17 percent say they won't have enough money for the basics when they retire, and another 24 percent say they'll be able to "just meet basic living expenses."

Whatever your financial or familial situation, generation or age, this book can help you get the upper hand on the generational sandwich. It provides the insights, information, and direction to prepare for—and financially and emotionally cope with—many of the issues that come with being a parent and having aging parents or grandparents at the same time. The issues may not always appear to be financial, yet their bottom line is money. We show you how to navigate the maze of pitfalls that you, your kids, and your parents invariably face. We explore the psychological and physical as well as the financial effects on the various generations because all are so intricately interwoven. We delve into what taking care of older parents means to you, your elderly parents and relatives, your kids, their kids' kids, and beyond, and the good and the not-so-good times associated with it all.

Throughout, we provide the questions and the answers, worksheets, and tips as a guide to help you make the decisions that are right for you. We use real-life scenarios and "Tips from Real Life" that can help you handle your own generational sandwich. We also tell you where to go for more information and provide a helpful glossary at the back of the book.

The book begins by discussing those emotional, physical, and related financial issues so intertwined in your life, no matter your financial responsibilities to parents or children. That is followed by an exploration of the finances and logistics necessary to make the decisions that are right for you and your family. This information provides an essential primer on surviving and thriving as a member of the Sandwich Generation.

Throughout, we mention organizations and Web sites that may be able to help you. We're not endorsing any of them, only trying to provide you with a starting point. Don't overlook local organizations in your area, either, which can be great sources of help, information, and advice.

Good luck, and let's get started.

# Welcome to the Sandwich Generation

## Chapter 1

**T**he squeeze is on for millions of Americans sandwiched between the financial, physical, and emotional demands of growing or grown children on one hand, and their own aging and often ailing parents on the other.

In many cases, these generations help support their parents or grandparents either physically or financially, save for their kids' college expenses, support their adult children, and, at the same time, try to save for their own retirement. All that is set against a backdrop of no-longer-guaranteed pensions, a rocky Social Security system, often sparse personal savings, and, until recently, near all-time low interest rates.

It's a daunting task for even the most resilient boomer. But you can take heart in the fact that you're not alone in being squeezed financially and otherwise. You can survive the sandwich with the right attitude and approach, and by taking advantage of all the programs, organizations, guidance, and assistance available. Success in navigating this pockmarked fiscal and emotional minefield begins with understanding the people, processes, and emotions involved.

Let's take a closer look at the layers of this generation sandwich.

## Who's Being Sandwiched?

**L**eading what's commonly known as the Sandwich Generation are the nation's approximately 76 million baby boomers. Alternately known as the beatniks of the 1950s; the hippies, radicals, and bra-burners

## WHERE TO START

Here are a few of the many organizations and agencies that can help when it comes to seeking physical, emotional, psychological, and even financial direction or support:

- AARP (www.aarp.org). Lots of information, tips, and direction on aging issues A to Z. Be sure to check out its list of hot links to Internet resources (www.aarp.org/internetresources/).

- Administration on Aging (www.aoa.gov). The federal advocate agency for older Americans provides a comprehensive overview of topics, programs, and services related to aging for seniors, caregivers, community service providers, and more. Click on "Elders and Families" for many additional resources. Its free Eldercare Locator (www.eldercare.gov) is an online tool to help locate all kinds of services for seniors.

- American Bar Association (www.abanet.org). The largest voluntary professional association in the world with more than 400,000 members, it offers links to finding legal help (click on "Find Legal Help" or "Lawyer Locator") as well as plenty of free information for the public on a broad variety of topics (click on "Public Resources").

- Area Agencies on Aging (visit www.eldercare.gov to find your local group). Counties across the United States have local offices that can provide information, services, and direction.

- Center for Medicare and Medicaid Services (www.cms.hhs.gov). From the U.S. Department of Health and Human Services, the official site for Medicare and Medicaid information and services.

- The College Board (www.collegeboard.com). The starting place for college, from finding a college to scholarships, SATs, navigating the financing, calculators, and more.

- Family Caregiver Alliance® National Center on Caregiving (www.caregiver.org). Caregiving and health information, advice, tips, and direction, as well as research. Check out "Caregiving across the States: A State-by-State Resource" for contact information and direction.

- healthfinder®/U.S. Department of Health and Human Services (www.healthfinder.gov). Easy-to-navigate source of tons of medical, health and wellness, fitness, and drug-related (including alternative medicines) information. Click on "Organizations" on its home page for alphabetical listings and hot links to a host of federal, state, professional, and non-profit organizations and agencies that can help.

- Kiplinger (www.kiplinger.com). Your trusted information source for everything involving money and personal finances, from auto and college funding to elder care, investing, Medicare, Medicaid, retirement, taxes, and more; free interactive tools available, too.

- Medicare (www.medicare.gov). The home page for the nation's medical program for seniors.

- *MedlinePlus (www.medlineplus.gov). A source of medical, drug, and health information from the U.S. Library of Medicine and National Institutes of Health. Includes links to directories of health care providers, doctors, dentists, hospitals, clinics, and physicians that are Medicare providers nationwide.*
- *MyMoney.gov from the Financial Literacy and Education Commission (www .mymoney.gov). A federal government Web site intended to improve financial literacy in the United States. It's designed to help navigate the money maze, from saving and investing to buying a home and paying for college and retirement.*
- *National Association of Elder Law Attorneys (www.naela.org). National organization of attorneys that focuses on the legal needs and issues of the elderly.*
- *National Association of Professional Geriatric Care Managers (www.caremanager.org). In-depth information and resources on geriatric care managers, professionals who work privately with older adults and their families to create a plan of care that meets the needs of the older adult. Check out its Care Manager Resources links, too.*
- *National Association of Social Workers (www.helpstartshere.org). A different look at issues and answers on health, wellness, and life in general for children, their parents, and seniors from members of the NASW.*
- *National Family Caregivers Association (www .nfcacares.org or www.thefamilycaregiver*

*.org). Provides education, direction, information, and resources for caregivers.*
- *National Institutes of Health SeniorHealth (www.nihseniorhealth.gov). Developed for older adults by the National Institute on Aging and National Library of Medicine, both part of the National Institutes of Health, this site contains lots of health and medical information. Also check out NIH's Web site (www.nih. gov).*
- *Seniors Resource Guide (www .seniorsresourceguide.com). Publishes senior resource guides in 22 markets across the United States that address issues ranging from housing and health care to services and community resources.*
- *Social Security Online (www.ssa.gov). The home page for the nation's Social Security Administration with all kinds of valuable information on life, disability, and death benefits and the qualifications to receive them.*
- *Society of Certified Senior Advisors (http:// society-csa.com). With a goal of helping professionals work more effectively with senior clients, the Web site includes helpful information for consumers, too. (Click on "Seniors and Family.")*
- *U.S. Administration on Aging (www.aoa.gov). An excellent online resource and link to services, organizations, and information on everything from Alzheimer's to housing, money matters, elder rights, volunteer opportunities, and more. Great links to off-site resources, too (www.aoa.gov/eldfam/More/More.asp).*

of the late '60s and '70s; and the activists and free spirits of the '80s, these boomers comprise the post–World War II and Korean War baby boom. And now, as with almost everything else they've done throughout the years, they're struggling to find the right course.

But it's not just the boomers who feel the generation squeeze. Blended and extended families, kids, younger adults, and older Americans must deal with it, too. Adult grandchildren with their own children can face the generation sandwich if, for example, their parents don't rally to help an aging parent either for physical or emotional reasons, says Sandra S. Swantek, MD, adult and geriatric psychiatrist, Stone Institute of Psychiatry, Feinberg School of Medicine at Northwestern University in Chicago. She's also chairperson of the American Association for Geriatric Psychiatry's Clinical Practice Committee. "It's important to remember that families come in all shapes and sizes, and even the Sandwich Generation isn't necessarily a boomer."

*"Families come in all shapes and sizes, and even the Sandwich Generation isn't necessarily a boomer."*

—Sandra S. Swantek, MD, chairperson Clinical Practice Committee, American Association for Geriatric Psychiatry

Estimates are that 21 percent of the nation's adult population, or 44.4 million Americans age 18 or older, currently provide unpaid care to someone 18 or older. That's almost 23 million households involved in caregiving today. Of those caregivers, almost 60 percent either work or have worked while providing care.

*44.4 million adults in the United States are involved in caring for another person age 18 or older.*

—"Caregiving in the United States" study, National Alliance for Caregiving and AARP

For 62 percent of those people, caregiving means taking time away from or quitting their jobs, according to "Caregiving in the United States," a study conducted by the nonprofit National Alliance for Caregiving and

AARP and funded by The MetLife Foundation. Almost one-quarter (24 percent) of recipients of care live with their caregiver.

The same study breaks down caregivers by age and shows clearly that boomers aren't alone in their multigenerational caregiving responsibilities. The breakdown of caregivers by age (percentages exceed 100 percent due to rounding of numbers):

- 18–24 years, 11 percent
- 25–34 years, 15 percent
- 35–44 years, 22 percent
- 45–54 years, 23 percent
- 55–64 years, 18 percent
- 65–74 years, 9 percent
- 75 and up, 4 percent

*The average length of time a caregiver provides care is 4.3 years, although 29 percent provide care for more than five years.*

—National Alliance for Caregiving and AARP

## Who Foots the Bills?

Let's look at a few more telling numbers about the Sandwich Generation, this time from the Pew Research Center's December 2005 report, "Baby Boomers: From the Age of Aquarius to the Age of Responsibility":

- Two in ten boomers provide some financial support to an aging parent.
- 13 percent provide some financial support to an elderly parent or parent-in-law as well as support a minor child or adult child.

And if that's not enough evidence of just how pervasive this generation sandwich is, consider that the value of services provided "free" by caregivers in the United States is estimated to be about $257 billion a year (Arno, P.S., "Economic Value of Informal Caregiving," annual

---

## THE FINANCIAL SQUEEZE

- *50 percent of all boomers are raising one or more young children and/or providing primary financial support to one or more adult child.*
- *Another 17 percent, whose only children are 18 or older, were providing financial assistance to one or more adult child.*
- *Of those boomers who have one or more adult child age 18 or over, 33 percent provided primary support, and 35 percent provided some support in the past year.*
- *20 percent of all boomers provide some kind of financial support to an aging parent.*
- *13 percent of all boomers provide some financial support to an elderly parent or parent-in-law and at the same time raise a minor child or support an adult child.*

**Source:** Pew Research Center

---

meeting of the American Association of Geriatric Psychiatry, Orlando, Florida, February 24, 2002).

## Snapshots

Let's look at a few typical snapshots of life for members of today's Sandwich Generation. Chances are if you're among the sandwiched, you'll recognize similarities to your own situation. We'll take a closer look at solutions to these and other dilemmas later.

Jay, 46, is a successful businessman and has been happily married to Diane, 36, for 12 years. They have an 11-year-old daughter and a 2-year-old son. Jay also has a 24-year-old son from a previous relationship and helps with his son's graduate school expenses.

Two years ago, Diane's mother, 72 and a longtime widow, fell and broke her hip. Since then, she's been in and out of the hospital and never seems to recover completely. She requires full-time caregiving that her meager Social Security checks don't cover. Diane, an only child, at first tried to provide that care but had to stop because of her responsibilities to the couple's chil-

## JAY AND DIANE'S FINANCES 2005

| | |
|---|---|
| *Income:* | $170,000 |
| **Adjusted gross income (AGI):** | $145,000 |
| **Estimated annual basic expenses:** | |
| **House** | |
| Mortgage @ $1,100/month: | $ 13,200 |
| Utilities @ $350/month: | 4,200 |
| Upkeep/expenses: | 2,400 |
| Health care (self-employed, including insurance): | 11,500 |
| **Transportation** (including two car payments): | 11,120 |
| **24-year-old son:** | 28,000 |
| **College savings** ($100/month per child): | 2,400 |
| **Federal/state income tax liabilities:** | 30,000 |
| **Share of Mom's care costs:** | 35,000 |
| **Food and entertainment** ($500/week): | 26,000 |
| **Total expenses:** | **$163,820** |
| | |
| *Income:* | **$170,000** |
| **Minus general expenses:** | 163,820 |
| **Total left for other expenses, saving, investing, emergencies:** | 6,180 |

## WHAT DO BOOMERS DO FOR AGING FAMILY MEMBERS?

According to a July 2001 national survey for AARP:

- More than 80 percent interact socially through telephone calls and personal visits.
- 45 percent do housework for older family members.
- 46 percent transport an older relative to the doctor or shopping.
- 44 percent do their shopping.
- 36 percent talk to their doctors.
- 33 percent handle paperwork or bills.
- 17 percent hire nurses and aides.
- 12 percent help with intimate care.
- 27 percent report they contribute financially to help pay expenses for parents or in-laws.

**Source:** AARP's "In the Middle: A Report on Multicultural Boomers Coping with Family and Aging Issues," by Belden Russonello & Stewart, Washington, D.C., and Research/Strategy/Management, Great Falls, Virginia

dren. Even though Jay and Diane make a good living, a year and a half of footing the hefty bill for home health care, combined with the weak markets and interest rates over the past few years, have taken their financial toll. Jay has had to take out a second mortgage; the couple no longer has a financial nest egg, and they worry about what certainly will be astronomical college expenses for their two other children when the time comes.

Joe, 39, heads a very demanding multinational business and lives in New York City. His mother is 70, and her mom is 89. Both women live together in a small town in South Dakota that's not easily accessible by airplane. Divorced, Joe has full custody of his 15-year-old son and foots the bill for his prep school as well as a full-time, live-in housekeeper, neither of which comes cheap in Manhattan. Joe is constantly worried about the safety, health, and security of the senior women in his life. The miles between them make matters worse. The duo refuses to move closer to New York; consequently, Joe must juggle their care needs long distance. Every time the phone rings after 9 PM, Joe's first thought is, "Who died?"

---

### TIPS FROM REAL LIFE

*Are you taxed for time to run errands for an elderly family member and keep your small business afloat too?*

- *What about getting a high school or college student to shuttle or help your parent and/or children a few hours a week? The dollar cost could be minimal, and the value of the help well worth it.*
- *Local community, senior, and religious organizations often provide or can help you find volunteers to help.*

**More Information:** *Ask friends and neighbors if they know of someone or an organization locally; talk to school guidance counselors, student council advisors, or college professors and dean's offices; call your local area Agency on Aging or religious organizations or check out www.eldercare.gov.*

---

Mym, 53, works six days a week, 12 hours a day, building up her struggling interior design studio. She's divorced, has virtually no savings, and has two adult children, one of whom is still in college. He works but requires significant financial support. Six years ago, Mym, who had no health insurance, was diagnosed with breast cancer and ran up huge medical bills as a result. Today she's cancer free but still pays a little each month on those medical bills—and probably will continue to do so every month until she dies. Her mom, 79, is in poor health, needs Mym's financial as well as physical help to get by, and is seldom gracious about asking for it. Mym's brother lives in the same town but has his own physical problems—he has a disability—and family responsibilities, so he can't run many errands for Mom. Stress is the norm, but although Mym rents only a tiny house and can afford few luxuries, she's optimistic. "At least my youngest is almost out of school and will start working full-time soon," she says.

Three years ago, Bob and his wife decided to let his 89-year-old mother move into the extra bedroom in their home. In what appeared to be failing health, she really couldn't take care of herself without help, couldn't afford to pay for an assisted-living facility or home health care, and didn't need a nursing home. Besides, Bob and his wife figured she couldn't live that long—or

---

**TIPS FROM REAL LIFE**

*Would you like your children and their children and beyond to remember the time spent with an aging family member?*

■ *Why not have that person, with the kids' help if possible, record their memories in a Family Book of Memories, on paper, in a video, or even an audio text. It's a great family project and a wonderful way to keep the memories alive for generations to come.*

*More Information:* www.publishingcentral.com, *click on* "Writing" (www.mylifestory.org).

could she? Today Bob's mom thrives, not only on the food she's finally eating again, but on the companionship and enjoyment of being a part of her grandkids' lives as they grow up. And, despite early trepidations, Bob and his family treasure the time with Grandma.

## Times Change

Advancements in medicine have meant longer lives for all of us today. A half-century ago, Mym likely would have died from her cancer; Joe's elderly grandmother and Bob's aging mother both probably would have died too, and Diane's mom would have been shuttled off to an easily affordable nursing home. (Jay's 24-year-old most likely would have had to forgo college on Dad's nickel, as well.)

---

### NUMBERS THEN AND NOW

**Aging Population:**

- In 1900, 3 million people age 65 or older lived in the United States. By 2000, that number had climbed to 36 million.
- In 1900, 100,000 people age 85 and over lived in the United States. By 2000, it was 4.2 million.

(**Source:** Federal Interagency Forum on Aging Related Statistics, Older Americans 2004)

**Rising Home Costs:**

- National median existing single-family home price was $210,000 in January 2006, up 13.1 percent from a year earlier. Average price for single-family home was $84,400 in December 1987.

(**Source:** National Association of Realtors)

**Climbing College Costs:**

- Average cost of one-year tuition and fees in 1976 at four-year private college or university: $2,534.
- Average cost of one-year tuition and fees in 2005 at four-year private college or university: $21,235.

(**Source:** The College Board)

**Soaring Health Care Costs:**

- 2005 nursing home national average annual cost tops $64,200 for a semiprivate room, and is more than $74,000 for a private one.
- 2005 home-health aide national average hourly rate is $19, up 5.5 percent from 2004. Homemaker/companion average is $17 an hour.
- 2005 assisted-living facility national annual cost averages more than $34,850.

(**Source:** MetLife Mature Market Institute®)

In 1950, the average life expectancy for males and females together was just over 68 years. In 2002, it had climbed to age 77. That means not only are we living longer, our parents and their parents are living longer too. That also means that our money potentially has to be spread across more generations and last for many more years in retirement. Add to the mix factors such as inflation, changing demographics, the soaring costs of housing, seemingly out-of-control health care costs, long-term care, insurance, college educations, and more, and the situation becomes a megawhammy loaded with obstacles that the sandwiched generations must navigate. Jay and Diane, Joe, Mym, and Bob have learned how to stay afloat, but not without a struggle. (We'll examine their strategies later in this book.) You, too, can learn the way with our help.

## Changing Demographics and Attitudes

In the mid–20th century, the perfect life for most people, based on TV scenarios such as those on *Father Knows Best* and *The Donna Reed Show,* meant graduating from high school, with the boys going off to college (some girls, too); graduating from college and moving back to the hometown; getting married; having a family, with Mom at home full-time while Dad worked until age 65; then retiring, and, not long afterward, dying peacefully surrounded by loved ones. Perhaps Grandma was alive, but only while you were young. Dual-wage-earning couples; divorce; blended families; adoption; second, third, and beyond marriages; kids and grandkids living thousands of miles away; double mortgages; and college costs that rival the price tag on a home were rare, as were concerns about taking care of several generations at the same time.

*38 percent of baby boomers have been divorced.*

—Pew Research Center report

But then somewhere along the way, things changed. Today, Pew numbers show that 38 percent of all baby boomers have been divorced. Many families have split, resplit, and remarried. Horizons have broadened. Many boomers grew up and moved out, often thousands of miles away from their families. Retirees, too, flew the coop—often to warmer environs. Both groups, in turn, built their own lives and families or extended families, and aren't willing or can't move back "home" when Mom or Dad grows old or infirm and requires a closer eye. Nor does proud Mom or Dad want their children to move or to "burden" their children with their care. (More on the independence issue in Chapter 4.)

The generation sandwich has changed too, says Susan Silk, PhD, a clinical psychologist in Southfield, Michigan, a suburb of Detroit. No longer is it a simple bologna sandwich with the meat (the Sandwich Generation) squeezed between two slices of white bread—elderly parents being one slice and your kids the other. "These days it's more like this great big deli sandwich with stuff lathered and squished out all over the place because everybody's lives are just so much busier," says Silk.

It used to be that your kids went to school and played in a neighborhood where, generally, their safety wasn't a major concern. Those students involved in after-school sports and other activities often were able to walk or bike the short distance to the ball field or the piano lesson and didn't need to be shuttled everywhere. At the same time, aging parents lived down the street or across town. Plenty of siblings, friends, and an established network of extended family could help with any caregiving or babysitting responsibilities.

Says Silk, "Today, we have households where all the adults are working. . . . So we have our day job; we have our job as a spouse; and, however willingly we do this, we have our job as an adult child of an elderly parent. Adding more layers of complexity, we're more committed to enriching our children's lives, and we have our own professional agenda."

From a financial standpoint, retirement doesn't automatically occur at age 65 anymore, either. Even the

---

## RETIREMENT AT 65 IS THE NORM NO MORE

*Even the nation's Social Security benefits system looks beyond 65 as the magical age for full retirement benefits. The following general table shows the age qualifications to receive full retirement benefits. For actual calculations, check out www.ssa.gov/OACT/ProgData/nra.html.*

| Year of Birth | Age | Year of Birth | Age |
|---|---|---|---|
| 1937 and prior | 65 | 1955 | 66 and 2 months |
| 1938 | 65 and 2 months | 1956 | 66 and 4 months |
| 1939 | 65 and 4 months | 1957 | 66 and 6 months |
| 1940 | 65 and 6 months | 1958 | 66 and 8 months |
| 1941 | 65 and 8 months | 1959 | 66 and 10 months |
| 1942 | 65 and 10 months | 1960 and later | 67 |
| 1943–54 | 66 | | |

*Note: Those born on January 1 of any year should refer to the normal retirement age for the previous year.*

**Source:** Social Security Administration

---

nation's Social Security system is phasing up its "normal" retirement age. Many people work well beyond that—either by choice or need—often to offset soaring health care costs, life savings lost as a result of catastrophic business failures, and/or the burst Internet bubble. Still others take early retirement and, in turn, lower benefits, with many forced into retiring by corporate cutbacks or because they're needed as child care providers for the grandchildren. Where Social Security and Medicare once might have covered many costs for older Americans, today they fall short. The average monthly Social Security check for a retired worker is about $1,000.

# (Some) Workplace Attitudes Change

*Businesses lose $11 billion to $29 billion annually related to their employees' caregiving responsibilities to those 50 and older.*

—National Alliance for Caregiving/MetLife study

Work-related issues add to the stress and strain of caregivers. Almost 60 percent of caregivers have worked at some time while actively providing care. Six in ten of those workers report having to work late, leave early, or take time off during the day to provide care.

Estimates are that the nation's businesses lose between $11 billion and $29 billion annually related to employees caring for those ages 50 and older, according to the National Alliance for Caregiving/Met Life study, "Employer Costs for Working Caregivers."

*For details on the Family and Medical Leave Act, check out www.dol.gov/esa/whd/fmla.*

## ELIGIBILITY FOR FAMILY AND MEDICAL LEAVE

*Below are a few of the eligibility requirements of the Family and Medical Leave Act. For more detail, check out the Department of Labor's Employment Standards Administration Wage and Hour Division (www.dol.gov/esa/whd/fmla).*

**Eligible Employee:**
- Worked for employer for at least 12 months.
- Worked for employer at least 1,250 hours over the previous 12 months.
- Worked at a location where at least 50 employees are employed by the employer within 75 miles.
- Full-time teachers in an elementary or secondary school system, or institution of higher education, or other educational establishment or institution meet the 1,250 hour test.
- Active-duty time of reservists and National Guard returning to civilian occupations counts toward eligibility for FMLA.

**Qualified Employer:**
- Generally, anyone who employs 50 or more employees within a 75-mile radius for each working day during each of 20 or more calendar workweeks in the current or preceding calendar year, as well as anyone acting, directly or indirectly, on their behalf.
- Public agencies and public, private, elementary, and secondary schools are exempt from employee number requirements.

**Immediate "Family Member":**
- Employee's spouse, children (son or daughter), and parents.
- Does not include a parent-in-law.
- Sons or daughters age 18 or over are not included unless they are "incapable of self-care" because of mental or physical disability that limits one or more of the "major life activities."

**Source:** U.S. Department of Labor's Employment Standards Administration Wage and Hour Division

But attitudes toward family caregivers are changing. Eligible employers are required by law to provide qualified employees time off without pay to care for a family member. The federal Family and Medical Leave Act of 1993 mandates that eligible workers may take up to 12 weeks a year of unpaid leave for a variety of reasons, including the care of an immediate family member (spouse, child, or parent) with a serious health condition. Eligibility, however, is the key and depends on the size of an employer (small businesses generally don't qualify), the length of your employment, and more. Check out the details at the Department of Labor's Employment Standards Administration Wage and Hour Division *(www.dol.gov/esa/whd/fmla)* first, and then talk to your company's benefits coordinator before making any assumptions.

Family-friendly and forward-thinking employers these days offer more workplace initiatives with caregivers in mind. Initiatives can include:

- Elder care and child care in the workplace and often on the premises
- Flextime and flex-place to provide workers "guilt-free" time for necessary caregiving for the young and old. Downsizing and high-speed Internet connections have helped fuel the remote-worker trend.
- Access to professional assistance and advice from psychologists or experts on various caregiving issues

*If your employer doesn't offer a specific caregiver or elder care benefit, consider pitching them the idea. They could be more open to the idea than you think, especially if your proposal includes the numbers and the issues.*

## New Challenges and Roles

All this and more have created unique challenges for the Sandwich Generation as well as their children and aging parents. Distance and a parent's age often exacerbate the potential for sibling rivalries, as do conflicts over money and inheritance. Long-distance caregiving presents its own set of travails and traumas that we'll address—along with the solutions—in Chapter 3. Another source of guilt (and responsibility) for the Sandwich Generation: then-healthy Mom or Dad may have moved away from other family members, friends, and their established network of helpers years earlier to help care for the grandchildren. Now Grandma and Grandpa are older and need help themselves.

Although many of the issues aren't necessarily financial, their ramifications are. What if Grandma moves in with the family and takes over Junior's room so that the family needs a second mortgage to finance home expansion? Or perhaps Mom must quit work to take care of Grandpa, so that Junior now must put himself through college. Or maybe Mom, stressed out by an argument with Grandpa, has an automobile accident and needs long-term care herself.

Whatever the logistics and geography, finding solutions to medical, housing, lifestyle, and other issues takes a gargantuan effort along with the right contacts to navigate the bureaucratic maze. Even if, in the beginning, all family members and partners involved are best of friends and all on board with who's doing what for whom, it's a road that's meant to be trod carefully. Where once no one minded if younger sister shuttled Mom around or if widowed Dad dated other women, the stakes suddenly have changed now that Mom's old and sickly or Dad is in assisted living. Today, younger sister might resent the fact that older sister never helps with Mom. Or what if Dad marries that other woman? What will happen to the inheritance? And why is *he* the one in charge—not me?

Mom, who lives 550 miles away, has a cold. Who will check to make sure she's OK? Who will bring her meals or cook for her? Did she remember to pay that health insurance premium due yesterday? She's gotten awfully forgetful lately. And what about the cost of Junior's college? Forget our retirement; how can we afford home-health care for Mom and come up with the money for school, too? All of these are questions that can plague the Sandwich Generation as they learn to chart a course through elder care.

# The Result

It sounds like a grim picture for a generation of adults once branded with such labels as the Now generation and the Me generation, and whose credos included "you can have it all" and "sex, drugs, and rock 'n' roll." Somewhere through the years, though, that's changed too. Despite the financial, physical, and psychological stresses and strains of this generational sandwich, the majority of boomers today is satisfied with their lives—of which caregiving for young and old plays a big part. Boomers recognize the irreplaceable value of family, and the wisdom and experience of their parents. They accept the responsibility of their roles. More than half 56 percent of boomers, believe it's their responsibility to allow an elderly parent to live in their home if she so desires, according to Pew numbers.

Sharing time together counts too. In AARP's multi-cultural boomers survey, 87 percent of the boomers surveyed strongly agreed that they enjoy spending time with their families and that family is the most important thing in their lives. The same proportion strongly disagrees that their families burden them.

*Moving beyond "sex, drugs, and rock 'n' roll,"*
*the vast majority of baby boomers today rate spending*
*time with their families as the most important thing*
*in their lives.*

In the more recent AARP study, "Caregiving in the United States," most caregivers say that their caregiving results in little physical strain (67 percent rate it 1 or 2 on a 5-point scale), emotional stress (44 percent give it a 1 or 2 on that same scale), or financial hardship (77 percent rate it a 1 or 2). Those levels of hardship, however, increase with the level of caregiving required.

Financial support and dependence isn't a one-way street either. Boomers aren't the only ones who shell out time, energy, and cash. Consider a few more statistics from the Pew 2005 report:

- 25 percent of boomers say their parents rely more on them for support, while 10 percent say they rely more on parents, and 11 percent say the reliance is equal.
- 33 percent of younger adults (ages 18 to 40) with a living parent report giving money to a parent in the past year.
- 42 percent of boomers who gave money to a parent in the past year did so on a regular basis.
- About 52 percent of boomers who gave money to a parent in the past year did so for special circumstances, while 47 percent received money from that parent during the same time period.

*"It's payback time, big time."*

—48-year-old businesswoman, mom, wife, and caregiver
referring to her 84-year-old dad

"My parents were always my best friends," says one 48-year-old whose parents lived at least 1,000 miles away ever since she struck out on her own. Her mom died 2½ years earlier, but Dad still is vibrant and remains in the distant town where she grew up. She's constantly fretting about his care and condition. Although he's never asked for money and would refuse to take any anyway, she worries about his finances, too. Will his money last? Finally he agreed to sell the big family home, and he now lives in a retirement apartment building where he can get meals prepared for him if he chooses. She regularly shuttles back and forth via a two-hour plane ride, her 2-year-old on her lap. Every little glitch in her dad's life is a crisis. She spends hours in long-distance phone conversations with agencies, organizations, and doctors struggling to resolve the latest problem.

"Sometimes my boss gets irked when my dad calls. Because of the time-zone change, the only time I can talk to him is during work. We talk every day, but only briefly," she says. "I think he's (the supervisor) jealous that he doesn't have such a good relationship with his dad.

"It's payback time, big time," she says, with a smile, of the struggles and stress in dealing with her dad and her own family. After eight hours at the office, she cooks dinner for her husband and child before heading out to a business meeting. "But I wouldn't trade these times with Dad for anything.

"Sure, it's difficult, and I get so irritated at my father. He's so stubborn, and I do have to put my foot down sometimes. But he really appreciates every little thing I do, and he gets such pleasure from my success, and from my daughter. She adores him, too. It's so great that he's been able to meet her. I wish my mom had."

# Remember:

- You're not alone in the generation sandwich struggle. Plenty of people, organizations, private groups, and professionals are available to help you if you know where to look.
- Sharing a parent's later years—whether socially, physically, or at a distance—can be a memorable and gratifying experience.
- Growing numbers of employers have begun to offer caregiving benefits ranging from related help and guidance to actual child care or elder care, flextime, and flexible work locations.
- Though many of the issues faced by the Sandwich Generation don't seem to be financial in nature, their repercussions are felt in the pocketbook.

# The Psychological and Emotional Impact

## Chapter 2

**T**oday's Sandwich Generation seems to epitomize the phrase "a roller coaster of emotions." Those being sandwiched are all too familiar not only with guilt, grief, fear, resentment, abandonment, and helplessness but with compassion, satisfaction, gratification, adoration, respect, and deep love as well. For many of the sandwiched—whether elderly, young, or in the middle—these seeming opposites on the emotional spectrum exist side by side in daily life. Sometimes it's tough to separate the guilt from the grief or the fear from the love, for example, because—as with other aspects of the sandwiched life—the emotions are so entwined.

Roles and relationships add to the emotional stew. Parents often have trouble accepting their children, no matter their age, as adults; conversely, children sometimes have a tough time accepting that their parents are aging.

And through all this, money and finances dominate options, decisions, and outlooks for boomers, their parents, and their own children. It's an expensive time of life with plenty of cash outflow and, in the case

---

**CARE COSTS**

*National average cost, according to The MetLife Market Survey of Nursing Home & Home Care Costs (September 2005):*
- *Nursing home: $74,095 annually for private room*
- *Hourly rate for home-health aide: $19*
- *Hourly rate for homemaker/companion: $17*

---

of most seniors, often very little inflow. Elder care at whatever level can cost thousands of dollars a month out of pocket. That's cash a parent or an adult child may not have readily available or available at all. All this further stresses already strained finances, emotions, and relationships across the generational sandwich.

## The Inevitable Guilt

Money issues aside, guilt is an automatic for the Sandwich Generation. Anyone who watches a parent or loved one age and decline feels guilty. Period. Whether the sandwiched is an active caregiver or not, whether he is in close contact with or seldom sees the aging person, guilt is likely to color the relationship.

It's tough to see Dad today, hands shaking, painstakingly struggling to knot his tie. Remember when he so easily taught you how to do it? What about all those Sunday afternoons when you and he played ball or built intricate model airplanes? And what about Mom? All those years you were so accustomed to her doing so much for you. Now it seems like the other way around. She doesn't even cook your favorite dinner when you're in town.

*"If you live far away from a parent, the guilt is even more pervasive."*

—Gary J. Kennedy, MD, geriatric psychiatrist

Every one of us has memories and images of loved ones in the prime of life. When those loved ones are long past their prime and showing their age, we all tend to feel guilt, which reflects our sense of responsibility and commitment and, to some extent, the realization that we can't quite do enough to stem the tide of time. Those older adults are going to decline no matter what we do. It's inevitable.

Such a situation is hard to accept, and it's hard to watch even when you do accept it, says Gary J. Kennedy, MD, a geriatric psychiatrist and expert on mental health issues of the aging. He's also director of geriatric psychiatry at the Montefiore Medical Center in the Bronx, New York, and author of several related books.

"Watching an older parent decline is just difficult. The aging person may have had a wonderful life. They may be wise and accepting of their decline, but that doesn't mean it's necessarily easy for the family to watch. If you live far away from a parent, the guilt is even more pervasive."

Olga and her oldest sister lived about 750 miles away in either direction from their aging mother. Both had full lives, were financially comfortable, and could visit their mom and the old homestead often. With her Social Security survivor's benefits (100 percent of their father's Social Security benefit) their mom had enough money on which to live. She used the money from their dad's $100,000 life insurance policy to pay off the house, bills, and make investments. She insisted, however, that the investments eventually were to be for her grandchildren, and she refused to touch them when things got tight. As she grew older and infirm, the role of primary caregiver fell willingly on her youngest daughter, who lived nearby. Olga and her other absentee sister provided money to help pay for their mom's extra health care needs. (All three siblings had agreed not to touch the investments or sell the house, out of respect for their mom's wishes.) They also stepped up their regular visits to provide their younger sister with needed relief from caregiving responsibilities. She also had a home-health aide come in one day a week to relieve her.

Their mom's dementia and physical condition eventually worsened to the point that she needed nursing-home care. The sisters were unable to find a facility that could take their mom immediately and that they collectively could afford. Even selling off all their mom's investments and combining them with her income would barely cover the cost of one year if the three girls picked up all the extra expenses (more on that later). They resisted selling their mom's home, per her wishes. Even if they had sold the assets hoping she would qualify for Medicaid, hefty out-of-pocket expenses

## OLGA'S MOTHER'S FINANCES*

**Assets (annual):**

| | |
|---|---:|
| Assessed value of house, mortgage paid off: | $150,000 |
| Dividends and earnings from investments ($50,000 invested with 5% return): | $ 2,500 |
| Social Security survivor's benefits, $900/month: | $ 10,800 |
| **Total income:** | **$ 13,300** |
| **Annual expenses:** | |
| Taxes, utilities, home maintenance: (including new exterior/interior home painting): | $ 10,400 |
| Home health care, $608/month (including $19/ hour for home-health aide one day/week): | $ 7,296 |
| Medicine, $300/month: | $ 3,600 |
| Health insurance/other medical costs, $350/ month: | $ 4,200 |
| Other living expenses (including food), $800/ month: | $ 9,600 |
| **Total expenses:** | **$ 35,096** |
| **Shortfall made up by Olga and her sisters** (divided three ways, $7,265/per sister): | **$ 21,796** |

\* General overview

would be incurred before the poverty-level medical coverage would kick in. (More on Medicaid qualifying and long-term care costs in Chapter 10.)

Exhausted and exasperated by the system and its lack of choices, the sisters finally were able to place their mom in a geriatric teaching hospital for observation. It was the only place that didn't have a long waiting list, says Olga. She and her sisters once again pooled their resources along with their mother's meager income to foot the bills.

As always, Olga visited regularly, and when she did, mother and daughter would dress up and go off to lunch, laugh, and enjoy each other's company. One weekend when Olga arrived, her mom was all dressed up and ready to go to lunch as usual. At the last minute, however, Olga's mom decided she didn't want to go out. So the two stayed in her room and talked instead. Olga spent the next week with her mom, had a great visit, and then returned home. Two days later Olga's mom died suddenly. That was a year ago. Olga still feels guilty that she wasn't there and feels she didn't do enough for her mom, even though she and her sister did everything possible for the elderly parent.

# Act with Reason, Not Emotion

No matter how tough it is to watch a parent or loved one age, it's important that you make decisions and act on them rationally rather than

---

## HELPFUL SOURCES

- *AARP (www.aarp.org). Click on "Your Health, Your Life, Long-Term Care" to find all kinds of valuable articles to help brighten your day and that of your loved one.*
- *Administration on Aging/Department of Health and Human Services (www.aoa.gov). Click on "Elders and Families" for information on caregiving, families, elder rights, and more.*
- *American Association for Geriatric Psychiatry (www. aagponline.org). News, facts, tools, and expert information for adults coping with mental health issues and aging.*
- *American Psychiatric Association (www.healthyminds.org or www.psych.org). Check out its "Resources Links."*
- *Children of Aging Parents/CAPS (www.caps4caregivers.org). Includes articles and support groups in a number of states.*
- *Family Caregiver Alliance (www.caregiver.org). A California-based organization with lots of information, advice, and direction.*
- *National Alliance on Mental Illness (www.nami.org). National grassroots support organization with information, education and training, and support.*
- *National Institute of Mental Health (www.nimh.nih.gov). A resource of information, direction, and links from the National Institutes of Health, part of the U.S. Department of Health and Human Services.*
- *National Mental Health Association (www.nmha.org). The nation's largest nonprofit organization that addresses all aspects of mental health and mental illness.*

---

**TIMELY TIPS**

*Get beyond the guilt; make a plan, and stick to it.*

out of guilt, cautions Kennedy. Create an effective plan for handling your loved one's care and realize that, generally, no matter what you do, you'll feel some degree of guilt—as Olga discovered.

You're not alone with your guilt either. Almost half of all baby boomers surveyed in a 2001 study for AARP ("In the Middle: A Report on Multicultural Boomers Coping with Family and Aging Issues") say they feel they should do or have done more for their aging parents. Those numbers don't change whether a parent requires a great deal of their time and effort, or very little.

## The Burden Issue

Knowing you have company in your angst may provide some momentary solace, but it doesn't alleviate the limitations imposed by certain situations. If you perceive that an aging parent depends on you— even if only to run an occasional errand or for the comfort of knowing you're close by in an emergency—you may feel unduly burdened, especially if it cuts into your own life, relationships, or finances. Those feelings can increase if, as clinical psychologist Silk suggested in Chapter 1, that parent initially gave up a strong support system in another town to move closer to you to help with the grandchildren.

Communication is essential in these instances, says Silk. Let the aging parent know you care, love them, and want to be there for them, but that your time is limited. Find out what's truly meaningful to them in terms of your time. That may mean Mom might have to take a taxi to the doctor occasionally so that you and she can go out to dinner and a movie instead. If you're also sandwiched by the responsibilities (and guilt) to your own kids, talk to them about the same things, says Silk, so that together you can determine what's most valuable to them.

And don't do things for either generation that they don't want or need you to do. It can be a meaningless waste of your limited time.

The stress of the generational sandwich also can be an opportunity to reassess some of those demands on your time, adds Silk. When it comes to the kids and shuttling them to various activities, ask yourself the real reasons why. Does a particular activity have true meaning for your child or is it just a "keep up with the Jones" scenario? If it's the latter, then drop it. That will give you more time that truly matters.

Louise, 54, knows of the burden issue firsthand. She's a divorced mother of two kids—one, now 26, is a successful lawyer, and the other is in his last year of high school. Finally, after years of hard work and lots of luck and timing financially, she's very comfortable with cash in the bank and even a retirement nest egg. Her youngest is heading off to college next year, so she's facing the prospect of becoming an empty nester. "I would love to get an apartment in New York City," she says. She's even found the perfect place, a relatively small condo on Manhattan's Upper West Side. The problem, however, is that right now she lives down the street from her 78-year-old mother, who, Louise says, relies on her being nearby. "My brother and sister already live far away, so I really can't leave my mom alone," she adds.

Should Louise leave? Should you leave if you're in a similar situation? The answer to that question depends on a variety of factors. Whatever your situation, it's important to act rationally and sensibly, not out of guilt or some other emotion. Discovering your answer begins with an honest assessment of the situation and frank questions and answers.

Louise, for example, first must determine if she really wants to sell her sizable house in Bratenhal, Ohio, a Cleveland suburb, and move to New York permanently. Can she really afford it financially? She has a large house—appraised recently at around $750,000, although it probably can bring in significantly more. But if she sells it, will the proceeds, combined with her comfortable savings and investments of about $750,000, be enough to pay for the kind of New York lifestyle she envisions? And even if it might be, what about the cost of ongoing home maintenance and living expenses in New York, taxes, insurance, and more. Is it even feasible?

## LOUISE'S FINANCES

Let's take a quick look at a few basic numbers relative to Louise's finances. Even without the details (fees associated with home sale, taxes, investment withdrawal penalties, and more) it's easy to see why Louise needs to scale back her expectations.

| | |
|---|---|
| Sale of home in Bratenhal, Ohio: | $750,000 |
| Value of savings/investments | $750,000 |
| Total funds: | $1.5 million |
| Cost of NYC condo: | $995,000 |

If condo paid for in full
| | |
|---|---|
| Amount left to invest and for expenses: | $505,000 |
| Annual earnings if invested at 5 percent return: | $25,250 |

**This amount is certainly not enough for taxes, maintenance, living expenses, and more in NYC.**

If condo is mortgaged with 20 percent down
| | |
|---|---|
| Down payment: | $200,000 |
| Amount left to invest: | $1,300,000 |
| 30-year mortgage @ 5.8854 percent * | |
| Monthly payments: | $4,714/month |
| Annual mortgage cost: | $56,568 |
| Annual investment earnings at 5 percent: | $65,000 |
| Amount left after mortgage: | $8,432 |

**This amount is certainly not enough to cover all other expenses for a year in NYC.**

\* Courtesy Mortgage Calculator from Realtor.com (www.realtor.com)

With all that and more in mind, perhaps Louise might decide to keep her Cleveland-area home and opt for an extended respite in New York instead or to pare down her image of the New York lifestyle.

She also needs to sit down and honestly and openly discuss the situation with her mom and siblings. Does her mom truly rely on Louise, or is it only Louise's perception that she does? Sometimes we like to think another person needs us when they really don't.

Has her mom, who is in good health, ever thought about moving closer to one of her other children? Has a sibling considered moving back home? How might Louise's siblings pitch in to help if Louise were to move? After all, unlike some siblings who might resent an elderly parent spending all their time with one sibling, Louise's brother and sister always have wanted to help but figured their sister had it covered. Perhaps Mom, too, has a long-suppressed desire to do something else but has stayed in the small town only because she assumed that's what her kids wanted.

If Mom's OK with a temporary leave of absence, Louise might consider renting out her home while she takes a sojourn from caregiving in New York. Or maybe one of her siblings could take over responsibilities for her mom on a regular basis so that Louise could get away for that needed long vacation. After all, caregivers at any level need time out to recharge their batteries. They need time and space where they're not preoccupied with the person for whom they're caring. That means, as a caregiver, you need to find a way to share the burden.

*Caregivers need vacations too!*

---

**TIPS FROM REAL LIFE**

*Do you feel the pangs of guilt over wanting to move away, and then regret that you can't because an elderly loved one counts on you?*

■ Honestly assess your desires and needs. Do you truly want to leave permanently, or is it just a need for an extended getaway?

■ Honestly assess your caregiving situation, as well. Does that loved one really count on you as much as you think? Ask her. The answer might surprise you.

■ Involve your siblings in your decision. Perhaps they're willing to shoulder more responsibility.

## Absentee Siblings

As Kennedy suggests, distance from an aging loved one only magnifies the guilt that all parties already feel. Regular and frequent visits back home, a successful career, raising your own children, and even grandchildren may not compensate for what we often perceive as our failure to do enough for an aging loved one who "needs" us. That feeling of not doing enough may surface no matter how much you participate in the care of a loved one, as Olga found out above.

Those who are estranged from an aging parent or loved one feel emotional pain in their own way; their role in an unhealthy or unresolved relationship is likely to add to their feelings of guilt. They are well-advised to make that visit or seek that reconciliation they've been postponing. Those who doubt such an approach should talk to others who didn't make the effort or take the time. A loved one's death forever closes the door to any attempt at acceptance and understanding.

If money is an issue, perhaps the aging loved one or their spouse or partner will help. Or, you might consider the cost of the trip factored out over the rest of your lifetime. That puts it all in a different perspective.

---

### MONEY IS NO EXCUSE

Is "can't afford it" the excuse for why you don't visit Mom? Consider factoring the cost of a trip over the rest of your life:

| | |
|---|---|
| Trip expense: | $2,000 |
| Your age: | 45 |
| Your life expectancy: | 77 |
| Cost factored out over the next 32 years: | $62.50/year* |

*\* Of course that doesn't include interest on your expense, but you get the picture.*

---

## Sibling Rivalries

So you thought that because you and your brother are finally grown with children of your own, the sibling rivalry that consumed you as children had ended? Think again.

We all know of situations in which one sibling shoulders the burden of an aging parent's care while the other leaves it to someone else or, worse yet, shirks that

## FAMILY BEHAVIORS

- *Some families recognize that problems and issues related to the care of an elderly parent are much greater than any of their petty sibling rivalries.*
- *An elderly parent's needs aside, other families are at each other's throats with rivalries, resentments, and more.*

physical or financial responsibility with a shrug. Their reasoning: I'm too far away, I don't have the time, I can't afford it, or I can't deal with it. Remember Louise, whose two siblings didn't get involved in their mom's care so they kept their distance? They assumed Louise could handle it. Even though she could manage the situation with ease, at times Louise resented her brother's and sister's freedom from responsibilities, especially because she had to limit her work and her own family time as a result.

Such behavior can be a manifestation of longtime sibling rivalry. Some rivalries, resentments, and reliances get acted out when parents are in need, says Kennedy, because rivalries of influence are amplified when a parent becomes more dependent.

Consider a situation in which a parent has Alzheimer's disease. It's a family event that seems to happen in slow motion as the elderly loved one's mental condition deteriorates. It's also a prime setting for family tensions and problems, says Kenneth M. Langa, MD, PhD, a general internist at the Department of Internal Medicine and Institute for Social Research at the University of Michigan in Ann Arbor, and an expert in public policy and health economics research.

"Guilt, resentments, and past problems and concerns from 20 and 30 years ago can come out as your parent is declining and needing more and more of your help, and more and more of the kids' help in general," Langa says.

Past issues can surface in plenty of other situations, too. Marge and her brother engaged in a fierce sibling rivalry growing up in California. After graduating from college, both had moved away and made lives of their own. The rivalry that so dominated their lives as youngsters faded. Then Mom and Dad grew old, Mom got sick, and the parents turned to Marge for emotional and physical help. The sibling rivalry resumed in force. Suddenly, once again, Marge and her brother were at each other's throats vying for parental attention and money, even after Mom died and Dad got sick. It wasn't until after Dad died several years later that the rivalry subsided. No longer was there anyone for the siblings to vie over for influence and attention.

In other situations, especially when money is involved, their rivalries may follow siblings to their graves or extend beyond that to younger generations. Family baggage indeed can make life tough for the Sandwich Generation.

Effie and Ed never liked their daughter's choice of husband. They felt him too irresponsible with money, so as they grew old and infirm, they looked to their son and his wife as caregivers instead. They also liberally dispersed money to their son and his family, more so than to their daughter. Resentful, their daughter stopped talking to her brother and his family, accusing them of turning her parents against her. Even after both parents died, the siblings didn't talk. They passed along their animosities to their children, too, so that even after Effie and Ed's daughter died, the dislike, distrust, and disdain continued. Today, neither side even knows why they aren't talking; they just don't talk.

> ## TIPS FROM REAL LIFE
>
> *Absentee son Rick kept putting off the trip back home to see his mom. He just couldn't bear to see her growing old and suffering from dementia. It was always "next Christmas," "next summer," or "as soon as I get through this crunch at work." Needless to say, Rick's mom died before that Christmas or summer materialized. That was five years ago. His guilt and her memory still haunt him.*

Conversely, though, sometimes a parent's dependency dissipates all the siblings' hostilities as they rally around. "They recognize that there is a problem to be dealt with that is much larger than any of their petty rivalries, so you will see families working remarkably well as a perfect team," says Kennedy. "Then you'll see other families that are just at each other's throats."

## Elderly Pangs of Guilt and Fear

Members of the Sandwich Generation aren't the only ones who feel guilt or fear, either. Many aging parents or loved ones often feel guilty over burdening their children. They desperately want their independence, and they don't want to overburden their grown children, who have other responsibilities. (More on the independence issue in Chapter 4.)

Marie's mom was 89 when she began exhibiting symptoms of dementia. Up until then she had led a vibrant, social, and busy life going from dance class to gym class and from luncheons to dinner parties. Money was no object, no matter the kind of care she wanted or needed. Shortly after her diagnosis, she and Marie were out shopping when Marie sensed something was wrong. Suddenly her mom turned to Marie and asked sarcastically but with a serious undertone, "Why don't you just put me in jail?"

Seniors also may feel guilty about hiring outside help or turning to others instead of their children for help. Often they feel guilty about spending money that they think they should be saving for their kids' inheritance. Another prevalent reason that is rarely mentioned out loud: an older parent might want to avoid the emotional baggage associated with asking his children for help. A frequent example of the latter is the elderly parent who doesn't get along with an out-of-town daughter, son, or in-law and dreads visiting them even though it means seeing the grandchildren. They just detest staying in that child's home. A vague sense of guilt, however, keeps the parent from staying in a hotel. "I just couldn't," the parent insists. "That would absolutely devastate my child."

*Guilt knows no generational bounds.*

Ruthie adored her grandchildren. She truly loved their father—her son—too. It's just that he was very difficult and overbearing at times. She didn't get along with his wife, either, and because they lived out of state, a visit meant having to stay at her son's home. Compounding the problem, his home was tiny and chaotic, and she had no privacy. For years, Ruthie dutifully made the trek because she felt that watching her grandchildren grow up was well worth any amount of stress. But as she got older, and admittedly slower, Ruthie found it more and more difficult to visit, especially because her son's house had only one small bathroom that his family of four—and any visitors—had to share.

Ruthie tried staying away for a time but was miserable. Finally, she confronted her son. He protested, but in the end understood her need for privacy and quiet, and he found a comfortable hotel nearby. Now Ruthie visits more frequently and enjoys the time with everyone,

---

### TIPS FROM REAL LIFE

*Are you uncomfortable staying in your grown child's home? Don't miss out on special adult and grandparent time spent together. Instead:*

- *Consider staying in a hotel down the street. Perhaps it has a pool so the grandkids can swim.*
- *What about a family vacation together somewhere else instead? If you're not up for multiple stops, try a destination resort.*
- *Try a multigenerational camping trip instead. (Note: Everyone gets their own tent.)*

*More Information:*
- *Hotel and resort listings or travel Web sites*
- *Visit www.familytravelforum.com; www.farhorizon.com; or www.aarp.org/families/grandparents*

including her son, and her grandchildren thrill at the wisdom and wit she shares.

Grandchildren, too, can be a source of guilt for the elderly. The time the children's parents spend helping to provide elder care is time spent away from the children themselves. Perhaps a grandparent feels that she doesn't spend enough time with a grandchild. Such guilt can be played upon by either generation. It's not unusual for a well-meaning grandparent to be caught in the middle of a parent-child battle—with the grandparent's finances often a casualty.

Sandwiched boomer Sam finally decided to cut off the cash flow to his 23-year-old college dropout son from his first marriage. The son not only had no job, but was making what Sam considered unfair and unreasonable cash demands. The most recent one—for a new SUV to replace his four-year-old Honda Civic in fine working order—was the last straw. Sam also was worried about the finances of his own business, saving for college expenses for his two younger children from his second marriage, and his own fast-approaching retirement age. At the same time, he was shuttling 1,000 miles back and forth to Florida, where his elderly dad was having medical problems—a situation that was very tough on Sam's frail mom.

So Sam cut the cash flow to his 23-year-old. Furious, the son turned to Sam's elderly parents for money. Other issues were involved, but the grandparents also felt guilty that their grandson had no "father" because of Sam's divorce and subsequent poor relationship with his ex-wife. They felt guilty that Sam had cut off his son financially. They felt guilty that the grandson was all alone in another city. They felt guilty that the grandson couldn't have all the things their son, Sam, had had at his age. The list goes on.

The grandparents, who were financially comfortable but not excessively so, blamed Sam, and they blamed themselves. Sam's son blamed his father and even felt a little guilty about going to his grandparents for money. But he still got his money. At last count the grandparents were still angry at Sam and still footing their grandson's bills despite the financial hardship it caused.

## Stressed Out

Increased friction with a spouse, significant other, sibling, stepparent, or child often goes with the territory for the Sandwich Generation. Studies show that two in ten boomers with direct responsibility for the care of parents and other older family members report this kind of stress as a result of the care needs of both sides of the generation sandwich (AARP's "In the Middle: A Report on Multicultural Boomers Coping with Family and Aging Issues"). The greater the level of care demanded of a caregiver, the more likely the caregiver will suffer higher levels of stress, too.

When people are busy with their elderly parents and that part of their life they represent, they're neglecting their current life, which can include a spouse and children. That's a very big thing, says care manager and psychotherapist Beverly Bernstein Joie, president of Elder Connections, a suburban Philadelphia–based elder-care management practice. She's a certified geriatric care manager, certified senior advisor, and expert in geriatric care management. "If it's temporary and you know there's an end in sight, that's one thing," says Joie. "If it's the kind of situation that has no perceived end in sight, it takes a tremendous toll on the entire family. After all, each person has only so much energy and time. Caregivers are torn between their parents and husband and children and find themselves on the short end of the stick."

Rebecca, small-business owner, wife, and mother of two, was the primary caregiver for her elderly grandfather, Bernard. Rebecca's own mother had many deep-seated differences with Bernard and refused to help him. Although Rebecca recognized (and at times sympathized with) some of her mom's issues with Bernard, he always had been there for her as child so she felt it her responsibility to be there for him now. Adding to the stress of the situation, Rebecca constantly fretted over taking time away from her own children to care for Bernard. She finally took her concerns to an expert, who suggested involving the children more in the caregiving of their great-grandfather as a valuable cross-generational lesson.

"Children learn what it's like to be old from their grandparents and their parents, and if and when they see their parents taking care of an older adult, that's how they learn that everybody is valued and loved," says psychiatrist Swantek. "Even when you're old and perhaps can't move too well and don't have a good memory, you're still a valuable and beloved human being. This is how we teach children to respect life, to respect their elders. Ultimately, we are teaching children—future adults—the important lessons that they will use when faced with their own aging parents and their needs. This is continuity of the generations."

Stress associated with caregiving also can mushroom if an elderly loved one suffers from dementia or Alzheimer's and has hallucinations or delusions. If an elderly person in that condition turns on you, don't take it personally, cautions Langa. "It's just so obvious, but sometimes people forget that what those elderly say and do isn't really aimed against them."

Often it's tough for a teenager to deal with the reality of Alzheimer's. They know Grandma has Alzheimer's, but why does she have to live with them and ruin their lives? Why can't they just leave? It's embarrassing to bring friends into the house with "her" there.

## Depression Is Not Normal

Do you or a loved one feel sad, tired, and worried all the time? Do you blame those feelings on the responsibilities of being sandwiched or getting old or something else? Those feelings could be a sign of the disease that is depression. Depression affects more than 19 million Americans every year. It can occur in caregivers or those receiving the care. But depression is not normal—for anyone. And it's treatable. (More on the disease in Chapter 10.)

An elderly mom in the early stages of dementia may develop depression as a result of realizing she's losing her independence. A caregiver might suffer from it as an outgrowth of his role in taking care of a declining loved one. Sometimes a person may have dementia-like symptoms that, in reality, are depression. Some experts call that condition "pseudo-dementia." Treat the depression, and the cognitive issues may dissolve, too, says Langa.

Whatever the situation, the disease that is depression often is overlooked, ignored, misdiagnosed, or misunderstood, especially in the elderly when other medical issues are present. The elderly may also refuse to get treatment because of a stigma attached to the disease. Others—family members and caregivers included—dismiss the depression as just another part of getting old. But, experts emphasize, depression is *not* a normal part of the aging process.

*Depression is not a normal part of the aging process.*

---

## LOOK FOR THE SIGNS

*If you or a loved one feels sad, tired, and worried most of the time, look at the following checklist from the National Institute of Mental Health and circle the signs that sound like you:*

- *I am really sad most of the time.*
- *I don't enjoy doing the things I've always enjoyed doing.*
- *I don't sleep well at night and am very restless.*
- *I am always tired. I find it hard to get out of bed.*
- *I don't feel like eating much.*
- *I feel like eating all the time.*
- *I have many aches and pains that don't go away.*
- *I have little to no sexual energy.*
- *I find it hard to focus and am very forgetful.*
- *I am mad at everybody and everything.*

- *I feel upset and fearful, but can't figure out why.*
- *I don't feel like talking to people.*
- *I feel like there isn't much point to living. Nothing good is going to happen to me.*
- *I don't like myself very much. I feel bad most of the time.*
- *I think about death a lot. I even think about how I might kill myself.*

*If you or your elderly loved one circled several of these signs, call a doctor. Take the list to show the doctor. You may need to get a checkup to find out if you have depression.*

**Source:** National Institute of Mental Health, National Institutes of Health, "Stories of Depression: Does This Sound Like You?"

Of course, not all caregivers or the elderly suffer from depression or other adverse emotional effects of their roles or of aging. Langa emphasizes that psychiatrists and mental health professionals tend to hear from those who are having difficulty in their caregiving situations. "We don't hear from the people who find caregiving rewarding and fulfilling and for whom the elder-care role fits into their lifestyle and the rest of the family," he points out.

Many people fall into the latter category. Every day they take care of millions of aging Americans, in many cases without extenuating issues or problems, and feel comfortable and content with the fact that they are sharing their lives and helping a loved one in need.

## Resolving the Anger

Although we've only briefly touched on it, anger often pervades relationships among parents and their children. And as with every other emotion, aging and dependency may only exacerbate the feelings.

If your relationship with an aging parent includes anger, consider ironing out your differences. The anger is unfinished business and contains negative energy that can breed illness and many other negatives in one's life, says Joie, also president of the Philadelphia Chapter of the National Association of Professional Geriatric Care Managers. She's spent 20 years helping others work through these issues.

Resolving the issues before a parent dies means there will be some closure, some completion in your life, which in turn will allow you to devote your energy to living your own life in the present rather than being contaminated by the past.

"Anger is an emotion just like joy or happiness or anything else, and it's just a question of coming to terms with those things. That's what life's about," says Joie. "That's what helps us grow up and let go of the past and move toward the future in an empowered position."

# Remember:

■ Providing elder care offers an opportunity for the richest emotions possible: love, gratitude, acceptance, consolation, even self-sacrifice.

■ Caring or not caring for an aging loved one naturally stirs up all kinds of emotions, some long-buried since childhood.

■ Everyone feels some degree of guilt, no matter the situation, the health of an aging loved one, or the family or friends involved or not involved.

■ Buried resentments between parent and child, as well as among siblings, may resurface; fresh resentments may be born.

■ Depression may add to the emotional stew as a caregiver becomes increasingly tired and stressed and/or as the elderly loved one declines more and more.

■ Openness and honesty with siblings and loved ones can ease some of the distress.

---

### SOURCES FOR MORE INFORMATION:

■ *Geriatric Mental Health Care: A Treatment Guide for Health Professionals,* Gary J. Kennedy, MD (Guilford Press, 2000)

■ *Successful Aging,* John Wallis Rowe and Robert L. Kahn (Dell, 1999)

■ *Suicide and Depression in Late Life: Critical Issues in Treatment, Research, and Public Policy,* Gary J. Kennedy, MD (Wiley, 1996)

# The Long-Distance Dilemma

## Chapter 3

The aging of parents and parents' parents who are hundreds—if not thousands—of miles away is one of the most troublesome by-products of the Sandwich Generation's new demographics. Those who watch Mom or Dad age firsthand from down the street, across town, or elsewhere relatively nearby might disagree with that assessment, and they also may complain that the long-distance sibling or family member doesn't carry his fair share of the caregiving responsibilities.

But the helplessness of being miles away while a parent declines can be overwhelming. The goodbyes after a visit with elderly Mom or Dad standing forlornly in the doorway can all but rip out the heart of an already guilt-ridden adult child. The long-distance family member must learn to live with the pervasive dread of that late-night phone call, as well as a sibling caregiver's dismissive answers to agonizing questions. And don't overlook the guilt associated with an adult child raising her own kids at a distance from grandparents who are unable to see the grandkids as often because of the miles between them.

In the turbulent times of an aging parent's failing health and decline, the new demographics and realized life dreams are of little solace. Just ask anyone who lives or has lived far from their aging parents.

For many, it's a cruel mix of guilt, fear, regret, and loneliness: guilt that you're not there with the aging loved one; fear that he won't be there a next time; regret that you ever left home; and loneliness for both you and the parent you've left behind.

## HELPFUL INFORMATION

- *AARP (www.aarp.org). Click on "Family, Home, and Legal" from the home page for facts and answers.*
- *Aging Solutions/Senior Solutions of America, Inc. (www .aging-parents-and-elder-care.com and www .todaysseniors.com). Florida-based company has several Web sites with plenty of interesting and helpful information.*
- *Area hospitals, medical centers, and geriatric care centers.*
- *Eldercare Locator (www.eldercare.gov). A free public service from the Administration on Aging, U.S. Department of Health and Human Services. The service is designed to connect older Americans and their caregivers with information on local senior services.*
- *Family Caregivers Alliance (www.caregiver.org). Helpful information on important issues for the at-a-distance caregiver; don't miss its online Handbook for Long-Distance Caregivers.*
- *National Association of Home Care (www.nahc.org). Trade association representing the interests and concerns of home-care agencies, hospices, home-care aide organizations, and medical equipment suppliers; click on "Consumers" for tons of information on the kinds of services available.*
- *National Association of Professional Geriatric Care Managers (www.caremanager.org). Nonprofit group offers an online tool to help you locate a professional near you.*
- *Physicians and other medical professionals. Contact an aging loved one's medical providers or related area organizations. Often they can head you in the right direction for services.*
- *Religious organizations. Many national and local faith-based groups offer their own or can direct you to reputable services, many of them volunteer.*
- *Visiting Nurse Association of America (www.vnaa.org). Official national association for not-for-profit, community-based home-health organizations known as Visiting Nurse Associations. Good information and links to home-health care and more. Click "About Home Health" or enter a zip code to locate a local Visiting Nurse Association.*

# Standard Panic

The gulf of distance magnifies many of the emotions, stresses, and strains on all parts of the generational sandwich—whether the grown children, their children, or, of course, the distant elderly family member. Too often in long-distance situations, family matters get blown out of proportion or the real problem becomes lost amid the fear and frantic phone calls of one trying to get answers.

It's 7:30 PM, you're in Phoenix, Arizona, and your 82-year-old dad is in Cincinnati, Ohio, where he lives alone. The rest of the family has moved away or died, and your dad's neighbors, who usually help out, are out of town. You call to make sure everything's OK, and Dad sounds strange on the telephone. Of course he says he's fine, but you're certain something is wrong. You decide to check on him in person, but you can't get to Cincinnati until the next afternoon; there are no earlier flights unless you charter a private jet. Even if you charter a jet—which is financially out of the question—the flight takes several hours, plus a three-hour time

---

**TIPS FROM REAL LIFE**

*If you're far away from an aging parent, don't rely on just one neighbor in case of an emergency.*
- Always have a backup. Talk to your parent's doctor or another of her professional advisors about alternatives in case something goes wrong. You may find unusual allies ready and willing to help.
- Ideally, find a paid caregiver you can trust who is willing to be there for an aging parent. It's money well spent in an emergency.
- Don't overlook old friends from your youth, either. Often they're ready, willing, and able to help, and not only in emergencies.

**More Information:** Retirement-living settings such as apartments, communities, and assisted-living facilities as well as physicians and other medical professionals may know of reliable and dependable caregivers available on a part-time basis.

---

zone change, so you wouldn't arrive until tomorrow afternoon anyway.

It's a familiar scenario. Your father could have forgotten to take his medicine and might be having a stroke, or worse, a heart attack. To whom do you turn? Will your father collapse, with no one finding him until it's too late? Oh, why won't he move out of that big house into a retirement apartment? Why won't he wear that emergency call button you bought him? Why do you have to be so far away?

Of course, as an alternative scenario, Dad could just be tired or experiencing a drug reaction or vitamin deficiency (a lack of B-12, for example, can produce dementia-like symptoms), or have heard some bad news about a friend. But you don't know for certain unless you or someone you know and trust checks it out.

Then there's Thanksgiving. Mom is 350 miles away and all alone since Dad died two years ago. You can't go to her home because you can't take time off from work both now and at Christmas. Mom's mad about that, too, because you're not coming to her house for Christmas this year; it's your turn to spend it with your wife's family. Or maybe your 17-year-old son is quarterbacking his high school football team in the state championship, and Mom doesn't understand why the family has to go to a game instead of visit her for the holiday.

How about the worst-case scenario? You're 1,000 miles away, and Mom is in the hospital, dying. But you're not sure when that's actually going to occur. Your employer allows only three days' bereavement leave, and you absolutely can't afford to take any more time off without pay because you've already missed so much work trying to help out with Mom. So how do you time your visit? Your sister, who's at Mom's side, is furious because you call every day and ask, "When is she going to die?"

Does any of this sound familiar? If you're a member of the at-a-distance Sandwich Generation it does, and that's whether your role is to provide moral, financial, or emotional support, or something else entirely. Even if you're estranged from an elderly parent, being far away is a tough load to shoulder.

---

> **TIPS FROM REAL LIFE**
>
> *Does an aging parent live alone with few friends and no nearby family?*
> - *Privately talk to longtime family friends about your parent's situation. Chances are they're not aware your parent is alone with nowhere to go on holidays. They'll often go out of their way to make sure he isn't alone anymore. Your parent may protest at first, but will truly appreciate your intervention.*

# Role of Friends

When trying to figure out who might be available to keep an occasional eye on your parents without requiring you to spend a lot of money and worry that the job is done right, don't overlook your childhood friends. Even if you haven't been close to them in years, bonds formed while growing up tend to be tight, and those friends often have fond memories of your parents, too. A call to an old friend can result in a friendly face occasionally looking in on an aging parent, or it might provide a welcome sea of calm in an emergency. A parent especially may welcome a visit from one of your childhood friends because, although there's a shared history, there's none of the emotional baggage that comes with family.

Jeff was Mark's best friend growing up. He enjoyed sitting and talking with Mark's parents, too, and often was invited to dinner. When the boys graduated from high school, Mark headed off to college out of state and went on to a successful career clear across the country. Jeff, on the other hand, opted to use his degree to start a career back in their hometown.

Mark usually went home at least once or twice a year and always called Jeff when he did. Although they seldom had much time to spend together, they occasionally managed to get together for a quick drink or cup of coffee. Then Mark's mom died, and his dad was all alone. Thousands of miles away with a family and responsibilities of his own, Mark worried constantly and felt that someone really needed to check in on his dad more often. On a trip back home, he mentioned his dilemma to Jeff.

*Childhood friends can be a reliable contact in an emergency.*

"No problem," said Jeff, obviously pleased to help. "I'll do it. It'll be fun. I always liked your dad."

Jeff's parents long ago had retired and moved to a warmer climate, and he missed the wisdom and perspective of older people. So the arrangement worked beautifully for all parties involved. But if he hadn't asked his friend, Mark never would have found the perfect solution to his caregiving problem. Neither will you find such a win-win if you don't ask. Experts agree, however, that the key is for friends and family to have a choice in the matter.

One often easy way to give them that choice is for an aging loved one also to have a part-time housekeeper. That helper can keep up the house and also keep a regular eye on a parent as well as perhaps cook a meal each day. Another option with low or even no cost to qualified recipients is Meals On Wheels or other similar home delivery food program that not only provides a meal but an extra set of eyes to look in on that elderly person. Churches and religiously affiliated organizations also often have programs that will send a volunteer to talk with or provide spiritual counseling (and that all-important check-in) for the aging. A local Roman Catholic diocese or church, for example, might have a program of volunteers to take Communion to and regularly visit a homebound individual.

# Aging Parents Feel Burdened, Too

Louise, the divorced, soon to be empty nester in Chapter 2, wanted to move to New York but felt trapped and believed she couldn't move because she had to take care of her aging mother nearby. It works the other way around, too. Retired elderly parents may want *finally* to get out of that town they've been stuck in for years but often feel they can't because their children call it home.

In the past several years, Emma's mom had slowed down considerably. Nonetheless she remained in the family's modest home where her two kids had grown up. Staying meant more housework and cooking than she really wanted to do, and more than once she had a few choice words about the situation. She also often mentioned how nice it would be to move closer to the grandchildren. Emma once asked her why she didn't move. "Because this is your home, and you kids always like to come back here. If I weren't here, where would you go?" she replied.

"Mom was right," says Emma. "It would hurt us if she sold our home and left."

## Distance Exaggerates Issues

Distance can magnify and confuse the issues too. Remember Sam, who stopped footing the bills for his adult son and whose own parents ended up angry with him? Unfortunately, all three parties were hundreds of miles apart and unable to sit down and discuss the real situation. Instead, everything happened via impersonal e-mails and emotional phone calls. Even Sam's ex-wife lived hundreds of miles from their son. As a result of distance and miscommunication, all the issues were blown way out of proportion.

*As with many other things, emotions cloud the real issues.*

Sound like a soap opera? Perhaps, but it's a very real example of how generational and physical distances can magnify differences and create chasms of emotion that are tough to deal with—not to mention the financial toll they can take.

Sam and his parents may have been comfortable financially, but it doesn't take long to blow through a decent retirement or prevent one from being amassed when the dollars are being shelled out thousands at a time. Before Sam ever learned about the $8,000 a

---

**ABOUT E-MAIL COMMUNICATION**

*E-mail doesn't come with an interpretation of what you wrote. That means people can read nuances into all kinds of comments all the time. Different people take different interpretations from the same content. That's human nature. E-mail is a great way to stay connected, but don't use it as your sole communications link. Follow it up with a phone call and even, if possible, an occasional visit.*

---

month stipend to his son, his parents already had sent their grandson close to $100,000. What if his aging dad—who recently had suffered a heart attack—suddenly had another and required full-time nursing care? (The average cost of a private room in a nursing home in Miami in 2005 was $219 a day or almost $80,000 a year, according to MetLife Mature Market Institute numbers.) Or what if a hurricane destroyed their $1 million beachfront condo in Florida and everything in it? Either scenario would require hefty financial outlays that could jeopardize everyone's future. Perhaps if the parties involved sat down face to face and spoke honestly, they could resolve their differences. Sam could avoid a confrontation with his dad. His son could get the resentments and guilt off his chest. And the grandparents could learn the real truth so they weren't acting out of emotion.

## Hidden Reality

"We never saw it coming." That's a familiar refrain from at-a-distance boomers taken aback by Mom's "sudden" dementia or Dad's "unexpected" heart attack. Many seniors deserve Oscars for their bravado performances during visits or on the phone with their distant children. Reality, meanwhile, is something quite different.

"By the time we recognized Mom's dementia, it was too late to move her somewhere near one of us," says Paul, 59, stressed out and exhausted after he, his wife, and his two siblings spent days trying to find a suitable place for his mom to live. Their kids, meanwhile, missed several days of school and had started to act up because they had been neglected too long. "Mom always insisted on staying put, and she always sounded so great and so normal on the phone," says Paul.

Luckily, Paul and his siblings were able to find a long-term care facility near their mom's home that was willing to take her. Most of the places they'd found had long waiting lists, and their mom couldn't wait. Unfortunately, though, the solution was miles away from any of the kids. Now they trade off visiting her regularly, and although their mom is comfortable and well taken care of, they constantly fret about her situation.

*Regular assessments of a senior's situation are essential to avoid unsettling surprises.*

If you, like Paul, have distant aging parents or grandparents, it's important that you or someone you trust checks regularly on that senior to assess whether her physical, emotional, and medical needs are being met. After all, those people who spend the most time with your elderly loved one are more likely to notice the slight changes in behavior that could signal possible trouble. "Regularly" means at least once a week or more, depending on the age or infirmity of the parent.

Don't feel as if you're snooping. You're not. You're simply doing what's necessary to ensure that your loved one is happy, healthy, and safe. And you can tell them so.

Simple things to look for range from the neatness of their home to their personal appearance, social life, and whether they're taking their medications. We'll get into the details on what to look for in Chapter 5.

## Distant but Not Alone

Technology in the form of personal medical alarms, "lifelines," and monitoring devices and services helps many distant and nearby boomers sleep easier with the fear that an aging parent may fall,

## MEDICAL ALARMS & MONITORING

*A few of the national companies that offer medical emergency "buttons" include:*

- *ADT Security Systems, Inc. (www.adt.com, click on "Home Security")*
- *AlertOne Services, Inc. (www.alert-1.com)*
- *American Medical Alarms, Inc. (www.americanmedicalalarms .com)*
- *Lifeline Systems, Inc. (www.lifelinesys.com)*
- *Personal Alert Systems, Inc. (www.personalalert.com)*

get hurt, or get into trouble with no one there to help. It also helps some seniors who understand the importance of lifelines to rest easier, too.

For a reasonable cost—generally around $25 to $35 a month or $320 to $400 a year—you or an elderly parent can buy a service with operators or contacts on call 24/7. That means if Mom or Dad falls, can't get up, or is having a heart attack, they can summon help, generally with the push of button on a waterproof or water-resistant device worn around the neck or on the wrist. Some services, for an additional monthly charge, even offer fall-detector devices designed to recognize a fall and immediately summon help.

Guardian Phone Center also has a 911 Guardian-Phone™, which is a small cordless phone that operates anywhere there's a touch-tone phone line and 911 service. It can be worn around the neck and is water resistant. In an emergency, the wearer touches the button and is connected with the local 911 service. It costs about $150, with no monthly fees other than for regular phone service (*www.guardianphone.com*).

Doug's dad was 78, vibrant, and in great health. But one day he fell in the bathtub and hit his head. He would have bled to death if his fishing buddy hadn't happened by to talk about their upcoming trip. That buddy also just happened to know where Doug's dad hid his extra key, and then also had the good sense to use it and check on him when no one answered the door.

Betty also fell, but she was much luckier. Ever since her husband died, she had lived alone, refusing to give up her home and move to a smaller, retiree-oriented community. The house was a 100-year-old, two-story farmhouse, and her daughter, who lived several hours away, worried all the time about her frail mom negotiating the stairs. Finally her daughter persuaded Betty to wear "the button." When the fall occurred, Betty pushed the button, heard a voice from a speaker box installed by the alarm company, and responded by describing what had happened. Quickly the necessary care was provided.

Both Betty and her daughter were thankful they had prepared for this contingency. Today Betty still is in the big house, and her daughter still worries about her, but at least they both sleep better at night, literally, knowing that if an emergency arises, help will arrive.

*"The end result of the terrible twos is kids grow out of it. The end result of where elderly parents are now is they die."*

—Beverly Bernstein Joie, certified geriatric care manager, psychotherapist

If a parent won't wear the button, try "compassionate manipulation," says Joie. Pay for the button yourself, and tell the parent whatever it takes to get them to wear it. It can be a lifesaver. That's what happened with Joie's mom, who resisted having the emergency alarm. She was having a stroke, and because she had the button, was able to summon help quickly and effortlessly. "It saved her," says Joie. "We can say they're stubborn. But at this stage of their lives, of course they want to hold onto life as they know it. The end result of the terrible twos is kids grow out of it. The end result of where elderly parents are now is they die."

## Have a Plan

Instead of agonizing over these and other possibly frenetic situations, cut out the stress, forget about acting out of emotions or panic, and devise a plan. If you live out of town from an aging loved one, make the situation easier on you and everyone else by putting together a plan of action that accounts for contingencies. Don't wait until that late-night phone call from Dad or someone else saying that something is terribly wrong.

Needless worry doesn't help anyone. Dad doesn't want you hovering around, driving him crazy day in and day out anyway. And Mom truly does enjoy her independence; it's just that every once in a while she needs to know you care and you're there. Your own children don't appreciate your taking the strain out on them, either. By planning up front, you can take care of your own family and your own life, while being assured that your parents are covered, too.

*Involve your aging loved one, his or her spouse or partner, your siblings, and your own kids in any emergency plan.*

Plenty of resources are available to help you formulate your plan of action. Of course, make plans with your parent and any siblings, too, so that it's not just your plan but one that has a high probability of working well.

---

## BRINGING IN PROFESSIONAL HELP

*If you're miles away from an elderly parent and not sure whether the expense of a geriatric care manager is worth it, check out a few numbers. Although the figures can vary considerably, you can get a good idea of the possible value of an expert.*

**Cost of one trip:**

| | |
|---|---|
| Airline ticket: | $400 |
| Airport parking: | $65 |
| Rental car: | $350 |
| Lost wages (one week): | $1,000 |
| Other expenses: | $300 |
| Total cost of trip: | **$2,115** |
| Cost of geriatric care manager assessment: | **$1,000*** |

*\*Generally, cost is well under this amount.*

Your family may offer ideas or directions you haven't considered.

Bringing in a professional geriatric care manager may make sense, financially and otherwise, even though they're private-practice professionals whose fees aren't covered by insurance. (Some long-term care insurance policies will cover at least a portion of their fees—more on that later). These experts will do a comprehensive assessment of all areas of a senior's life, including their health, finances, family, social network, safety, and more, then analyze the overall situation and propose an individualized care plan and action plan. Fees vary widely, and can be per assessment (probably under $1,000 and possibly much less), or hourly, typically $80 to $200 an hour. Their services also may be available on an hourly consulting basis.

Because these managers work in the locale where a loved one lives, they should be familiar with services, contacts, and logistics available there. All of these considerations can be tough to handle from a distance. And, if you compare the cost of a care manager with that of a last-minute airline ticket and everything else required for you to make the trip, it may be a small price to pay.

*Don't overlook a professional geriatric care manager as a way to help you assess the situation and design the right approach to caregiving at a distance. Their cost can range from $80 to $200 an hour, or, on a per-complete-assessment basis, probably well under $1,000.*

If you don't want or can't afford to bring in an outside care manager, get a copy of the senior resource book for your parents' town or city. Most areas offer these books, which are chock-full of services, centers, and organizations that are good starting points for virtually any situation. Look on the Internet, ask Mom or Dad to pick up one, or call a local office on aging for information on where and how to get the resource book for your parents' area. Hospitals, physicians' offices, and HMOs often have copies available, too.

## FINANCIAL OVERVIEW

Here's a typical financial assessment from a geriatric care manager.

### Financial Assets

| Asset | Financial Institution | Account # | Amount |
|---|---|---|---|
| Real Estate (Own Home) | | Home in Charlot | $375,000.00 |
| Stock Portfolio | Edward Shamath | 65-981243 | $445,000.00 |
| Real Estate (Vacation) | | Nantucket | $855,000.00 |
| Automobiles | | | $120,000.00 |
| Jewelry | | | $68,000.00 |
| Real Estate (Rental) | | Montana | $325,000.00 |
| Real Estate (Rental) | | Florida | $275,000.00 |
| 401K | | 123-45-7896 | $125,000.00 |
| | | **Total Assets:** | **$2,588,000.00** |

### Estimated Monthly Income

| Income Type | Source | Estimated Monthly Amount |
|---|---|---|
| Dividends | Central Industries | $2,416.67 |
| Pension | Central Industries | $5,000.00 |
| Social Security | | $1,850.00 |
| | **Total Estimated Monthly Income:** | **$9,266.67** |

### Estimated Monthly Expenses

| Payment Type | Payee: | Estimated Monthly Amount |
|---|---|---|
| Auto Fuel | | $83.33 |
| Groceries | | $500.00 |
| Housing | WS Financial, Inc. | $3,100.00 |
| Insurance | Worldwide Insurance | $83.33 |
| Newspaper | | $16.67 |
| Pet Supplies | | $100.00 |
| Utilities | | $500.00 |
| Vacations | | $500.00 |
| | **Estimated Monthly Total Expenses:** | **$4,883.33** |

**Source:** Courtesy of JewelCode Corporation, www.jewelcode.com.

Another great resource that people often overlook is social workers. They and other nonphysician medical professionals sometimes are available through an elderly patient's physician's office or health care plan. Many large companies with employee assistance plans (EAPs) include services that help families with the issues of aging and elderly care. Other resources and support groups like Alzheimer's and multiple sclerosis (MS) societies may provide occasional help, too. An elderly loved one's local/county Agency on Aging, if requested, generally will send a social worker to assess that person's physical, mental, and health situation, and then provide suggestions for placement, assistance, and care. If so prescribed by a physician, Medicare will pay for a visiting nurse to educate and provide a loved one with skilled care on an occasional basis. But there are limitations on the latter, so check with your insurance provider, Medicare, and your parent's physician.

If a parent is hospitalized, take advantage of social workers and other professionals on staff. Talk to them about the issues and ask for suggestions. Older patients often welcome physical therapists who help them win back their independence, while social workers are received with somewhat less enthusiasm by patient and family. But keep in mind that these experts are familiar with the resources of their community and can provide valuable input into a workable caregiving plan. If prescribed by a doctor or other qualified medical professional, their services may be covered by Medicare or other health plans, with limitations.

These professionals also know well the problems faced by long-distance family and may be able to connect you with unusual or out-of-the-way care services that are highly dependable and reputable nonetheless. Don't overlook talking with other medical professionals too. They're valuable sources of direction. After all, they do this all the time.

Missy, 42, lived more than 900 miles from her elderly dad, who had been hospitalized twice in the past two years. He was going in yet again for what was supposed to be routine surgery to implant a pacemaker. Swamped

---

### TIPS FROM REAL LIFE

*Are you worried about what will happen to a loved one once they're out of the hospital?*

- *Talk to hospital social workers. They're there to help you, along with the patient, put together a workplace, living, and caregiving plan.*
- *Local senior resource books provide a snapshot of what's available in the community.*
- *Ask other medical professionals if they know of any private service providers. Some may even provide services themselves when not working in the hospital.*
- *Talk to various religious-affiliated organizations. They may have or know of volunteer services to fit your needs.*

---

with the responsibilities of her 11-month-old son and her job, Missy had decided and her dad had agreed that she would not come for the surgery and instead would visit later when she could be of more help to him at home.

Of course, the surgery was anything but routine and her dad ended up hospitalized for nearly three weeks. Because Missy couldn't do anything for him during that time, she stayed at home with the baby. When her dad was ready to go home, Missy couldn't schedule a flight in time to take her dad home from the hospital, and no one seemed able to offer a solution. But in talking with nurses on her dad's floor during his previous hospitalizations, Missy had learned of a small private nursing/home-health care service run by a doctor's wife. Missy had spoken with the woman and learned that she was a former nurse and hired only other nurses or licensed practical nurses (LPNs).

The business owner even had asked Missy about her dad's personality to be sure that if and when their services were needed, she could match Missy's dad with a compatible care provider. Missy also had checked on the business by asking numerous medical professionals, including her dad's doctor, about its reputation. The service had impeccable credentials, and so Missy had found a fallback in case of an emergency. This was it, so she called the service. It was able to provide the perfect person to take her dad home from the hospital—and to provide more services later—and the health worker knew ahead of time how to handle the difficult aspects of her dad's personality. The cost: $17 an hour for an LPN. The trip home from the hospital cost Missy's dad $61. He gave the caregiver an extra $10 because she was so nice.

This was a small company that the hospital social services people hadn't thought to mention, and Missy never would have found out about it if she hadn't asked others for guidance and suggestion.

# Often-Overlooked Resource

Today's Internet-wired world aside, absentee family members should make sure they have an old-fashioned telephone book of the paper variety with business listings from the town where their loved one lives. They're free for the asking. It's worth its weight (including shipping) in gold when it comes time to find a provider or service late at night. The last thing you want to deal with is an automated information directory when you can't quite remember an exact name or address—if you ever knew it at all.

As basic a suggestion as this sounds, people often don't think about having a phone book. But a handy dandy Yellow Pages immediately will make your long-distance caregiving life easier—whether you need the number of a doctor or a dry cleaner—when checking on something for an aging parent. Online phone directories (*www.anywho.com* or *http://yp.yahoo.com*) are great but can be cumbersome and terribly time consuming if

---

**LOOKING FOR A BUSINESS OR SERVICE?**

*Get a Yellow Pages telephone book for the city where your loved one lives. It will make your life easier in the long run.*

---

you don't know where to start. They're also not always as complete as their paper counterparts. Additionally, beyond listing a phone number, many Yellow Pages ads can offer a quick answer to important questions about a business, such as how long a company or provider has been established in the community; whether it's licensed or accredited, if applicable; if it takes a particular insurance; who uses it; and more.

## Details of Your Plan

Once you know who or what organizations can help you look in on or care for an aging distant parent, write down all their contact information on a sheet of paper and put it in an easy-to-access location. At the office or at home isn't good enough. Neither is on the computer. What happens if the computer is down, or if the information is somewhere that's not accessible 24/7? Or what if it's at home and you're at the office? The key is for the information to be readily accessible at a moment's notice wherever you might be. Write down the numbers for your elderly parent, too, and then put the list in an easily accessible place. (Note: Write it B-I-G so a parent can read it easily in an emergency and perhaps even without her glasses.)

Also, write down contact information of important people and places you might need in the event of an emergency. Not only will it be more convenient to locate them, but writing down the information helps to formalize the plan.

## Planning for Emergencies

Your plan of action for an aging family member also should include contingency plans for how you will reach that person both by phone and in person in case of an emergency. Your list of pertinent phone numbers needs to include several friends and neighbors of a loved one, and their cell phone numbers, if they have them. Even if an aging loved one refuses to get a cell phone, buy the service and give him the phone anyway. You may be surprised. Despite their grousing, generally they'll use the phone in an emergency.

Special cell phones designed for kids that hold programmable numbers could be an option, too. The Firefly™, for example, has five buttons and can handle 20 preprogrammable numbers. You can pick it up at Target for under $100 and it comes with 30 minutes' free air time. More pay-as-you-go time is available, too. Besides, Grandma just might like its fancy colors.

*Don't forget to establish how an aging distant loved one will contact you in the event of a major natural disaster that might destroy normal communications channels.*

---

## CHEAP TRAVEL

***Trying to find less expensive travel options either because of a commuting caregiving responsibility or simply to get home more often to see aging parents?***

- *Regularly surf online travel sites for last-minute or fast deals that disappear quickly. An inexpensive ticket literally could vanish between the time it takes to close out a screen and open it again.*
- *Check Web sites of airlines that serve your specific destination for low-cost deals to that destination.*
- *Consider flying to optional destinations near your real destination. That gives you flexibility, and a willingness to drive the extra distance can mean cash savings. Perhaps a sibling or friend would be willing to pick you up.*
- *Do you qualify for any travel discounts, such as rental cars or hotels?*
- *Check bulletin board or Internet postings for rides to your destinations. But always thoroughly check out anyone before accepting a ride.*
- *Don't overlook want ads for qualified drivers. Businesses and individuals often look for individuals to drive cars to certain destinations. Alternatively, talk to local car dealerships about offering your driving services.*

Don't overlook contingency contact plans for a natural disaster or some other tragedy, either. In the aftermath and devastation of Hurricane Katrina along the Gulf Coast, for example, thousands of families and loved ones lost track of each other and were frantic because they had no emergency contact plan in the event of failed standard forms of communication, including cellular phones.

If you have aging parents at a distance, the availability of emergency cash—no matter your financial situation—also has special urgency. If you don't have emergency cash, or can't get to it, you may forever rue being unable to be there when an elderly loved one truly needs you or when it's time to say good-bye. How much cash should you have ready access to? That's up to you, but it should be enough to comfortably pick up the expenses of an emergency trip to visit an elderly parent.

# Remember:

- Plan for contingencies before you're in a panic and stressed out by an emergency.
- Write down your plan, complete with contact information for the important people, places, and organizations you might need to access.
- Emergency access to cash is critical if you're a long-distance adult child of aging parents.
- Look to old friends of yours and your family as possible sources of help occasionally or in an emergency.
- Social workers, geriatric care managers, and other medical professionals can make the job of at-a-distance caregiving easier in the long run. Some fees even are covered by health insurance.
- Get a Yellow Pages directory for the city where your distant loved one lives. It's an invaluable resource.

# The Independence Issue

**Chapter 4**

Whatever our age, we all enjoy independence and mobility, whether it means lazing around the house on a sunny day, driving ourselves to the doctor's office for a morning appointment, or deciding whether to meet friends for a late lunch at the mall. Seniors, too, enjoy charting their own course on their own time.

"This [notion of] independence or getting along without anyone's help is a very American way of looking at things," says public and health policy researcher Langa from the University of Michigan. "That sense of being able to get on like you have in the past, be independent, and not be a burden on other family members clearly seems to be one of the most important things on people's minds. It's not as prominent, however, on the minds of older folks in other cultures, like Africa and Asia," he adds.

In American culture, independence definitely is lauded as a virtue—hardly surprising in a nation born as a result of a war of independence. We value people who pull themselves up by their bootstraps, stand on their own two feet, and think for themselves. No wonder so many seniors try so desperately to hold onto their independence as long as they can.

## Consider Senior's Viewpoint

One of the biggest mistakes many in the Sandwich Generation make is to assume that aging parents can't live without their children, or that automatically their parents will need them and want to move closer to and be more dependent on them as they age.

*"Independence is a very American way of looking at things."*

—Kenneth M. Langa, MD, PhD

Not so, say experts and seniors who live their lives miles from their adult children and their families. "I have my friends," says divorced, widowed Ella, 84, "and I'm not leaving here to live somewhere where I don't know anyone."

## SOURCES FOR MORE INFORMATION

- *AARP (www.aarp.org/families/driver_ safety). Plenty of helpful information.*
- *American Association for Geriatric Psychiatry (www.aagpgpa.org). Nonprofit professional organization offers news, information, and resources for consumers.*
- *AAA Foundation for Traffic Safety (www .aaafoundation.org). Nonprofit educational and research organization has free information and brochures on variety of topics, including issues with elderly drivers (click on "Products").*
- *American Dietetic Association (www .eatright.org). An organization of food and nutrition professionals, ADA promotes optimal nutrition, health, and well-being. Click on "Food and Nutrition Information" for lots of good reading.*
- *Eat 5 A Day (http://5aday.nci.nih.gov). From the U.S. Department of Health and Human Services, National Institutes of Health, and National Cancer Institute, this site provides all kinds of information about healthy and nutritious eating. (Also check out www .healthierus.gov.)*

- *Fifty-Plus Lifelong Fitness (www.50plus.org). Nonprofit begun at Stanford University 26 years ago with the mission to promote an active lifestyle for older people. Check out its resources/links on the home page.*
- *Fitness Over Fifty (www.fitness-over-fifty .com). Includes lots of helpful articles and information, workout programs, and more about getting older and getting better.*
- *Geriatric Mental Health Foundation (www .gmhfonline.org). Nonprofit includes plenty of consumer information and resources as well as a locator tool; also offers free brochures on alcohol and substance abuse in late life, healthy aging advice, and more.*
- *Meals on Wheels Association of America (www.mowaa.org). Nonprofit association serving organizations that provide local senior meal programs throughout the country. To find a Meals On Wheels organization near you, use its locator on the home page.*
- *National Center for Family Friends (www .family-friends.org). Under the auspices of The National Council on the Aging, this intergenerational volunteer program matches men*

"This is the family's home, a place where you children can come to visit. Why would I want to leave?" says Sol, 89, who still lives in the same home in the same town where his kids grew up.

"I'm just not going to do it," says Liz, 72, recovering from a massive heart attack. "I may not be able to get around much, but if I moved I wouldn't know anyone. I'd be alone. And what happens if the kids move again? Where does that leave me if I've picked up and moved cross-country to be near my children and grandchildren? No. I won't do it!"

and women over 55 with families that have children with disabilities and chronic illnesses to provide social and emotional support as well as advice and help.

■ *The National Council on the Aging* (www .ncoa.org). *A national network of organizations and individuals dedicated to improving the health and independence of older people and increasing their contributions to communities, society, and future generations. Check out the "Seniors' Corner or Mature Worker" links on the home page.*

■ *Project Enhance* (www.projectenhance.org). *Includes two senior community-based health programs for older adults, EnhanceWellness and EnhanceFitness. For more information or to find a wellness project in your area, contact your state and local senior services organizations.*

■ *ThirdAge, Inc.* (www.thirdage.com). *An online direct marketing company focused exclusively on serving the needs of midlife adults—generally those in their 40s, 50s, and 60s; includes articles on health, money, beauty, relationships, and more.*

■ *Senior Corps* (www.seniorcorps.gov). *From the Corporation for National and Community Service, this organization helps retirees and those over 55 volunteer as mentors, coaches, or companions to people in need or contribute their job skills and expertise to community projects and organizations.*

■ *SeniorNet®* (www.seniornet.org). *A nonprofit with information and reading on everything from education, books, and money to health, volunteering, and more.*

■ *Senior Solutions of America* (www .aging-parents-and-elder-care.com *and* www.todaysseniors.com). *These sites include plenty of useful information from Elder Care 101 to the elderly and their pets, prescription drugs, living solutions, checklists, and more.*

■ *SilverSneakers®* (www.silversneakers .com). *A health and fitness program for older adults that combines physical activity, healthy lifestyle, and socially oriented programming; offered through various organizations and fitness clubs around the country.*

Psychotherapist Joie suggests that this seemingly obstinate attitude may stem from what she and other professional geriatric care managers see as a prevalent end-of-life theme among seniors. "They're dealing with the loss of their identities—who they know themselves to be—the loss of their independence, the loss of their health, and the loss of their friends. And when dealing with so much loss, people want to hold on to life as they know it. So there's a tremendous amount of resistance to moving someplace different, because it's the unknown, and somehow people feel that there is safety in familiarity. What you hear seniors saying is, 'I want to be independent.' They believe on some level that that means not changing anything. So they set themselves up to become dependent because they don't allow help in before an emergency occurs . . .

"Seniors typically are not proactive. And the people who hire care managers are their children who understand what's happening and what to do about it."

## Seniors and Autonomy

However they define it, seniors want their independence, agrees geriatric psychiatrist Kennedy, also a former president of the Bethesda, Maryland–based American Association for Geriatric Psychiatry. And for some, that independence may be rooted in a stable level of depending on others.

Seniors often feel guilty about burdening family members, yet many are afraid of losing their autonomy and independence if a home-care worker comes to their house. So, despite the guilt, they turn to family members for help, somehow thinking that in doing so they're preserving their independence. That, of course, isn't true. To complicate matters further, family comes with interpersonal baggage—psychological dynamics, old history, rivalries, resentments, and problems—that outside help doesn't carry.

Other seniors, hoping to avoid the family issue, turn outside the family for help, care, or assistance. Remember Ruthie, the grandmother in Chapter 2 who had

---

> ### VOLUNTEERS TO HELP
>
> *Senior Companions is a program from the Corporation for National and Community Service's Senior Corps in which volunteers, age 60 and over, help adults in the community maintain their independence in their own homes by helping them with shopping and light chores, interacting with doctors, or just making a friendly visit. (Go to www.seniorcorps.gov or type "Senior Companions" into a search engine to find local organizations.)*

issues with her son, didn't get along with her daughter-in-law, and didn't want to stay in their home? Even though Ruthie was healthy and spry, she didn't like the dependence inherent in staying under their roof. Finally, after years of discomfort in their home, she did what she wanted and stayed in a hotel. In doing so, she ditched the family baggage, reclaimed her autonomy, and thoroughly enjoyed the visits to see her grandchildren. Many other elderly aren't as fortunate in finding a quick and affordable solution.

Liza's mom, Marie, 70, was vibrant, still working, and adored her job and her life. She lived in the home where Liza and her two sisters had grown up, and she spent time gardening, dating, and socializing with her neighbors. Marie also enjoyed sharing time with her teenage granddaughters—she exchanged letters frequently with one who lived out of town—and she had good relationships with her three grown daughters as long as she didn't visit too often. They, like Marie, were strong personalities themselves, and whenever any of them got together, each one vied for control. Marie and her daughters were quite happy with the status quo; there were no regrets, nothing but minor squabbles, and, most of all, everyone enjoyed their independence.

*Actively involve a senior in decisions and discussions about his future.*

The situation came crashing down suddenly. While crossing the street on the way to a doctor's appointment,

Marie tripped and fell, hitting her head. She was hospitalized for three weeks, and then, disabled, moved into Liza's home. Marie wouldn't hear of assisted living or a nursing home, even temporarily. Her independence shattered, she became depressed, unhappy, and difficult, and her health went downhill fast.

## The Compromise

Liza's mom had other options. She simply was unwilling to listen to what they were, even though Liza tried to include her mom in decisions about her future. In the end, the family was miserable because of Marie's unhappy living situation. Liza's long-distance sisters weren't spared, either. They had to listen to the rants and raves of both Liza and their mom.

Kennedy suggests that one approach to helping older adults maintain their independence yet recognize and accept the help and care they need is to talk to them and explain that if they want to extend their independence, they need to be flexible and let someone help them preserve it. Tell them, "To have your independence for the longest time possible, you may need to cede minor aspects of it to other people." If Liza's mom had done that up front, she wouldn't have been so miserable later. Eventually, as we'll discuss later, she did relinquish bits of her independence, and the overall situation and her health improved dramatically.

*"To have your independence for the longest time possible, you may need to cede minor aspects of it to other people."*

—Gary J. Kennedy, MD, geriatric psychiatrist

Some older adults have major home-health needs, such as a regular insulin injection, yet their vision is too poor or they're too arthritic to manage the syringe and draw up the medication themselves. They might truly need to move into a family member's home in order to receive that needed assistance on a regular, affordable basis. In such a situation, it's important that the caregiver get help and a respite, even if only occasionally. Again, it's all about exercising that right of choice. (We'll talk more about how to determine the proper level of care and independence in Chapter 5.)

In some cases, it's necessary for family members and caregivers to negotiate with an elderly person so she understands that other people besides family members will be helping to provide for her needs. For example, says Kennedy, the negotiations could be as simple as, "Yes, I'll be here in the evenings, but during the day you will need someone else to come in."

## The Driving Dilemma

At some point, anyone with an elderly or aging family member frets about that person getting behind the wheel of a vehicle: How can Mom or Dad still drive? They'll get killed. Worse yet, they'll kill someone else. How can we get them off the road? They're a menace to public safety. These all are familiar refrains of children whose parents insist on driving past their ability to do so. Their auto insurance rates can climb dramatically, too, and if they've had a number of accidents, even if they're just fender benders, it can be difficult for them to get coverage.

> *Many seniors recognize their driving limitations.*
> *Others refuse to acknowledge them and don't quit*
> *until it's too late or they're forced into it. It's that issue*
> *of independence again.*

Of course, just because someone is older doesn't necessarily mean he is incapable of driving or that they won't use common sense about whether to drive. Also, younger drivers often tend to have an impatient attitude toward older drivers.

Many seniors quietly recognize that their reflexes are slower, they can't see as well at night, and perhaps their hearing is fading. On their own, they'll cut back their driving by no longer driving at night, staying off freeways, and driving only familiar routes to nearby places when necessary. They may even turn in their car keys.

The latter often happens as a result of a scare on the road—perhaps they narrowly missed getting in an accident—or maybe they are simply afraid because they know they really can't see well enough to be a responsible driver.

## CHECKLIST FOR SAFE ELDERLY DRIVING

*Watch for telltale signs of decline in the elderly person's driving abilities. Does she:*

- *Drive at inappropriate speeds, either too fast or too slow?*
- *Ask passengers to check if it is clear to pass or turn?*
- *Respond slowly to or not notice pedestrians, bicyclists, and other drivers?*
- *Ignore, disobey, or misinterpret street signs and traffic lights?*
- *Fail to yield to other cars or pedestrians who have the right of way?*
- *Fail to judge distances between cars correctly?*
- *Become easily frustrated and angry?*
- *Appear drowsy, confused, or frightened?*
- *Have one or more near accidents or near misses?*
- *Drift across lane markings or bump into curbs?*
- *Forget to turn on headlights after dusk?*
- *Have difficulty with glare from oncoming headlights, streetlights, or other bright or shiny objects, especially at dawn, dusk, and nighttime?*
- *Have difficulty turning head, neck, shoulders, or body while driving or parking?*
- *Ignore signs of mechanical problems, including underinflated tires? (One in four cars has at least one tire underinflated by eight pounds or more; low tire pressure is a major cause of accidents.)*
- *Have too little strength to turn the wheel sharply in an emergency, such as a tire failure, a child darting into traffic, etc.?*
- *Get lost repeatedly, even in familiar areas?*

*If the answer to one or more of these questions is yes, you should explore whether medical issues are affecting your loved one's driving skills. It may be time to discuss giving up the car.*

**Source:** www.AgingSolutions.info
© 2006 Senior Solutions of America, Inc. Reprinted with permission.

Arnie was a spry 83-year-old. His mind was sharp even though he had slowed noticeably and his eyesight had faded a bit since his wife died. He lived in a retirement home—its parking lot filled with dented and dinged vehicles—and still had his car, or so his at-a-distance children thought. The idea of their dad driving was a constant worry. But they long ago had given up nagging him to stop driving. One day on a visit to see her father, Elise decided to broach the subject yet again. No sooner had she opened her mouth than Arnie casually informed her that he had sold the car two months earlier! Sometimes even the most stubborn elderly parent can still surprise his offspring.

Not everyone, however, is as sensible as Arnie. Richard, 92, was slow to react and had trouble seeing—actually he was blind in one eye and cloudy in the other—yet he kept driving. His wife, also elderly, and their kids used to protest constantly but finally gave up. Then one day the dreaded accident happened. Richard never saw the other car with the right of way in an intersection and he broadsided it. Luckily he never drove faster than 25 miles per hour on any street, and this time was going even slower. The two children in the car he hit weren't hurt, and their mother, who was driving, suffered only a couple of cracked ribs; it could have been far worse. That incident was enough for his family, but not for Richard. He had no intention of giving up his right to drive until his insurance company dropped him, but that, combined with his family's insistence, forced him to relinquish his license.

If you hit a belligerent wall with a Richard-like elderly parent, you do have recourse other than waiting for an accident to happen. His insurance company may be willing to listen to you. Also, try confronting an elderly parent en masse—kids, other family members, even a social worker, and concerned friends. What if Richard had killed those kids in that car? How would he have felt? What would that have done to the kids' family? To Richard's family? And from a bottom-line perspective, how might that have affected Richard's family's financial future?

---

## TIPS FROM REAL LIFE

*Do you have an aging loved one who shouldn't be driving but won't quit?*

- *Take a compassionate and patient yet firm approach. That may include adjusting your attitude toward older drivers who drive the speed limit!*
- *Try the reasoning that it's not safe for him as well as others on the road. Don't be accusatory. All that does is create confrontation.*
- *Refuse to ride with that person.*
- *If your parent still won't quit, suggest ways in which she might limit her driving, such as not driving at night or on highways, driving only to nearby places on familiar roads, and more.*
- *Consider the gift of nominal tuition for a driver's refresher course either through AARP (it's just $10 per person) or some local organization.*
- *If all else fails, disable the car or physically take it away.*

---

If those approaches still don't work, take the car keys, pull the battery, or do anything else to keep the car from moving.

Also, keep in mind that while *your* primary concern may be for the safety of a parent and others on the road, to that elderly person, driving symbolizes independence. Without it, many reason they may as well just sit around and wait to die. When you approach the subject of driving, don't be accusatory or condescending. Perhaps consider getting an outsider or nonfamily member to objectively assess your senior loved one's driving abilities' before you demand he stop driving. Sometimes our assessments are jaded by the fact that someone we love *has* slowed down.

It's also essential that if you do take away someone's right to drive, you replace it with other options for personal mobility. One reason Arnie gave up his car so willingly was that he had an outside caregiver who came three times a week to help him. She would do the laundry and housework, drive him places, help him with the grocery shopping, and more.

Other mobility options could include everything from hiring a full-time chauffeur to finding a high school or college student or even a stay-at-home mom willing to drive an aging parent around occasionally in exchange for a few dollars an hour. Local area offices on aging, senior centers, and religious-affiliated organizations also generally can direct you to free or low-cost, to-your-door transportation that's usually reliable. Regional transportation districts often have Access-a-Ride–type services that not only get a senior or handicapped individual where they're going when they want to go, but provide a welcome, smiling face while doing so.

*If a senior loses her right to drive, replace it with other personal mobility options.*

Note, however, that the initial contact and setup of many free or low-cost services requires jumping through a few hoops that may be tough for a senior to negotiate on his own. Be sure an adult child or family friend is available to help smooth the process.

Often, seniors can benefit from driver safety refresher courses. AARP *(www.aarp.org)* offers one open to those age 50 and up. Also check out the AAA Foundation for Traffic Safety's Senior Driver Web site *(www .seniordrivers.org)*.

## Healthy Aging

Regular physical activity helps all of us—kids, caregivers, and the elderly—maintain our health, relieve stress, and prevent decline as we age. It can be free, too. All you have to do is walk down the block and back or around the corner and back regularly. Exercise of some kind is especially important for older people who want to maintain their independence, mobility, and mental acuity for as long as possible.

"This seems quite obvious when you think about it, but continuing to be out and about and moving and walking as much as possible does seem to keep people independent both physically and mentally," says the University of Michigan's Langa.

Plus, studies show that physical activity has significant potential to reduce health care costs nationally by $77 billion annually (in 2000 dollars), according to "The State of Aging and Health in America 2004," a report from the nonprofit Merck Institute on Aging & Health and the Centers for Disease Control.

*By getting out and getting active, Americans have the potential to cut health care costs by $77 billion annually!*

Physical activity also can
- help prevent development of diabetes, high blood pressure, and colon cancer;
- cut the risk of dying prematurely;
- help maintain healthy bones and muscles, increase joint mobility, and improve functional capacity of those with osteoarthritis; and
- help alleviate symptoms of depression and anxiety for other causes and improve the quality of life of older adults by enhancing their psychological well-being.

(**Source:** U.S. Department of Health and Human Services report, "Physical Activity and Health: A Report of the Surgeon General," Atlanta, Georgia, U.S. Department of Health and Human Services, Centers for Disease Control and Prevention, National Center for Chronic Diseases Prevention and Health Promotion, 1996)

*The brain is a muscle. It needs exercise, too.*

—Gary J. Kennedy, MD, geriatric psychiatrist

If you're still not convinced that a physically active lifestyle makes more sense than a sedentary one for a senior, research also shows that inactive adults have significantly higher direct medical costs than active ones, and that the costs associated with physical inactivity increase with age (Agency for Healthcare Research and Quality, CDC report, "Physical Activity and Older Americans: Benefits and Strategies," June 2002).

So get out there and get active, caregivers and care recipients alike. If an aging parent or family member resists your help and insists on going it alone, work on convincing them of the importance of staying physically fit. It's a double dose of good sense for all of us as we age. The more active we are, the better our physical and mental states, and the less likely we are to need help now or later. That translates to lower costs of health care for everyone!

The brain is a muscle, too, so exercise it as well as your body, says Kennedy. Seniors need to be active intellectually, socially, and spiritually, as well as physically. Suggestions on how to do that include encouraging an elderly parent to take classes or courses—many free or at a low cost—from local community colleges or senior centers, learn a new language, play bridge or Scrabble, do crossword puzzles, and more. Some public colleges, community colleges, and even universities will allow seniors to audit courses free of charge.

"I preach involvement, involvement, involvement," says psychologist Silk. She urges her senior clients who often mention loneliness as a concern not to sit at home waiting for things to happen. Instead, whether they're institutionalized or have health issues, they should consider doing volunteer work or taking classes as ways to bring more meaning in their lives. "I work in one assisted living setting where the seniors work in the dining room: they set the tables, they clean up, and the people that are doing that are the least depressed and the least lonely."

If an elderly parent is religious but no longer attends religious services—perhaps because they can't get there—look for ways to help them get involved again in their church, mosque, or synagogue. The social and spiritual stimuli are good for the brain. It also could be a good way for the younger generation—your kids—to spend more quality time with the older generation.

Jack is 82, a physician, and still teaches courses at the medical school near his home. He lives with his 81-year-old wife in the same large home where his kids grew up, gardens and walks regularly, constantly has a new carpentry project, drives the hot car he couldn't afford as a kid, and travels in between all that activity. He's planning his 83rd birthday bash, just signed a new two-year teaching contract, and hasn't slowed down at all.

Sure, he has a few aches and pains. Who wouldn't at his age? But no one would know it, not even his family. In fact, recently his daughter and her adult son learned that he's had prostate cancer for almost a year. His positive attitude and busy lifestyle go a long way toward keeping him young, active, and in no way a burden on anyone.

*Even those with limited mobility can get exercise via calisthenics in a chair.*

Exercise is more important to seniors than it is to others, adds Kennedy, because seniors have less physical reserves so they must maintain a level of conditioning. Of course there are limitations to what seniors can do physically, based on overall health and medical conditions such as arthritis or heart disease. But exercises are adaptable. If mobility is an issue, try calisthenics in a chair. If a parent much prefers watching TV to walking around the block, try exercises designed for couch potatoes. Type "couch potato" and "exercise" into an Internet search engine, and you will find plenty to keep your parent busy in front of the TV for days. The Arthritis Foundation even offers a wealth of resources and information on exercises for those suffering from arthritis. (Visit *www.arthritis.org/conditions/* and click on "Exercise and Arthritis.")

*Attention couch potatoes: Move over. It's exercise time.*

Plenty of senior exercise programs—from simple stretches to water aerobics, marathon training, and mall walking—are available almost everywhere across the country, many free or at a low cost. Check out community centers, senior centers, fitness centers, or local community organizations, clubs, and more.

Remember Liza and her unhappy, dependent mother, Marie? One way Liza finally was able to help get her mother out of her funk and back into living again was to sign her up for a senior health and exercise program called SilverSneakers at her fitness center. (The program is offered at various facilities around the country; it's free to those people whose health insurance participates; otherwise, it's often just the cost of membership in the facility or health club. Visit *www .silversneakers.com*.) Once Liza's mom was in the company of her peers and mentally and physically challenged again, she started to return to her old self. Ordinary doctor-prescribed physical therapy just wasn't enough, says Liza.

For those who can't or don't want to spend the money for a formal exercise program, look into free community activities, or dress appropriately, wear comfortable shoes, and head out for a walk. Do it regularly.

Mall walking is a popular option, too, especially for those who don't like to brave the elements. Many malls even have informal walking clubs that usually meet mornings before stores open. A senior not only gets her exercise, but camaraderie and mental stimuli, too. Mall walking also could be a great social pastime with a grandchild or adult child. Do your formal walking, then afterward wander and windowshop together.

Swimming is another excellent exercise—no impact and no stress on aching joints. If your loved one is overweight, no problem either. The water will help support him as it provides needed resistance and exercise. Many pools even offer water exercise or aerobics tailored to seniors. Some private pools also may have free community days if, for example, a city or municipality donated the land for the facility in exchange for the community service.

---

### WISE WALKING WAYS

- *Make it a regular morning routine.*
- *Try a half-hour at a conversational pace.*
- *Walk with a partner, because that's added incentive.*
- *Have that conversation while walking.*

**Source:** Gary J. Kennedy, MD, geriatric psychiatrist

## Other Ways for Seniors to Stay Active

Older generations have much to offer the world, no matter their age. Their skills, vision, experiences, wisdom, and knowledge helped define who we are as a nation as well as who we are as individuals.

Plenty of volunteer opportunities exist for the aging to share their skills and wisdom with others. Private, public, nonprofit, religious, business, and other organizations have all kinds of programs from grandparenting to tutoring, construction to gardening, and simply visiting other seniors. Some may even offer small stipends. Talk to your parent's local Agency on Aging for opportunities in their community.

If you're a caregiver for an elderly parent or loved one, consider ways in which that person might get involved, including with their own family members. Such activity is good for mind, body, ego, and soul. Encourage your children to spend time with your parent or parents. Not only will they learn about your family and enjoy the interaction with a different generation, but also chances are they'll look and learn. That learning can include recognizing the importance of planning ahead and saving as a means to having options in their own old age.

## Eat Right

Physical activity should be combined with good nutrition for optimal health and well-being of both caregivers and the cared-for. That means eating right, eating regularly, and avoiding what's not good for you. Nutrients that are especially important to seniors include vitamin D and calcium, whole grains, omega-3 fatty acids, and antioxidants. Seniors, along with almost everyone else, also need to pay special attention to breakfast. A nutritious morning meal is a perfect way to kick-start energy levels for the day.

The elderly, particularly if they live alone, can become depressed and may not eat regularly or properly, and can become sick or rundown as a result. Remember

Bob and his wife from earlier in the book? Bob's failing mother moved in with them and suddenly perked up when she started eating regularly. She had simply lost interest in cooking for herself and eating alone.

If a senior seems uninterested in eating, you might also consider getting her teeth checked. Loose teeth, ill-fitting dentures, and other dental problems can make chewing difficult or painful. Also, proper dental hygiene helps ward off infections of the mouth and gums, which can lead to serious health problems. Of course, dental hygiene is just as important for the other half of your generational sandwich. Helping your children establish good dental habits—including regular checkups and daily flossing—can prevent major dental problems, and expense, further down the road.

*Check out the government-sponsored Web site*
*"Eat 5 to 9 Servings of Fruits and Vegetables a Day*
*for Better Health"* (http://5aday.nci.nih.gov/)
*for information on healthy eating.*

Clarice was 77 and obviously slowing down. She had health issues, but generally they were under control, and barring any unforeseen issues, she could expect to live for many more years. But Clarice lived alone and admittedly was lonely, especially for companionship at mealtimes. For a time she and her neighbor shared meals, but then the neighbor moved away. Eventually Clarice, who had spent her life cooking for a crowd, lost interest. "Who wants to cook for just one?" she lamented. Luckily, a thorough chewing-out from her daughter, more frequent shared meals with her family, and some unusual and interesting cookbooks revived Clarice's enthusiasm for food. She started paying more attention to eating properly and regularly and began to feel like her old self again.

If an aging loved one seems lethargic and uninterested in eating, perhaps a nutrition or cooking class may get them back on track. Local senior programs, hospitals, and other organizations often offer low-cost classes. The Internet and sites like those of the American

Dietetic Association *(www.eatright.org)* and the National Institutes of Health *(www.nih.gov)* and its various Web sites also are valuable sources of free nutrition information. Programs such as Meals on Wheels may be able to help, too.

## Remember:

- Decisions about someone else's future should not be made unilaterally. Include that person and his spouse or partner as well as your siblings in any major decision making.
- In order to maintain their independence longer, seniors sometimes need to recognize that they must compromise and give up a little.
- Poor driving ability is not synonymous with aging, but it's important to pay attention to how well a senior drives. She may no longer be safe on the road.
- Don't belittle or accuse when addressing the driving issue with an older loved one. Instead, be compassionate and understanding.
- If a senior loses his ability to drive, help them by offering other options for personal mobility.
- Physical activity is essential for caregivers and the elderly alike to promote health and well-being now and in the future.
- Physical inactivity can lead to higher medical bills for the aging.
- Exercising your brain is every bit as important as physical activity. The brain is a muscle; use it!

# Knowing What's Right for Your Situation

## Chapter 5

**D**etermining the right choices for an aging parent can be agonizing for everyone involved. Whatever decisions you make will have emotional and fiscal (direct or indirect) repercussions across the generational sandwich, too.

Truthfully, there probably isn't any single answer for any given situation but, instead, myriad approaches to myriad issues. It's no easy task to identify the pertinent issues and then choose the appropriate combination of solutions that will work for your elderly loved one, you as the adult child and/or caregiver, and your children, if any.

The process can be an emotionally and physically draining catch-22. What might work best for one of the parties involved often fails to satisfy the needs or concerns of the others. These decisions, after all, will affect the rest of someone's life and beyond—and money is invariably an issue. Adding to the stress of the situation is the fact that it's tough for grown children to accept a loved one's aging and for the senior to accept his loss of independence, as well.

But you can take certain steps to help ensure that your aging loved one, you, and the rest of the family make choices that are financially, physically, and emotionally sound. Let's look more closely.

## Involve Everyone in the Decisions

**W**e've said this before, but it's worth saying again. Because these decisions affect everyone, everyone needs to be involved in the

## SOURCES OF INFORMATION

- *AARP (www.aarp.org/families/). Plenty of helpful information.*
- *Area Agencies on Aging (www.eldercarelocator.gov). Counties across the United States have local offices that can provide information, services, and direction.*
- *AGS Foundation for Health in Aging (www.healthinaging .org). A national nonprofit organization founded by the American Geriatrics Society to advocate on behalf of older adults and their special health care needs. Click on "Public Education" for resources and information.*
- *CarePlanner (www.careplanner.org). A free service of the Centers for Medicare and Medicaid Services, this online interactive tool can help seniors or caregivers understand different living options.*
- *Eldercare Locator (www.eldercare.gov/ Eldercare/Public/Home.asp). A service from the U.S. Administration on Aging, it connects older Americans and their caregivers with sources of information on senior services.*
- *Elder Connections (www.elder-connections .com). A suburban Philadelphia–based, elder care management group.*
- *Health in Aging (www.healthinaging.org). From the American Geriatric Society, full of helpful health and aging resources.*

- *Local mental health associations (www .nmha.org/affiliates/directory). Chapter locator from the National Mental Health Association.*
- *National Association of Home Care (www .nahc.org). Trade association representing the interests and concerns of home-care agencies, hospices, home-care aide organizations, and medical equipment suppliers; click on "Consumers" for tons of information on the kinds of services available.*
- *National Association of Professional Geriatric Care Managers (www.caremanager.org). A nonprofit organization of professional practitioners committed to working toward quality care for the elderly and their families through education, advocacy, and high standards of professional practice.*
- *SeniorNet® (www.seniornet.org). A nonprofit with information and reading on everything from education, books, and money to health, volunteering, and more.*
- *Senior Solutions of America (www .aging-parents-and-elder-care.com and www.todaysseniors.com). These sites include plenty of useful information from Elder Care 101 to the elderly and their pets, prescription drugs, living solutions, checklists, and more.*

decision-making process, especially the person whose future you're deciding. That sounds pretty elementary: let's ask Mom and Dad what they would like to do with their own lives. But that doesn't always happen among the Sandwich Generation. The reasons vary, and the blame doesn't lie only with the sandwiched.

Elderly parents or grandparents often are afraid to speak up, either out of fear or that "I-don't-want-to-be-a-burden" guilt syndrome. Also, as discussed earlier, the elderly can be averse to change, thinking somehow that the status quo and familiarity equate to independence. Sometimes they also are confused or simply take longer to think things through—a normal part of aging—and are badgered into accepting decisions they wouldn't have chosen for themselves.

Even if the senior is asked for her opinion and offers one, it may be ignored. "They're old. What do they know?" or "They're out of touch" or "I know best" are familiar, albeit unfortunate, refrains. And, of course, there's always the adult child who insists that an elderly loved one's options are limited because of finances. In many cases, the options are limited because the child won't allow the parent's or grandparent's home to be sold to pay for care. For those adult children, the home represents their inheritance—not their loved one's retirement.

Instead of the impatient or unfair approach, talk to your aging parent or loved one. Be respectful of them and their dignity. Their opinions do matter, and they deserve a say in their future. Put yourself in their place and think about how you would feel in a similar situation. In talking with them, give them choices rather than simply asking them what they want to do. The latter may be too broad and too confusing.

Nate and Judy had it all planned. They would stay in the family's home together until one died, then the surviving spouse would sell the house and use the proceeds to move into Gateway Acres, a lush retirement community nearby. The only problem was, as Nate found out after Judy died, that the plan was unrealistic.

When he presented his plan to his two adult kids, they crunched the numbers for him, and he realized he couldn't afford the high cost of Gateway Acres even with their help. In fact, because he didn't have savings or investments other than proceeds from the home sale—and no long-term care insurance—Nate couldn't afford to live in any acceptable facility without his adult children's financial help. Luckily, though, his children were able to help him, and they found Shady Home, a

## NATE'S FINANCES

**Proceeds from home sale**

| | | |
|---|---|---|
| Sale price: | $ 450,000 | |
| Less expenses | | |
| Real estate agent fee: | $ 22,000 | |
| Repair-for-sale costs: | $ 7,000 | |
| Moving expenses: | $ 2,000 | |
| Closing costs: | $ 10,000 | |
| Home equity loan: | $ 37,000 | |
| | $ 78,000 | |
| **Balance left:** | **$372,000** | |

**Annual income**

| | | |
|---|---|---|
| Return on investment, 5% rate: | $ 18,600 | |
| Social Security, $1,200/month: | $ 14,400 | |
| | $ 33,000 | |

**Retirement living choices**

| | Gateway Acres | Shady Home |
|---|---|---|
| Monthly fee: | $ 9,000 | $ 4,320 |
| Monthly spending: | $ 400 | $ 200 |
| Medical costs (Rx inc.): | $ 320 | $ 320 |
| **Total:** | **$ 9,720** | **$ 4,840** |
| **Annual cost:** | **$116,640** | **$58,080** |
| **Shortfall:** | **$ 83,640** | **$25,080** |
| **Cost to children (each):** | **$ 41,820** | **$12,540** |

quiet, albeit smaller and less flashy community that together they could afford. If only Nate, Judy, and their kids had talked about their ideas for future living arrangements sooner.

Sadly, little more than half of boomers talk with their parents about their living arrangements, according to the Pew Research Center's 2005 baby boomers study. The percentages of boomers who discuss other issues with their parents are broken down as follows:

- Parents' health, 85 percent
- Parents' living arrangements, 53 percent
- Parents' financial situation, 52 percent

- Parents' treatment wishes regarding terminal illness, 47 percent
- Parent's will, 44 percent
- Boomer's financial situation, 42 percent

Even fewer of the Sandwich Generation discuss their living arrangements with their adult children, according to Pew. What do boomers talk about with their adult kids?

- Kid's financial situation, 60 percent
- Boomer's financial situation, 43 percent
- Boomer's health, 57 percent
- Boomer's will, 37 percent
- Boomer's living arrangements, 36 percent
- Boomer's treatment wishes if terminal illness, 35 percent

*Beware the 'I-don't-want-to-be-a-burden' syndrome in an elderly person. It often clouds their true feelings.*

To ensure that whatever choices are made for a loved one really and truly work for all involved, include everyone—even your own children—in major decisions. Hold a family meeting to talk about the issues. After all, family dynamics play a big role in successful caregiving. It may make perfect financial sense to bring Mom, who suffers from dementia, home to live with you, but what if that alienates your teenage son or daughter? What if you didn't realize the ramifications of the severity of Mom's illness? What if your husband's salary gets slashed in an across-the-board corporate move and you have to return to work full time?

You must address these and more questions honestly before any decisions are made.

Lou, who supported his 67-year-old, relatively healthy mom, knew she had memory problems. In fact, her doctors had said they thought she had the "beginnings" of dementia. But she appeared relatively OK other than forgetting things occasionally, and continued to live alone in a nice house near Lou that he had purchased for her several years earlier. One night he got the call from a trucker in Chicago. It seems his mom had gone out for groceries six hours earlier, had gotten lost, and ended up driving the wrong way on Interstate 94 outside of Chicago, which was 170 miles away. Luckily no one, including Lou's mom, had been hurt. Once Lou realized the severity of his mom's condition, he talked with her and her doctors, and she relinquished the car and moved to an assisted-living facility.

## Educate and Assess

Before making any decisions regarding an aging parent's living situation (more on living alternatives in Chapter 6) or how that parent should handle his life and finances, first educate yourself on the issues. You probably are well aware of many of them. After all, what has brought you to this point of decision making? Mom or Dad has fallen, has slowed down, is sick, has shaky finances, is afraid to leave the house, or is in some other tenuous situation.

*Leave out the emotion when assessing a loved one's situation.*

Start by considering the general concerns of the elderly such as health, health care, mobility, nutrition, caregiving, living options, and more. Plenty of organizations and Web sites, as well as printed material—including this book—can help you understand these issues and become familiar with the outside help and support services available.

Don't get into too many specifics, however, because at this point you are simply getting a working overview so you can better understand the issues and ask more pertinent questions of potential providers. More detailed research comes a bit later in the process.

Talk to your parent's medical providers, too. What, if any, medical issues are involved? When it comes to their health, elderly parents often don't truly understand their medical condition, refuse to accept it, or avoid being totally honest about it with their children. Ask these medical professionals what they think of your parent's current living situation and what makes the most sense strictly from their patient's point of view. Also ask for any suggestions. Lou's mom's doctor might have suggested closer supervision for his patient as a way to avoid incidents like the interstate debacle. Doctors and other health professionals often know of out-of-the-norm solutions or unadvertised but highly sought-after and excellent caregiving options.

Now you're ready to make an honest, unemotional, and straightforward assessment of your aging loved

## LOOK AT WHAT'S OUT THERE

*Many Americans mistakenly hesitate to turn to government resources for help in determining what's best for an elderly parent. Here's a look at some of the information available from the U.S. Department of Health and Human Services Administration on Aging Web site (www.aoa.gov) and many local area Agency on Aging offices:*

- *Adult day care in centers that provide companionship, interaction, and health-related services to the aging in a protected setting*
- *Caregiver programs such as the National Family Caregiver Support Program, which offers programs and services for caregivers of older adults and some limited services to grandparents raising grandchildren*
- *Case management, in which experts will work with you to assess your and your senior's efforts for her to remain independent, including arranging for any further services if needed*
- *Contact and safety checks of seniors by trained volunteers*
- *Elder-abuse prevention programs that include investigating allegations of abuse, neglect, and exploitation of seniors*
- *Financial assistance that begins with benefit counseling programs*

- *Home health care when it's needed*
- *Home repair and modification programs that help older people maintain their homes; this can involve volunteers, grants, loans, or other assistance*
- *Identifying available senior housing options*
- *Information and referral assistance to link you with available resources*
- *Legal advice and representation to those age 60 and up for some legal matters such as government program benefits and consumer problems or tenant rights*
- *Nutritious meals through services such as Meals on Wheels for the homebound*
- *Personal care to help those with functional impairments ranging from dressing to housekeeping, supervision, and walking*
- *Respite care from the constant/continued supervision, companionship, therapeutic, and/or personal care of a person with a functional impairment*
- *Senior center programs for active and less-active older people*
- *Transportation options to qualified elderly or individuals with disabilities*
- *Volunteer options for seniors*

one's existing situation. Objectively assess their physical and mental health, finances, physical abilities, capabilities, and existing support system. What kinds of services or care, if any, do they need to remain independent, or

## TIPS TO EASE THE STRESS

The nonprofit National Association of Professional Geriatric Care Managers offers a few suggestions for adult children in dealing with their aging parents:

■ Be honest. If you are concerned about their needs, say so. State this in an "I" message much the same way you do with young children. For example, "I am concerned about your diet. You seem to be losing weight." Or, "I noticed that you call me often and forget we have just talked. Are you concerned about your memory? I am."

■ When parents frequently call long distance and complain about vague symptoms, sometimes they are telling you that they are scared or lonely. Try to get to the underlying issue and don't focus so much on the vague symptoms. All medical complaints need to be evaluated by a health care professional.

■ Tell your parent that you respect their autonomy. Wanting them to be independent and to support their independence, you need to know about a few important items to help them when and if and emergency presents itself:

— What kind of legal planning have they done? If they become disabled, could you or another party take over your parent's affairs without going to the court system? This means your parent has a trust and durable powers of attorney for health and finances in place.

—Talk about your parent's finances. What is her monthly income? Where does the in-

come come from? What are his assets? Get a list of bank accounts and brokerage accounts. Is the income sufficient to meet your parent's needs? Your parent could be entitled to some government programs if he or she is low income or even middle income.

—What medical insurance does your parent have, and what are the account numbers of those policies? What is your parent's Social Security number? Does he have life insurance policies or long-term care policies? If so, get the names and phone numbers of the companies.

—Has your parent prepaid for funeral and/or burial expenses? Where has she done this? What is the phone number of the mortuary and/or cemetery?

—Who is your parent's doctor(s)? What medications is your parent currently taking? List them all and ask what each medication is for. Ask if your parent takes any over-the-counter medications, vitamins, or herbs.

—How often does your parent see friends? Do you have the name and phone number of a friend he visits with often?

—Is your parent drinking alcohol? If yes, how much?

—Is your parent driving safely? Does she have convenient transportation?

**Source:** National Association of Professional Geriatric Care Managers (www.caremanager.org); reprinted with permission.

is a change of living situation in the offing? Ditch the emotion and be blunt with yourself, your spouse or partner, your siblings, your children, your elderly parent, his or her medical professionals, and any other experts involved.

This also may be a good time to bring in an outside trained professional, such as a professional geriatric care manager, to help analyze the situation. Your local area administration or Agency on Aging generally will provide someone to do an assessment and provide a list of available services and providers. A professional geriatric care manager, on the other hand, will perform that comprehensive assessment of a senior's situation that we discussed earlier. (Remember, that includes an evaluation of all areas of a senior's life—health, finances, family, social network, safety, and more—followed by an analysis and a proposed individualized care plan and action plan.) Even a brief consult with a manager could be money well spent. These professionals not only are expert at solving problems like yours; they also provide an objective voice amid the emotion-filled universe of family and loved ones.

## Less Formal Alternative

Discovering if and how much assistance an older adult needs doesn't have to be an Inquisition-like process. It could be as simple as you, a friend, or a health professional dropping by one day. (Medicare usually covers the cost of a visiting nurse service's safety check and educational visit for an elderly person, if prescribed by a physician or qualified health professional.)

Make note of your general impressions. Is your parent's home in good array? Is his appearance neat or disheveled? Does she appear to be moving around easily, or is mobility labored? Can he get up easily, or does he need help? Can she see what she's doing, or are actions based on memory and familiarity? Also, ask if your parent is taking his medications on schedule, or you can check the pill box. If the box is labeled with the days of the week, is it being used and, if so, used properly?

Pay attention to what you've observed. If a parent has trouble moving and can't function well on his or her own, you may want to consider an environment with caregiving available, or even a move to your own home. If he or she has medical issues too, that could signal the need for a full- or part-time health care provider in their home, your home, an assisted-living facility, or some other assisted environment. If the parent is disheveled and the house in disarray, that could signal something more serious—perhaps a mental health issue such as depression, dementia, or Alzheimer's, or some physical limitation.

Don't lose sight of the fact, however, that even though a person may have difficulty seeing or even moving, he or she may function perfectly well in his own environment and does not need to move elsewhere.

At 97, Sarah's mind was sharp as a tack. Her eyesight wasn't as good as it once was, but her glasses compensated for that. Her arthritic knees were another story. She had great difficulty walking upright and on her own. But she had learned to move from room to room by holding onto chairs, tables, and other furniture strategically placed throughout her two-story house. The stairs weren't an issue either. Years earlier she and her now-deceased husband had had an elevator installed so he could get up and down easily. The end result was that she got along quite well.

Sarah's daughter lived 250 miles away but came up each week to see her mom. Sarah also had an active social circle of much younger people whom she thoroughly enjoyed. She even took a water aerobics class twice a week. Also, Mary, 70, came in five days a week to keep Sarah company and help out with the chores. As Sarah put it, "We're both too old, so we help each other."

For Sarah, her home was the perfect environment despite her disabilities and her advanced age.

Remember that any assessment is weighing the safety, quality of life, and long-term survival of a loved one, not necessarily what a sandwiched boomer sees as "what's best" for Mom or Dad. Each person must be acknowledged for who they are and the choices they make, says care manager Joie. "You do not have the right to tell them how to live their life. People—even old people—have the right to make poor decisions. And you as the adult child must come to terms with accepting what's so."

## Beyond Dollars and Cents Decisions

As is often the case, the best solution for your aging loved one's situation may not be the cheapest available. Any decision about what's right from a caregiving or living standpoint needs to take into account personalities, relationships, and the "normal" lifestyle of that aging relative. It also must include, if at all possible, the participation, preferences, concerns, and needs of the elderly person involved.

Remember Liza's mom, Marie, whom we mentioned in Chapter 4? Robbed of her independence by a fall, Marie had to depend on others for even simple things like eating, and she despised her situation. Compounding the problem, Marie moved in with Liza and her husband, refusing even to consider an assisted-living facility or nursing home. Liza didn't put up much of an argument either because after figuring her mom's finances (we'll talk more about that in Chapter 7), she decided the family couldn't afford the cost of a suitable assisted-living facility. Because of financial and other qualifications and restrictions, Medicaid would not have covered the cost. (More on that later.)

*Family emotional baggage should not figure into your decision on what's right for an elderly loved one.*

Perhaps Liza should have looked more closely at other options like home-health care or splitting her mom's caregiving with a part- or full-time housekeeper or even her own siblings.

From the beginning, sharing her home with her mom was a bumpy ride. Liza's mom wanted her independence and her own home back. The demands of caregiving forced Liza to pare back her work hours to part-time, cutting deeply into her family's income.

Liza and her mom fought constantly. It got so bad at one point that Marie screamed at Liza, calling her a Nazi and her home a concentration camp. That was the final straw that finally persuaded Liza to look at alternative living situations. She talked to her two sisters, who agreed to help financially, and together they found a nearby retirement community that offered varying levels of care—from retirement apartments with choice of meals provided, to assisted living and nursing home care.

The move was an immediate success. Marie was thrilled not to burden Liza with her care. She had her "independence" back. She started out in the assisted-living facility, but within a year—with the help of physical therapy and an active senior exercise program—she was able to move into her own apartment within the community. Today she's happy, healthy, and enjoying her family as a vibrant, independent human being. It's a bit of a financial stretch for Liza's family, but because Liza immediately was able to return to full-time employment, the move is definitely worth the extra effort.

As a bonus, Liza's sisters, who live out of town, don't feel as much animosity toward her now that their mom doesn't depend on her so much.

## To Move or Not

Trying to find the best situation for an elderly loved one can be a time of psychological upheaval for everyone involved. It can be a time of financial upheaval, as well. "People are spending an absolute fortune on end-of-life issues," says Joie. For example, a nursing home can cost $250 a day; assisted care can cost $3,000 to $5,000 a month; and home-health care runs $20 an hour or about $200 a day for a licensed, bonded, insured caregiver. And don't forget you're dealing with seniors. Not only did many of them grow up during the Depression, but they are now typically at a time in life where, financially, everything is going out and nothing is coming in. As a result, most seniors, whether they have money or not, are reluctant to spend—or "waste"—money.

Jane's aging mother, Ronda, is worth millions of dollars, yet Ronda refused to spend money for the home-health care she desperately needed. The only way Jane could persuade her mother to accept a home-health aide was by picking up the tab herself and saying the caregiver was from the county Office on Aging.

This and countless, similar scenarios have nothing to do with being cheap or stingy, says Joie. It's about fear. "Rich or poor, the elderly tend absolutely to be threatened when it comes to money expenditures for themselves."

## Remember:

- Educate yourself about the situation, then either make a formal assessment yourself or bring in an expert to do that.
- Be objective and honest in the assessment.
- Watch for red flags that might indicate a parent needs greater care, including changes in weight, short-term memory, usual routine, or speech or ambulation; bills unpaid; entering contests; refusing to go out with friends; refusing or agreeing to everything without considering the consequences; mood swings; and more.
- The solution to your aging loved one's situation involves much more than dollars and cents.
- Treat elderly loved ones with compassion and respect. Ask their opinions. They do matter.
- Don't automatically assume that the best solution means moving an elderly parent out of his or her longtime home.
- Don't make decisions out of emotion. Base your decisions on reason and reality instead.

# Planning Ahead: Documents and Decisions

**Chapter 6**

For members of the Sandwich Generation, surviving and thriving amid the stress and strain of today's big dollar squeeze requires planning. We plan to buy houses, cars, that big-screen TV, to pay for the kids' college, to try to save for retirement. We also need to plan for end-of-life issues—ours and those of our loved ones. Those plans should include building in cash and control for contingencies as well as accounting for and financing everyday life. Putting the plan into action sooner is better than later. But it's not too late to start now, either. If your elderly loved one didn't plan ahead and can't or won't do so now, do it for them. Otherwise, the financial burden can cripple you and your children.

Americans just don't do a very good job of planning much ahead, says Charles Sabatino, director of the American Bar Association's Commission on Law and Aging. That's especially true when it comes to supportive services and long-term care for the aging.

Forget the automatic response, "I can't do it." You can. Whatever your age and whether you have aging loved ones or children of your own or both, you (with the help of a professional, if necessary) can fill out the proper forms to have the necessary information in hand at the appropriate time. By handling certain matters today, you can spare yourself and your loved ones financial and emotional burdens later. And you needn't spend a fortune to put the basics in place.

Consider a few facts:

■ No matter what anyone tells you, the government will *not* pay for it all. If a couple retires today at age 65, they'll need $200,000 in savings just to supplement

Medicare and cover out-of-pocket health care costs in retirement unless they have an employer-funded retirement plan (based on Fidelity Employer Services Company study, 2006). And that doesn't even factor in annual 8.5 percent to 9 percent increases in health care costs, says wealth planner and NBC TV's *Talk About Money* host Jim Barry, CFP® and a Boca Raton, Florida–based wealth manager.

- Companies—like US Airways, United Airlines, and Bethlehem Steel, to name a few, are pulling out of employee "lifetime" pension plans. Companies also are going under or being sold off. Of course, the government's Pension Benefit Guarantee Corporation guarantees the pensions, but with limitations. The maximum guaranteed benefit as set by law for single-employer plans ended in 2006 is up to $3,971.51 a month (or $47,659.08 a year) for workers who retire at age 65. (The amount is lower for early retirees or survivor's benefits, and higher for those retiring after age 65.)

- The national average annual cost of a private room in a nursing home is more than $74,000, or $203 a day (according to "The MetLife Market Survey of Nursing Home & Home Care Costs," September 2005).

- The national average hourly rate for home-health aides is $19, and for homemakers/companions, $17 ("The MetLife Market Survey of Nursing Home & Home Care Costs," September 2005). If a loved one requires a health aide only three hours a day, seven days a week, the cost will be about $21,000 a year. Full-time home-health aide assistance will set someone back more than $166,000 a year!

It's easy to see that with the soaring costs of health care, retirement, living options, education, and life and death in general, we can't afford *not* to take the steps now to protect ourselves and our loved ones financially today and tomorrow.

People don't like to talk about the very real possibility that they will contract a chronic or debilitating condition or that they may need help as they age. "Although

## FOR MORE INFORMATION

- *Aging With Dignity (www.agingwithdignity .com). Its renowned low-cost ($5) Five Wishes health care directive form can be ordered on site.*
- *American Bar Association (www.abanet .org). To find an attorney, click on "Find Legal Help" or "Lawyer Locator." Lots of valuable information under Public Resources.*
- *Caring Connections (www.caringconnections .org). An informative Web site from the National Hospice and Palliative Care Organization.*
- *Davidow Davidow Siegal & Stern LLC (www .davidowlaw.com). Click on "Services and Resources" for helpful information. Downloadable free Health Care Proxy available under Resources.*
- *Family Caregiver Alliance® (www.caregiver .org). Community-based nonprofit with lots of helpful information on the issues. Click on "Fact Sheets & Publications."*
- *Financial Planning Association (www.fpanet .org). The membership organization for the financial planning community offers lots of information and an online tool to help you find the right professional to help you with your personal finance needs.*
- *Insurance Information Institute (www.iii .org). Nonprofit dedicated to improving the public's understanding and knowledge about insurance.*
- *Insurance rating organizations: A.M. Best Company (www.ambest.com); Standard & Poor's (www.standardandpoors.com); Weiss Ratings, Inc. (www.weissratings.com).*
- *Kiplinger (www.kiplinger.com). A source for all types of information on money and per-*

*sonal finances; free interactive tools available, too.*
- *Lawyers.com (www.lawyers.com). From highly reputable Martindale-Hubbell, get information or find an attorney.*
- *MetLife, Inc. (www.metlife.com). A leading provider of insurance and other financial services whose nonprofits include The MetLife Foundation and MetLife Mature Market Institute. Extensive information on a variety of issues, including Alzheimer's.*
- *National Academy of Elder Law Attorneys (www.naela.org). Five thousand–member organization of attorneys focusing on legal needs of the elderly. Click on "Public" for directories and resources.*
- *National Association of Insurance Commissioners (www.naic.org). Go to www.naic .org/state_web_map.htm to access links to state insurance department Web sites.*
- *National Elder Law Foundation (www.nelf .org). Nonprofit organization that offers certification for attorneys specializing in elder law. Click on "Find a CELA" to locate a certified elder law attorney.*
- *National Hospice and Palliative Care Organization (www.nhpco.org). Nonprofit with helpful information on advance directives as well as other end-of-life issues.*
- *Nolo (www.nolo.com). From a leader in do-it-yourself legal solutions and information for consumers, Nolo offers more than 300 books, software, and e-products including downloadable forms, and valuable free information. Click on "Family Law & Immigration," "Wills & Estate Planning," or "Resource Center."*

most of us like to think that we'll just go to sleep one day and not wake up the next, that's probably not going to be the case," says Sabatino. "But there are things you can do ahead of time, at least in terms of making sure your affairs are managed well," he adds.

## Do It Now

Sit down with your aging parent or parents and talk finances openly and honestly. As much as Americans dislike discussing money, it's essential to do so. Remember, as we mentioned in Chapter 5, just more than half of boomers willingly talk to their parents about their finances. It's especially important to have the talk while a parent still is healthy and mentally sharp. Don't wait for a crisis, when a parent might not be lucid, can't understand the issues, is overwhelmed, or no longer cares, says Barry, who's been among the sandwiched and now is a senior himself.

> *"Communicate, communicate, communicate with parents. Do it now while their minds are still sharp."*
>
> —Jim Barry, CFP®, wealth manager and host of NBC TV's Talk About Money

Two years ago, elder law specialist Lawrence Davidow suddenly found himself in the position of caregiver when his father developed an infection and had to be hospitalized. Until that time, the elder Davidow had been active and thriving. A lawyer like his son, at age 82 he still worked regularly. The junior Davidow is managing partner with Long Island, New York–based Davidow, Davidow, Siegel & Stern LLP, and president of the National Academy of Elder Law Attorneys.

"All of a sudden it was thrown on me, and I'm an hour and a half away trying to run a business—not to mention all the stuff I do with the National Academy of Elder Law Attorneys and three kids. It was my first wide-eyed view of what my clients had been going through," Davidow recalls.

Davidow's father remained hospitalized for a month and then required several months of at-home recovery. "He needed me," says the junior Davidow. "He needed me to coordinate things. He needed me to make sure his bills got paid. He needed me to talk to the doctors, especially in the beginning. And when it all started, I didn't even know what medications he was taking. Although I have his power of attorney and I have his health care proxy and his living will—I have all those documents in place—I didn't know where his assets were or how he had invested them."

In other words, Davidow, like many adult children thrust into the caregiving role when their aging parents fall ill, wasn't totally prepared. With many of the general documents in place, he was steps ahead of most Americans, but he still hadn't done enough.

---

**TIPS FROM REAL LIFE**

*Are you and/or your aging parents worried about paying for the future?*

- *Talk to each other now about finances and documents before you're in crisis mode.*
- *Ask for specifics, such as: How much is the house worth? What investments do you have and what are they worth? How much do you have in savings?*
- *Find out and list names, account and policy numbers, and contact numbers.*
- *If a parent hasn't prepared the necessary documents and can't afford to do so now, pick up the tab for them. You can't afford not to.*
- *While you're talking money with your parents, ask yourself whether you're prepared—with the right documentation in place—to accept any inheritances without complications.*
- *If any potential inheritance is meant for a specific child or use, do you need any special trusts in place?*
- *Do you have the proper financial advisors?*
- *Do you have a will, powers of attorney, health care directives, and trusts so that your own estate can avoid probate?*

---

The end result, says Davidow, is that he demanded his father get more organized, and he now insists his clients do the same.

"The assumption by adult children that Mom or Dad's affairs are pretty much in order so we really don't need to sit down and talk about it is a fantasy," adds Sabatino. "There's a need for a lot more communication than I think takes place until a crisis arises and then people realize how disorganized things really are, especially around capacity issues" pertaining to the ability of an individual to make his or her own decisions and manage their own affairs.

Let's look more closely at what needs to be done, beginning with the necessary documents, decisions, and paperwork.

## A Will

A will is a legal document that designates how someone's possessions, assets, and property will be disbursed after death. In other words, who gets what. If you die without a will—called dying intestate—the state will decide how your assets are divided based strictly on its property distribution formula. The absence of a will adds to the headaches, heartaches, and squabbling that can engulf families after a loved one dies. It doesn't matter if the fight is over who gets the silk scarves or the Jaguar.

Wills generally should be drawn up by a lawyer. If you do it yourself, at the very least have it reviewed by an attorney to ensure it conforms to the legal requirements of your state. Also, make sure it's notarized and that the notary's commission hasn't expired.

For the do-it-yourselfers, will forms are available at some stationery and office supply stores, and also are downloadable off the Internet; some sites will even walk you through the process of filling them out *(www.lawdepot.com; www.allaboutlaw.com; www.medlawplus.com; www.legaldocs.com)*. Kiplinger *(www.kiplinger.com)*, for example, offers a "Your Family Records Organizer," which includes copies of necessary forms.

*Choose the executor of a will carefully. Family politics and differences can get pretty ugly after a parent dies.*

Besides specifying who gets what, a will also names an executor, a person designated by the testator (the person making the will) to carry out his wishes and oversee the administration of the estate. Executors generally receive a stipend for their time, although it's not required. Stipend amounts vary, and are subjective, often depending on the size and complexity of the estate.

Wills also should name a backup executor to take over the responsibilities in case the person who is first choice must step aside or can't serve.

The choice of an executor for an estate is totally up to the testator. But it may not be quite as simple as it sounds. Before Mom or Dad automatically names you, an older brother, or sister as executor, they may want to think again. Remember all those family dynamics we've talked about? After a parent dies, especially when money is involved, personality differences, accusations, dislikes, and more can exacerbate an already difficult situation. A parent may want to consider naming a nonfamily member—or, at the least, a nonheir—as executor. Or, that unbiased person could serve as coexecutor. That way, an heir must bounce ideas off the other coexecutor and, in effect, keep a lid on the situation, suggests Phillip E. Cook, CFP®, and a Torrance, California–based financial planner, investment counselor, author, and lecturer.

"A lot depends on the maturity and relationships among siblings," adds Cook. "When adult kids don't have money, that's when the feeding frenzy occurs. The more unemotional a parent can be about assessing the personalities and the amount of money each should get—and the more realistic she can be—the better the decisions they will make."

Parents can help their children avoid falling prey to the vulture syndrome. If an aging parent knows in advance of something a particular child would like to have, he can specifically designate it for that child in the will. Another suggestion: Divide the inheritance equally among your children, no matter their financial or marital status. That will go a long way toward diffusing anxieties and tensions among family members.

A few other points to remember:

- Different states have different property and probate laws.
- If an elderly loved one moves to another state, the will must be reviewed to make sure it conforms to the laws of the new state.
- Assets such as life insurance policies, pension plans, and POD (payable on death) certificates of deposit generally are handled outside of the will and paid directly to the beneficiaries (unless a beneficiary isn't specified, and then they become a general asset handled by the will).
- Keep several copies of the will in different places other than a safe-deposit box, which is sealed when a person dies and not opened until well into the probate process.

# Durable Financial Power of Attorney

This legal document designates an individual— perhaps the caregiver—to make financial and legal decisions for someone else, such as an elderly loved one, and to make financial transactions on their behalf. It goes into effect on signing unless it's designated as a springing power of attorney, which delays its implementation until such time as the loved one becomes incapacitated in some way and can't make financial decisions. If your parent opts for a springing power, be sure the document is clear on how the "incapacitation" will be determined and by whom.

Again, make sure that your parent or loved one understands the importance of choosing an agent with durable power carefully. This is, after all, someone who will control his or her monies. Horror stories abound about the caregiver or family member who, once given the control, abused the privilege. The classic story is that of the wealthy man who lies helpless in a double room in a second-rate nursing home while his son, who holds the purse strings, and his family live comfortably on Dad's money.

*An individual must be competent to execute a durable power of attorney. If his or her cognizance could be in question and the power challenged, have a qualified physician certify the individual's competence.*

Financial power of attorney designation ends when the other person dies. His or her assets are sealed, too, until the will has been read and an executor named. If you're concerned about possible payment-due expenses immediately after a parent's death, talk to that parent while he or she is cognizant about perhaps setting up a separate bank account in your name for just such a purpose. Another option is that the parent could take out a POD certificate of deposit to you or someone else—the child with financial concerns, perhaps—so that shortly after the parent's death, the money could become available.

If an individual becomes incapacitated, can't make decisions, and doesn't have a designated power of attorney or anyone with legal authority to make decisions, the courts will appoint a conservator to take control of that person's assets. This conservatorship also ensures the court's continued oversight that those assets are being handled correctly for the benefit of the incapacitated individual.

# Health Care Proxy

Known by various names including health care proxy, durable power of attorney for health care, and health care directive, this document designates another individual or agent to make health care and medical decisions for someone in the event they can't make them for themselves.

Generally it is separate from a living will, although some living wills also may name an individual as having health care power of attorney. Make sure your loved one also designates a backup or alternate individual with health care power of attorney in case the primary person can't act on their behalf. Life-and-death decisions often can be extremely difficult in emotional circumstances.

NAELA's Davidow goes one step further with the proxy to ensure it's readily available anywhere. Each of his clients fills out the form (see Figure 6.1), which is then shrunk down to wallet size and put in a protective plastic case. Davidow also asks his clients to include in the case the names and phone numbers of their doctors and a list of medications they're taking with the dosage and times. "That's critical information that can save somebody's life," he says.

More tips from Davidow:

- Do not designate your doctor as the one to make your health care decisions. A physician cannot be your attending doctor and agent at the same time.
- Give your health care agent or surrogate a signed copy of the proxy and make sure that she also knows your feelings about life-support systems and artificial nutrition.
- An individual who has a health care proxy can make his own health care decisions until he's no longer capable.

## Living Will

Aliving will is a document that stipulates in writing what a person does or doesn't want with regard to artificial life support and treatment in the event he or she becomes incapacitated. Its importance was magnified in 2005 with the notorious case of Terry Schiavo, the Florida woman kept alive by an artificial feeding tube literally for years while her husband and parents fought over removing it. Though Schiavo reportedly had told her husband she never wanted life support, her wishes weren't written down.

Discuss with your elderly loved ones their feelings about artificial life support, artificial resuscitation in the event of respiratory failure, the issue of pain control,

**FIGURE 6.1 POCKETSIZE PROXY**

# Health Care Proxy

**(1)** I, _____, hereby appoint _____, residing at _____, whose telephone number is _____, as my health care agent to make any and all health care decisions for me, except to the extent that I state otherwise. This proxy shall take effect when and if I become unable to make my own health care decisions.

**(2)** Optional: I direct my agent to make health care decisions in accord with my wishes and limitations as stated below, or as he or she otherwise knows.

*This health care proxy contains no limitations. I have discussed my wishes with my Agent and Substitute Agent and each knows my wishes concerning artificial nutrition and hydration.*

**(3)** Optional: I hereby make an anatomical gift, to be effective upon my death of: (check all that apply)

☐ Any needed organs and/or tissues
☐ The following organs and/or tissues: _____
☐ Limitations: _____

If you do not state your wishes or instructions about organ and/or tissue donation on this form, it will not be taken to mean that you do not wish to make a donation or prevent a person, who is otherwise authorized by law, to consent to a donation on your behalf.

**(4)** Name of substitute or fill-in agent if the person I appoint above is unable, unwilling or unavailable to act as my health care agent: _____, residing at _____, whose telephone number is _____.

**(5)** Unless I revoke it, this proxy shall remain in effect indefinitely, or until the date or conditions stated below. This proxy shall expire (specific date or conditions, if desired): _____

**(6)** Signature: _____

Address: _____

Date: _____

**Statement by Witnesses** (must be 18 or older and cannot be the health care agent or alternate): I declare that the person who signed this document is personally known to me and appears to be of sound mind and acting of his or her own free will. He or she signed (or asked another to sign for him or her) this document in my presence.

Witness 1 _____

Address _____

Witness 2 _____

Address _____

**DAVIDOW, DAVIDOW, SIEGEL & STERN, LLP**

| | |
|---|---|
| **One Suffolk Square - Suite 330** | **13105 Main Road** |
| **1601 Veterans Memorial Highway - Islandia, NY 11749** | **Mattituck, NY 11952** |
| **Tel (631) 234-3030  Fax (631) 234-3140** | **Tel (631) 298-9600 • fax (631) 761-0370** |

*Executing the above health care proxy form does not in any way take the place of legal advice from a qualified elder law attorney. The above health care proxy form does not in any way take the place of a well thought out estate plan. It is only one element of incapacity planning and should be used in conjunction with a more complete estate plan.

*continued*

**FIGURE 6.1 POCKETSIZE PROXY, continued**

# HEALTH INSURANCE PORTABILITY AND ACCOUNTABILITY ACT

## HIPAA Release Form

I, _____, hereby authorize the release of my individually identifiable protected health information to my "personalrepresentative" pursuant to 45 C.F.R. Section 164.502 (g)(2).

I intend that my "personal representative" be treated as I would, with respect to my rights regarding the use and disclosure of my individually identifiable protected health information and/or any other medical records.

I authorize any physician, health-care professional, dentist, health plan, hospital, clinic, laboratory, pharmacy, or other health care provider, insurance company, Medical Information Bureau, Inc. (or other healthcare clearing-house), or any other health care provider that has provided treatment or services to me or that has paid for or is seekingpayment for such services; to give, disclose and release to my "personal representative," without restriction, all of my individually identifiable health care information and medical records regarding past, present or future medical or mental health conditions.

This authorization shall supersede any prior agreement I may have made with my health care providers to restrict access to or disclosure of my individually identifiable health information. This authorization has no expiration date and shall not require any re-authorization by me at any particular time interval and may be revoked by me in writing and delivered to my health care provider.

For purposes of this release, the term "personal representative" shall include but shall not be limited to the agent under a "Health Care Proxy."

_____
Signature

_____
Date

Witnesses:

_____

_____

**DAVIDOW, DAVIDOW, SIEGEL & STERN, LLP**

| | |
|---|---|
| **One Suffolk Square - Suite 330** | **13105 Main Road** |
| **1601 Veterans Memorial Highway - Islandia, NY 11749** | **Mattituck, NY 11952** |
| **Tel (631) 234-3030 • Fax (631) 234-3140** | **Tel (631) 298-9600 • fax (631) 761-0370** |

*Executing the above health care proxy form does not in any way take the place of legal advice from a qualified elder law attorney. The above health care proxy form does not in any way take the place of a well thought out estate plan. It is only one element of incapacity planning and should be used in conjunction with a more complete estate plan.

and whether they want to receive certain drugs but not others. All this and more can be included in a living will. Be very specific about what is and is not acceptable. (See Health Care Decision Planning, below.)

Of note, however, unless specifically addressed in writing, artificial resuscitation will occur in the event of respiratory failure. If an elderly loved one does *not* want to be resuscitated, he or she must have a specific do not resuscitate (DNR) order. Also make sure that a living will is specific as to what types of life support are acceptable and what types aren't.

Several organizations offer guidance, documents, and help with living will preparation. Aging With Dignity, a well-known nonprofit organization, offers its Five Wishes document for $5 (*www.agingwithdignity.org*).

Once the living will is completed, make sure it's easily accessible and that your loved one's doctor has a copy and is aware of her wishes.

For three years, Kathy and Ray had watched their best friend waste away on feeding tubes and respirators and had vowed not to let the same thing happen to each other. They had their attorney draw up living wills that specified in the event of respiratory failure do not resuscitate and no respirators. Period. They also stipulated no life support of any kind. They thought they had it covered.

But they had made one big mistake that proved costly financially and emotionally. Kathy and Ray put the signed documents in their safe-deposit box at the bank without giving copies to their doctor or keeping a copy at home with them. The result: Ray had a massive heart attack and was rushed to the hospital in the middle of the night. He didn't have his living will with him, his doctor didn't have a copy nor did anyone else, and so the hospital officials connected him to life support. A drawn-out court battle ensued, and he finally was removed from life support a year later. Kathy and their children watched in agony as Ray hung on in a vegetative state for a year.

Beyond the emotional toll, the ordeal cost Ray's widow a sizable amount of cash. Although Medicare and

---

## HEALTH CARE DECISION PLANNING

*Following are questions to consider as part of your health care decision making, according to the National Academy of Elder Law Attorneys:*

- *What are your desires with regard to artificial nutrition and hydration?*
- *Who will serve as your agent for health care? Who will serve as the alternate?*
- *Do you wish to limit transfusions to blood provided by family members and/or friends?*
- *Do you wish to state your preference between home care and nursing home care, or will you allow your agent for health care to make placement decisions?*
- *Are there certain medical treatments or pain control measures that you would like to be sure to have and others that you would like to refuse?*
- *Do you wish to refuse treatment if it means greater dependency upon others?*
- *Do you wish to refuse treatment if it means having to suffer chronic pain?*
- *Do you wish to take pain medication that will reduce or eliminate the ability to communicate?*
- *Do you have any particular wishes regarding specific health care facilities, religious preferences, disposition of your body, donation of bodily parts for transplant or research, etc.?*

**Source:** *National Academy of Elder Law Attorneys (www.naela.org); reprinted with permission.*

---

the couple's supplemental or "Medigap" insurance picked up much of the cost, Ray was in a private room and had other extras like a private nurse that weren't covered by their insurance.

## Pet Directive

Does an elderly parent have a trusted four-legged companion or, for that matter, even a bird or an exotic pet? If so, the pet's care needs to be accounted for in the event its master becomes incapacitated, hospitalized, has to move to assisted living or a nursing home, or is uprooted in some other way.

Talk to aging parents about their wishes regarding their faithful companion. What would they like to happen to the pet if it no longer can live with them? Who should care for the pet? How will its care be financed? Who is the pet's veterinarian, where is the vet's office, and what is the contact number? Does the parent have any special requests for when the pet dies? As insignificant as all this may seem to some non-pet owners, what happens to an adored pet is a very big deal to an aging individual who may live alone. Making the arrangements now can go a long way toward providing your loved one with welcome peace of mind.

## Funeral Directive

"My mom took care of her funeral before she died—the cost and all the details down to the music, the Scripture, and the headstone. It made it very easy for us. I thank her so much for it," says one 50-something sandwiched child.

*The nonprofit Funeral Consumers Alliance (www.funerals.org) can help families and loved ones better understand their choices and rights when it comes to choosing an affordable funeral.*

At the other end of the spectrum, another 50-something child recounts his nightmare after his mom died. "Choosing the casket was the hardest thing I've ever done in my life," he recalls. "I was overcome."

More people today are preplanning their funerals with the help of funeral directives that stipulate the details down to the minutiae, if desired. In some cases, economics prompts the planning. Funeral homes and cemeteries often offer discounts if someone prepays. Prepaid funeral expenses also can be one way to spend down an elderly person's assets so that they qualify for Medicaid (more on that later). For others, it's simply a way to close their lives in the manner they desire.

Many of us find it difficult to confront our mortality. But talking about end-of-life issues such as a funeral directive is one way an elderly parent can help his or her adult child cope with the parent's eventual death.

## HIPAA Documents

We're all becoming accustomed to it these days. Every time you visit a medical provider, they thrust that HIPAA document at you to sign yet again. HIPAA stands for the Health Insurance Portability and Accountability Act, and it's the law passed by Congress in 1996 that governs the privacy, security, and electronic data interchange of health records. Providers are required to inform their patients that they're in compliance with the law, which is why we sign and sign again. That includes elderly patients.

HIPAA also requires that Mom or Dad sign another form authorizing the provider to talk with a family member about the parent's health. It sounds simple enough, but again, that's not always the case.

Jeannie Newman, who has worked in the fields of social work and business for more than 20 years and is a consultant with Caliber Associates, an ICF International consulting company in Fairfax, Virginia, recounts the tale of her parents. Both have been diagnosed with cognitive impairment disorders, one with vascular dementia and the other with Parkinson's and senile dementia. Nonetheless, when her parents visit their physicians, they, too, are required to sign the HIPAA release form authorizing the doctor to talk to Newman about their health. Although both parents are very willing to sign the form, it is, nonetheless, a hassle every time they visit the doctor, says Newman. She has to call ahead and remind the office staff that her parents have cognitive issues and that the form already has been signed. Naturally, there are mix-ups at times, so that means more hassles. And because both she and her sister live a long distance from their parents, the situation creates more stress and strain on them as well as their already confused loved ones. It's an unfortunate situation in which the best interests of the elderly seem to fall through the cracks.

## Do It Yourself or Not?

Although some people prefer to go it alone, it can pay huge dividends financially and emotionally to bring in the experts. One mistake can cost you or your loved ones literally hundreds, thousands, and even tens of thousands of dollars and up—whether in lost or overlooked benefits, taxes, inheritances, retirement gains, and more. Beyond the dollars, one wrong or missing document, overlooked tiny loophole, or slight mistake, and you or your parents can lose control of their lives, their choices, and their finances.

Most of us have heard or experienced the nightmare stories: the elderly and unmarried partner of a loved one left out financially or turned away at the hospital by unsympathetic family members because the right documentation wasn't in place; the forgetful retiree who misses the deadline to roll over his or her retirement monies in time to avoid tax penalty; or the family and their parent who always had counted on Medicaid, but when they needed it to care for elderly Mom, discovered they had failed to realize all its qualifications, grace periods, and limitations. Forced to pay out of pocket with their meager incomes, everyone suffered.

## Legal Help

Although some people may protest the idea, hire a qualified attorney—preferably up front—to advise you and ensure that all the legal requirements of particular decisions and documents are met and that the documents are executed properly. Even if you're a do-it-yourselfer, have an attorney take a look at what you've done. The complexities of the laws, situations, options, and qualifications involving the elderly are so great, and the ramifications of something done improperly are so devastating—financially, emotionally, and even physically—that an attorney's fee pales in significance.

You and your loved ones can't afford not to get the right kind of legal assistance up front. After all, decisions now concern your aging parent's future, your future, your family's future, and because inheritances are involved, your children's children's futures and beyond.

*At the very least, have a qualified lawyer review your elderly loved one's essential documents. It's preferable, however, to work with that qualified attorney to draft the documents, too.*

## Finding the Right Lawyer

Finding a "qualified" lawyer involves more than simply going to your family attorney or a neighbor.

Consultant Newman, the social worker and former banker, recounts what happened when she and her sister turned to their family's lawyer to help with the documents necessary to care for their elderly parents. At the time, her father had been diagnosed with vascular dementia, and her mom was suffering the early stages of cognitive impairment. Because her father also was in the early stages of his disease, he appeared relatively normal in the meeting with the attorney. "The attorney didn't want to deal with the fact that Dad had dementia. I think he thought of us as hysterical females," says Newman.

In other words, although her dad acted normally, in reality he was and is cognitively impaired. Also, the attorney considered himself her father's attorney because they have been colleagues and friends for more than 30 years, Newman says, and therefore he was looking out for what he perceived to be the best interests of his client—not those of the family as a whole. "I trust him as an attorney," says Newman, "but I don't trust him to do what's best for the family overall."

All this added to the angst and issues that Newman and her family already had to deal with. If she had to do it again, Newman says she would find a good attorney who specializes in family and elder care issues.

An elder law attorney is another option. Many belong to the 5,000-member National Academy of Elder

Law Attorneys. Whether they belong to NAELA or not, however, they focus on the legal needs of the elderly, including age discrimination; durable powers of attorney; elder abuse; estate planning and probate; long-term care; health care decisions; Medicare, Medicaid, and other public benefits; and trusts. Others simply have special expertise in issues affecting the elderly. Check out the American Bar Association's Web site to help you find the right attorney for your needs.

- *"The average person cannot afford not to go to an elder law attorney and get their affairs in order because the costs they leave behind are far greater than attorney's fees."*
- *"Middle-class people who end up getting the wrong disease will lose everything they worked a lifetime to acquire, and the small amount they would have paid to an elder law attorney will pale in comparison."*

—Lawrence Davidow, member of the Sandwich Generation and president of the National Academy of Elder Law Attorneys

Why bother with an attorney specializing in elder law? "For the same reason that when you need a heart transplant, you don't go to your regular doctor. This is a specialty," says NAELA's Davidow, who also has earned the Certified Elder Law Attorney (CELA) designation, which requires education, training, and a 6½-hour bar exam. There are approximately 360 CELA attorneys nationwide. Their costs for service, he says, are similar to those of other well-qualified attorneys, $200 to $300 and up per hour, depending on where in the country they practice. Some elder law attorneys also offer fixed fees (approximately $250 and up) to prepare certain documents such as a living will, health care proxy, and durable financial power of attorney, or a package price for all three.

An attorney specializing in elder law understands the unique issues, problems, and solutions facing seniors and their families; knows the law as it relates to all that; is aware of the services that are available to help; and will be your advocate, adds Sabatino. Most good elder law attorneys also work with geriatric care managers to further ensure their clients' needs are met.

Whatever attorney you're considering to help with documentation and planning, Davidow suggests interviewing potential candidates, checking out their credentials, and talking to other clients for references. Nonprofits and charitable organizations like those associated with Alzheimer's and Parkinson's diseases also may be aware of the best elder law attorneys in the community.

## Beyond Must-Have Legal Documents

In addition to making sure all the necessary documentation is in place for a loved one, here are some other tips that can make a big difference and cut the headaches.

**KNOW YOUR LOVED ONE'S SOCIAL SECURITY NUMBER.** The world of finances, benefits, and filings begins with these nine numbers. Be sure that if you have aging parents, you keep their Social Security numbers in a safe place. Storing them on your computer isn't the right place. What happens if the call that something has happened to Mom or Dad comes in the middle of the night, and your computer is at the office or the person on the other end of the phone can't wait for you to sign on to your home computer?

---

### QUESTIONS TO ASK POTENTIAL ATTORNEYS

*Whether you opt for an elder law attorney or not, interview potential candidates. Check out their credentials and references. Reasonable questions to ask, according to Lawrence Davidow, president of the National Academy of Elder Law Attorneys, include:*

- *What percentage of your practice is elder law?*
- *How long have you been practicing elder law?*
- *Have you ever written or spoken on elder law?*
- *Are you a member of the National Academy of Elder Law Attorneys?*
- *How many trust documents have you drawn up?*
- *How many Medicaid applications have you been involved in?*

**ADD YOUR NAME ON BANK ACCOUNTS.** As an adult child, also be sure that your name is on your elderly loved one's or parent's accounts as a signatory. Then, as a joint account holder, you will have ready access to the money if your parent needs it and is unable to sign his own checks or is incapacitated in some way. That's especially important if, for example, a parent gets sick, is hospitalized, and suddenly requires something that takes an outlay of cash that you as the caregiver might not have readily available. A jointly held account would enable you to immediately access the needed cash. The joint account doesn't take the money out of the parents' taxable estate but does make it easier to help them while they're alive.

With joint accounts, however, tread carefully. If a parent or child in some way faces a liability issue—a lawsuit, perhaps—jointly held assets are fair game. That means if your parent has a big chunk of his retirement savings in a jointly held account with you, and you're sued, your parent's retirement savings are at risk because they're in a jointly held account.

One way to avoid either scenario is for an aging parent to hold only a small portion of her savings jointly with a child. Those "emergency funds" then could cover essential or last-minute expenses.

*Be sure you have a list of all your parents' or loved one's bank account and safe-deposit box numbers and locations. Ditto with credit cards (know where they are, along with the house and car keys, too), investment accounts, insurance policies (including supplemental health or Medigap insurance), and professionals who work with your parents, including any accountants, doctors, tax preparers, lawyers, and brokers. And don't forget to write down their Social Security numbers, either. Kiplinger offers its "Your Family Records Organizer," available in CD-ROM and print versions, that can help (www.kiplingers.com/store/organizer).*

**DON'T PUT YOUR NAME ON A CAR TITLE.** Because of the same liability issues mentioned with bank accounts, it's not a good idea to own a vehicle jointly with an elderly parent.

*DO* **HAVE OR KNOW WHERE TO FIND THE CAR KEYS.**
When his dad had a massive heart attack and was hospitalized, Al rushed across the country to be with him. After an exhausting several days, it looked like his dad was going to be OK, so Al decided to head back to his dad's house to finally get a good meal and some sleep. He took a cab there, figuring he could grab his dad's car keys and run out to the store to pick up some food later. The only problem was he had no idea where to find the car keys. Luckily, however, he did have a key to the house.

**ADD YOUR NAME ON CREDIT CARDS.** Have you ever called to make a payment by phone on an elderly or ailing loved one's credit card account and been told you're out of luck because your name isn't on the card? Imagine that, a credit card company turning away money. But they do. Consider putting your name on that per-

---

## TIPS IN GENERAL

- *Make sure any documentation is signed and notarized as indicated. Is the notary's seal valid, or has his commission expired? If it's not valid, neither is the document that required it.*
- *With bank accounts, insurance policies, safe-deposit boxes, and more, be sure you have a list—all in one place—of the numbers, locations, and any other pertinent information.*
- *It's a good idea to have legal documents such as wills and powers of attorney, at the least, reviewed by a lawyer familiar with statutes in a loved one's locality to make sure the documents are valid. Some states have special requirements for various documents. Not all form letters or document forms are valid in every state, either.*
- *Make sure copies of the documents are easily and readily available both to you and the aging loved one. Check out Kiplinger's "Your Family Records Organizer" available in CD-ROM and print versions (www.kiplinger.com/store/organizer), as a simple way to get the forms you need and help keep track of them.*

son's account before she becomes incapacitated. It could make at least the aspect of paying their bills easier. Of course, remember that it's up to the elderly loved one whether to allow your name on their credit cards.

**HAVE ART AND ANTIQUES APPRAISED.** Many insurance companies require formal appraisals by qualified experts for high-end items including jewelry, art, and antiques. This can be a costly, confusing, and sometimes unexpected expense for an elderly person's heirs or caregivers if something is to be sold.

> *Be cautious of antique shop appraisers and those with hidden hourly fees.*
>
> —Chicago Appraisers Association

How can you determine who is a real expert and if a valuation is correct? After all, even the experts can make mistakes. And, of course, how could you afford the appraisals? (Costs vary, but qualified appraisers generally provide free estimates.) Perusing eBay isn't the answer either. Too many variables and too much fraud—either unintentional or deliberate—are involved where *objets d'art* are concerned. The Web does, however, provide a few good places to start when seeking an appraiser:

- American Society of Appraisers *(www.appraisers.org)*. Click on "Find an Appraisal Expert."
- Chicago Art Appraisers Association *(www.chicagoappraisers .com)*. Check out its information on the basics of identification and appraisal of artwork, furniture, sculpture, china, and more.
- International Society of Appraisers *(www.isa-appraisers .org)*. Click on "Find an Appraiser."
- Local art museums. Curators often will do appraisals in their areas of expertise for a fee.

**HAVE YOUR LOVED ONE CREATE AN ETHICAL WILL.** Also consider asking an elderly parent or relative to write an ethical will. Although not a legal document, it's an open book of someone's life, a way to share their thoughts, feelings, attitudes, and more with generations to come.

If you're unsure where to begin your own ethical will, or life's story, many books, seminars, and Web sites can help; for example, *www.ethicalwill.com* and *http://yvm.net/vme/ethicalwills.*

## The Trust Issue

We'll talk more about trusts, how to set them up, and their value as a financial and estate planning tool in Chapter 11.

## Remember:

■ Bring in qualified professionals to work with you and your elderly loved ones to determine what's best for their situation. Consider hiring an attorney specializing in elder law and a geriatric care manager. Remember, the cheapest approach is not always the least expensive or the best in the long run.

■ Consider creating one or more trusts to handle specific needs for a family and loved one. Those needs could include avoiding probate court, shielding assets, or providing for the care of someone else.

■ Must-have documents include:
– A notarized will
– Health care proxy naming a person to make health care decisions on your behalf (also a backup person)
– Living will including, if desired, a do-not-resuscitate order to specify that a parent does not want to be kept alive in a vegetative state by artificial means
– Durable financial power of attorney naming an individual, and a backup, to make financial decisions on your parent's behalf
– Signed HIPPA documents that allow physicians to release health care information on a parent to you as a loved one

■ A few other important steps to take:
– Make sure you have all the important numbers in a parent's life, including Social Security number, bank

account numbers, health insurance policy numbers, and more.

- Have your name included on a parent's accounts so you can access cash in case of an emergency.
- Write down and have easily accessible important contact names and numbers for an aging loved one. That should include doctors, neighbors, hospitals, and emergency contact numbers.
- Find out where your parents keep their car keys! It can save time in an emergency.

# Finances for the Sandwiched

## Chapter 7

**N**o matter what the issues, the cost of end-of-life choices isn't cheap and is only going up. Have you priced a funeral lately? As of 2004, the average cost was $6,500, not including cemetery costs, according to the National Funeral Directors Association. At that price, the $255 Social Security death benefit won't go far.

The costs of raising kids, paying for their education, and, for many baby boomers, ongoing parental responsibilities for adult children keep soaring, too. The tab for junior's four-year college easily can set you back $100,000. And your child is likely to need your help buying their first home, because median single-family house prices now exceed $200,000.

And what's the cost of your retirement? We'll talk details later, but, as we all know, that's also heading toward the stratosphere along with the cost of getting old.

The end result: The Sandwich Generation, their kids, and their aging parents all need to take the right approach, make the right choices, and plan ahead to stay ahead—or at least afloat—today and in the future.

## Telling Numbers

**L**et's take a closer look at some of the demands for sandwiched baby boomers' limited dollars. We've talked about some of the costs of aging, but what about growing up? At the other end of the generational sandwich, the estimated expense of raising a child from birth to age 18 (not including college costs) ranges from $127,080 to $254,400, depending on a family's income (based on "Expenditures on Children by Families, 2002," U.S. Department of Agriculture Center for Nutrition Policy and Promotion, Miscellaneous Publication No. 1528-2002). That's no small amount of pocket change!

Looking at more statistics from the Pew Research Center's baby boomer survey from December 2005:

- Fully one-third of boomers with grown children provide those children primary financial support.
- 62 percent of those providing support say it's because their adult children are in school; 34 percent cite other reasons.
- 66 percent of boomers consider paying for their children's college a parental responsibility.
- 27 percent see saving for an inheritance as a parent's responsibility.
- Almost three in ten boomers (29 percent) who have a living parent have provided financial support to that parent in the past year.
- 42 percent of boomers who gave money to a parent in the past year did so regularly.
- 19 percent of boomers with a living parent report receiving financial support from that parent.
- 57 percent of boomers with a financially independent adult child say they have provided some financial assistance to that child in the past year.
- 33 percent of younger adults (ages 18 to 40) with a living parent report giving money to a parent in the past year.

With these financial pressures and more, it's a must for the Sandwich Generation to make the time to talk about money—with their aging or elderly parents and with their growing or adult kids. They can't afford not to.

*"The reality about money and seniors is that whether or not you have money determines a great deal about how the end of your life plays out."*

—Beverly Bernstein Joie, geriatric care manager

Adding to the financial squeeze, fewer people are putting aside savings. The Federal Reserve Board's Survey of Consumer Finances reveals that between 2001 and 2004, the proportion of families saying they saved in the previous year was down 3.1 percent to 56.1 percent. At the same time, retirement tops the list as the reason why Americans save, with 35 percent saying it's their main reason for saving, up from about 24 percent in 1995. Other reasons Americans say they save, according to the survey, include liquidity—saving for emergencies, possible unemployment, and illness—30 percent, and education, 11.6 percent.

## Getting Started

Whatever the demands on your money, it's tough to meet your own obligations and have money left over to help someone else—whether that's your children, your aging parents, or both—without first getting a clear picture of where you stand financially. When elderly parents are involved in the equation, as is often the case with the Sandwich Generation, you need a clear picture of their finances, too, so you'll know if, when, and/or how much financial or physical help they may need now or later.

You'll also need to think about your own financial goals and objectives, those things you would like to accomplish in the short term, intermediate term, and long term. Getting an elderly parent who needs assistance settled in an assisted-living center as soon as possible might be a short-term goal, saving for your 15-year-old's college education could be an intermediate one, and putting aside enough for your retirement would be a long-term goal. Thinking about time frames for goals helps provide a measure of your progress toward achieving them.

Once you have an idea of the goals you would like to achieve, we can tackle clarifying your own financial picture. Then, after you're better versed in what it takes to achieve goals, you can weigh in on the financial picture of your aging loved ones. You'll have an idea of the specific questions you'll need to ask them. The right questions can make the process more direct and less

## SOURCES FOR MORE INFORMATION

- *America's Health Insurance Plans (www.ahic .org). National association representing nearly 1,300 member companies providing health insurance coverage, including long-term care insurance providers. Click on "Consumer Information."*
- *Financial Planning Association (www.fpanet .org). The membership organization for the financial planning community offers information and an online tool to help you find the right professional to fit your personal finance needs.*
- *Insurance Information Institute (www.iii .org). Nonprofit dedicated to improving the public's understanding and knowledge of insurance.*
- *Insurance rating organizations: A.M. Best Company (www.ambest.com); Standard & Poor's (www.standardandpoors.com); Weiss Ratings, Inc. (www.weissratings.com); Moody's Investors Service (www.moodys. com); Fitch Ratings (www.fitchibca.com).*
- *Kiplinger (www.kiplinger.com). Your trusted information source for money and personal finance, from auto and college funding to elder care, investing, Medicare, Medicaid, retirement, taxes, and more; free interactive tools (click on "Tools") available along with reasonably priced organizational and informational CD-ROMs, brochures, financial records help, and more.*
- *Microsoft Money (www.microsoft.com/ products). Web site for one of the popular personal finance software packages.*
- *Mymoney.gov (www.mymoney.gov). The federal government's Web site with a wealth of information aimed at helping Americans understand more about how to save, invest, and manage their money. Free "My Money Tool Kit" also available.*
- *NASD (www.nasd.com). Primary private-sector regulator of America's securities industry offers information on investing, investments, and brokers. Click on "Investor Information" for links to college-related savings information.*
- *National Association of Insurance Commissioners (www.naic.org). Check out its free brochures, including "A Shopper's Guide to Long-Term Care Insurance" and "Choosing a Medigap Policy."*
- *Nolo (www.nolo.com). From a leader in do-it-yourself legal solutions and information for consumers, Nolo offers more than 300 books, software, and e-products, including downloadable forms, as well as valuable free information. Click on "Family Law & Immigration," "Wills & Estate Planning," or "Resource Center."*
- *Quicken by Intuit (www.quicken.com). Web site for one of the popular personal finance software packages.*
- *Smart About Your Money (www .smartaboutmoney.org). From the nonprofit National Endowment for Financial Education, the site has free downloadable materials to help you learn more about money and your life. Check out its free "Wealth Care Kit."*

stressful for both of you when talking about intimate details of their financial situation—a conversation that often makes many of their generation uncomfortable.

Yes, it's time for a crash course in Financial Planning 101. Get out your shoebox of receipts, old tax returns, pay stubs, and notes; grab a pencil (so you can easily erase any mistakes) and a large pad of paper; and let's get started. You may want to download or pick up a copy of the latest software version of Quicken by Intuit (*www.quicken.com*), Microsoft Money *(www.microsoft.com/products),* or some other personal money management program that will help you organize your finances and walk you through the following exercises.

## Do It Yourself or Not

Alternatively, with records in hand (either the shoebox or computer printout), visit a Certified Financial Planner™, your accountant, or other qualified planning professional to help you with the financial equation. Some people insist on going it alone, while others opt to bring in experts well-versed in the issues and, it is hoped, the answers. As we've talked about previously, professionals—including qualified geriatric care managers, elder law legal specialists, lawyers, and more—can be a great help when trying to sort through the maze of complicated choices facing the Sandwich Generation.

The same is true when it comes to figuring out your financial picture today and planning for the future. It's essential, however, that if you do decide to bring in a professional, make sure he has the expertise in the area you need. As with any other goods or services, do your homework, get references, and check them. Does the person have the necessary credentials? Does she have any credentials at all? Anyone can call himself a financial planner or a geriatric care manager.

Even if you decide to rely on a professional, you first may want to do the following exercise on your own because it can help you understand what's involved in the total picture. So read on.

## Your Net Worth

It sounds scary, but it really isn't. Determine your net worth or the combined net worth of you and your spouse simply by writing down all your assets (what you have) in one column, all your liabilities (what you owe) in another, and then subtracting total liabilities from total assets. *Voilà!*

| | |
|---|---|
| *Total assets* | _____ |
| *Minus total liabilities* | _____ |
| *Your net worth* | _____ |

It sounds simple enough, but, of course, there's a catch or two. Be as thorough as possible in your determinations, but don't go overboard with the minutiae. This isn't an application to take out a mortgage. This is a worksheet designed to help you. Be honest with your valuations. If, in the assets column, your car is three years old, use the midrange resale price, not the one that's so high you'll never get it. Ditto for your spouse's car.

Let's consider your assets. Write them down, along with their estimated value, in one column. Assets include:

- Current assets such as income (before taxes), checks and commissions due you, cash in bank accounts, money market accounts, certificates of deposit, savings bonds, alimony and child support, and other forms of income easily convertible to cash. Don't overlook an expected tax refund either.
- Personal property such as your vehicle; recreational equipment (including a boat, snowmobile, or RV); art, antiques, and collectibles; jewelry; computers and other electronic equipment, including the plasma TV and your iPods. If you have an itemized list of possessions for your homeowners' or renter's insurance, that's a great way to expedite compiling the list. With furniture and clothing, guesstimate based on resale value.

- Real estate, including your house, timeshares, vacation homes, shares in vacation homes, and other property. If you have a recent appraisal for tax or mortgage refinancing purposes, use that figure. If not and the only appraisal is outdated, check prices in the neighborhood to see what comparable properties are selling for and then guesstimate the value of yours.
- Securities such as stocks, bonds, and mutual funds
- Long-term assets, including your pension, 401(k), or other retirement account; IRAs; Roth IRAs; shares in a private business; 529 plans or other education savings accounts; life insurance policies (in some cases these could be a valuable saving tool if, for example, you or an elderly parent have a whole life insurance policy and decide to borrow against its cash value); and more

Now total all the numbers from that column; that amount equals your total assets.

Next, figure your liabilities. List them in another column with the dollar amount beside each item. Again, be honest about your situation. This is designed to help you achieve your goals. Liabilities include:

- Current liabilities such as utility bills; medical bills; phone bills (don't forget the cell phone bill); child support and/or alimony; high school activity costs and fees, including uniforms and sports equipment; college costs, including tuition, room and board, and spending money; and elder care costs, if applicable, including that extra $100 you slip Mom's home-health aide every month just to make sure she provides her extra special care
- Real estate liabilities, including the mortgage or rent; second mortgage, if applicable; home equity loan; timeshare and/or vacation home expenses; and any other expenses related to real estate holdings
- Credit and loan liabilities such as your credit cards, auto loans, bank loans, overdraft loans, personal loans (that includes the $5,000 you owe your brother), and any other outstanding loans

- Taxes due, including federal and state (estimated if you're self-employed), property, and capital gains taxes
- Retirement plan contributions if not automatically withheld in your paycheck

Total the liabilities. Then go back through both columns to make sure you didn't miss anything.

Now you're ready for the good news/bad news. Subtract the liabilities total from the assets total. Don't despair if the net worth number is negative. After all, this is an expensive time for the Sandwich Generation, and this exercise is designed to help you assess where you stand. You may think you know where you stand, but it always helps to write it all down in one place. That way, you can get a clearer picture of how much money you will need to meet your obligations and where you might be able to cut back. Then you'll be able to determine, with the help of an investment professional and qualified financial advisor, what it takes to achieve your goals. After all, the secret to surviving the multigenerational sandwich is planning—for yourself, your children, and your aging loved ones.

## Cash Flow

Next let's look at your cash flow, which is the difference between what's coming in and what's going out each month. Again, it's back to the lists. Write down on one side of the paper all the money coming in each month—your income—from all sources. Don't overlook regular dividends from securities and investments, alimony, or child support. On the other side of the paper, list all your monthly expenses or outflow of cash. Then subtract the outflow from the income, and that's your cash flow. If your cash flow is positive, congratulations. You have discretionary income to put toward accomplishing your financial goals. If it's negative, it's time to reevaluate, prioritize, and figure out where you can cut back.

Don't despair if you and your family aren't rolling in extra cash. As we've mentioned, this is a costly time in your life. And this book is designed to help you understand your options, then plan ahead to get ahead.

## Your Parent's Finances

It's now time for that "talk" about money with your aging loved one. If you and your elderly parent haven't discussed finances before, don't worry or feel guilty. As the Pew numbers show, you're not alone. Instead, view this as a wake-up call to do it, and do it now. Remember Lawrence Davidow, the elder law expert, and how, although he and his aging father had all the necessary legal documents in place—powers of attorney, health care proxy, living will, and more—he still had no idea about his dad's finances and investments? When the crisis occurred, Davidow had to scramble to get the answers. Rather than reacting frantically in a crisis, you can get the answers now. Besides, if you plan ahead, you, your family, and aging loved ones no doubt will sleep better at night knowing there's one less thing to worry about.

When you approach elderly loved ones about their finances, keep in mind all that we've mentioned before. Put yourself in their position; treat them with respect, and be gentle but firm. Remember, too, that they may not always truly need your financial help or even want it. Also, they may not realize they do or don't need

---

**TIPS FROM REAL LIFE**

*Are you worried about whether your elderly parents or loved one can afford their lifestyle?*

- *Talk to them about their finances*
- *Ask for details, but at the same time assure your parents that your primary concern is that they don't outlive their money*
- *If they're willing, help them determine if they're getting all the financial benefits due them*
- *Are they forgoing something out of fear they can't afford it? Perhaps a financial assessment on paper is all it takes to reassure them of their sound financial condition*

---

help. After all, as we mentioned, many older people just don't spend their money on themselves out of fear. The majority of them grew up and developed their subsequent attitudes toward conserving money during the Depression. They're also reluctant to talk about how much money they have or about making changes.

"Money is a very strange phenomenon at this time in life," says Beverly Bernstein Joie, the certified care manager and a certified senior advisor. "People don't like to talk about how much money they get or have, and so it's hard to do a care plan without that."

Your financial conversation with elderly parents may not have to be as detailed as your own exercise to determine where they stand financially. It could be that by asking a series of simple questions, you will get the answers you need. As you ask the questions, though, write down the answers on a pad of paper. The end result, as with your own financial figuring, is that you want an idea of your elderly parents' assets versus their liabilities, as well as their cash flow, so that you can determine what they realistically can or can't afford and whether you'll need to step in to help. Your financial conversation should include the following issues:

- What's the house or condo worth? What would you like done with it eventually?
- Would you consider a reverse mortgage (using the home's equity to pay for expenses)? (More on that later.)
- What's the value of other special possessions, such as antiques or artwork? Have you had formal appraisals of them? What would you eventually like done with those possessions? Whom, as in special experts, have you worked with or who do you know that could handle a sale or other disposition of those possessions?
- What investments have you made? What's their current value? Where are they? Where are contact names and numbers? What would like you done with those investments if something happens to you?
- What is your monthly income, including income from investments as well as Social Security, pensions, and any other income?

- What kind of insurance coverage do you have—health insurance, including Medigap supplemental insurance; long-term care insurance; and life insurance? If you have life insurance, is it a term or whole life policy? If it's the latter, have you borrowed against the policy's cash value? If not, would you consider that? Even if you have a term policy, you may be able to get a lump sum of cash through a new option called a "life settlement," where you sell your policy to a third party and they continue the premiums and collect the life insurance when you die.
- What documents do you have and where? Check out Kiplinger's Web site *(www.kiplinger.com)* for tips, tricks, and data to make the job easier or consider picking up a copy of its "Your Family Records Organizer."
- Have those documents been reviewed by an expert to make sure they've been prepared correctly and contain no loopholes? Are they signed? Are they notarized? (Not all states require notarization, but it's generally a good idea.)
- What would you like to happen if you become incapacitated?
- Do you have trusts in place to help defray costs to your estate at your death and preserve your money for your heirs?
- Do you have adequate health, life, and long-term care insurance? If not, how can we help you get it?

Middle-class boomers can't afford the financial repercussions if they or an elderly parent haven't prepared for eventual disability or infirmity. You must step in and take steps now to protect your family and your financial future. The same holds true for your siblings. Just as two or more people might pool assets to buy a piece of real estate, siblings also can pool assets to pay the cost of their parents' long-term care insurance premiums, says Barry, the NBC TV host of *Talk About Money*. (More on long-term care insurance later in this chapter.)

Siblings Roger and Eloise constantly worried about their elderly dad's finances. After all, his apartment in the retirement community cost him about $3,000 a month, and he had high medical bills that his insurance didn't completely cover. All this was happening at a time when his income was little more than his $2,300 monthly Social Security check—at least that's what his kids thought. They fretted, literally, for years. But every time the siblings separately or together tried to approach the money issue with their dad, he sidestepped the conversation. It wasn't until their father died that Roger and Eloise discovered he had sizable investment income combined with a comfortable Keogh, or retirement plan; savings; and an IRA that he'd been drawing down slowly. If only they had had that "talk," they could have spared themselves years of needless anxiety.

## DAD'S FINANCES: A SNAPSHOT

**Income:**

| | |
|---|---|
| Social Security: | $2,337/month |
| Sales commission residuals: | $823/month |
| Investment dividends and income: | $1,000/month |
| IRA withdrawal (10% of remaining $45,000): | $4,500/year or $375/month assuming an 8% return |
| Keogh (H.R. 10) plan (qualified retirement plan for the self-employed): | $87,000: $5,600/year or about $467/month assuming an 8% return |
| **Monthly total income:** | **$5,002** |

**Expenditures**

| | |
|---|---|
| Room/board: | $2,950 |
| Utilities (phone, cell phone): | $150 |
| Entertainment: | $400 |
| Transportation (via caregiver): | 0 |
| Caregiver/companion ($12/hr, 4 hrs/day, 5 days/wk): | $960 |
| Medical (Medicare, Medigap, Rx, Physicians, etc.): | $240 |
| Other: | $100 |
| **Total expenses:** | **$4,565** |
| **Surplus:** | **$437** |

# What Now?

By now you have a pretty good idea of the current financial picture for both you and your aging loved one. But that's not enough. What's the prognosis for two, five, or even ten years down the road? A parent may be able to afford her lifestyle today, but what about in ten years? Even if that parent is 65 and healthy, will he be able to come up with the necessary tens of thousands of dollars needed just to supplement Medicare for the rest of his life? Roger and Eloise's dad died at age 84 without really tapping into much of his retirement savings. But what would have happened if he had lived another ten years or had a catastrophic illness? It wouldn't have taken long to deplete his savings. He had no long-term care insurance either.

We'll talk more about Medicare and Medicaid later, but first let's look at what you and/or your parents can do to help simplify finances for your elderly loved one, and to help defray costs down the road.

# Get Organized

Whether or not you're in charge of your elderly loved ones' finances, you can take a few easy steps to help simplify their recordkeeping and help avoid missed or forgotten bills and checks. Tread carefully, though, and remind your aging parents that this isn't about taking away control of their money. It's about making the situation easier for everyone.

**SET UP DIRECT DEPOSIT.** If your elderly parents still handle their own finances, talk to them and help them understand that direct deposit of regular checks like Social Security, securities dividends, and pensions is a smooth, dependable way to save time and effort—theirs and yours. It also avoids lost or forgotten checks, no matter anyone's age.

**SET UP AUTOMATIC BILL PAYMENT.** Arrange for automatic withdrawals from checking or savings accounts to pay regular household bills. That will streamline the process; and your loved ones will gain peace of mind, too, because they won't have to worry about whether or not a particular bill was paid.

**SET UP A BUDGET.** Working with parents in control of their finances—or on your own, if you control their finances—put together a monthly budget of your parents' income and expenses. That way, you easily can see where they are financially at any point in time. That can be especially important if money is tight and unexpected expenses crop up. It also will help you plan your own finances if you know that two or three months down the road you must come up with a certain amount of cash to help your parents. (Search for the words *budget worksheet* on the Internet to find lots of free sample budget help or check out the government's informational Web site, *www.mymoney.gov.*)

**SET UP A REVOCABLE LIVING TRUST FOR AN AGING LOVED ONE.** A revocable living trust is established during a person's lifetime with them as the trustee and in full control of the assets. This type of trust avoids probate for all the property in the trust and keeps personal affairs personal and private by addressing what happens to the assets on the trust owner's death. Plus, the trust dictates what will happen should that person be unable to function as their own trustee because it designates a successor trustee. For tax purposes, earnings and losses in a revocable living trust show up on the individual's tax return. A trust is also one more layer of protection from anyone who might challenge someone's wishes for disbursement of their assets. A word of advice, however; if someone sets up a trust, they must also follow up by actually transferring assets into it, and that can be a time-consuming process: It means retitling a house and stocks, bonds, or other assets to be placed in the trust. "The biggest mistake people make in setting up a trust is never transferring the property into it," says elder law attorney Sabatino.

**TAKE ADVANTAGE OF SENIOR DISCOUNTS AND SAV-
INGS PROGRAMS.** Many organizations and groups offer
special programs and discounts for seniors. Many programs are free; others may have a nominal cost of
membership that's quickly recouped by the dollar savings they provide. Retailers often offer regular senior
discount days, and movie theaters long have offered
ticket discounts for seniors. AARP *(www.aarp.org)* offers
its members discounts on everything from cellular
phones to travel, prescription drugs, and more. Cost of
membership is $12.50 a year, which includes your
spouse or partner.

National prescription discount programs and seniors' organizations can be other cost savers for aging
parents (and you and your family, too). H2U *(www.h2u
.com)* is a discount and prescription drug program and
health information source that works with hospitals in
more than 15 states across the country. It's designed to
meet the unique health and financial savings needs of
people age 50 and over, and to help its members save
money as well as manage their health and enjoy a healthy
lifestyle. H2U—which stands for health, happiness, and
you—also offers free online health assessments in conjunction with participating hospitals, lots of health information, special VIP hospital benefits, discounts on
local attractions, and much more. Membership is just
$15 a year, which is more than offset by its many bene-
fits—including the free upgrade from semiprivate to private room at participating hospitals.

For prescription drug discounts, H2U taps into
Caremark, the nation's largest prescription discount
drug card program (it replaces the old programs Ex-
pressScripts and ScriptSave) that can be used at more
than 59,000 pharmacies nationwide for savings of up to
50 percent. Participating pharmacies include CVS, Eck-
erd, Kmart, Wal-Mart, Sam's Club, and Walgreens.

Before buying into a discount program, make sure
a parent is not duplicating services. An existing membership in an organization like AARP or even an insurance plan may already provide a discount drug program
that a parent isn't aware of or hasn't used.

Even if a senior is eligible for Medicare's new Part D prescription drug program, compare the total costs of using any discount drug program with that of Medicare Part D, including the cost of the monthly premium, to determine which provides better savings.

## Reverse Mortgages

A reverse mortgage allows an elderly person (age 62 and up) to tap the equity in her home to stay in that home and to generate needed cash for whatever purpose, whether home remodeling, medical bills, or basic living expenses.

*Much free information on reverse mortgages is available on the Department of Housing and Urban Development's (HUD) Web site (www.hud.gov). Click on "Information for Senior Citizens." Or check out the National Reverse Mortgage Lenders Association (www.reversemortgage.org).*

Unlike a regular mortgage, which the homeowner pays monthly, a reverse mortgage provides the homeowner a cash payment from the lender for a specified amount and period of time. He can take the payment in a variety of ways ranging from a line of credit to monthly disbursement and more. These can be structured differently depending on the lender, so before a parent signs, shop around for the program that fits your needs.

Qualifications for a reverse mortgage loan are *not* based on income and debt, as with a traditional mortgage, second mortgage, or home equity line of credit. The amount a person may borrow depends on her age, the value of the home, interest rates, and more. Some reverse mortgages also can be for a fixed time period, thus increasing the amount of the monthly payments. If a borrower outlives the term of the reverse mortgage, the payments stop, but the borrower can remain in the home without making payments as long as they keep up payments on insurance and taxes. When the borrower dies or no longer lives in the home, the home is sold and the loan repaid.

A reverse mortgage does not affect someone's Medicare reimbursement, but the cash it produces can affect the senior homeowner's Medicaid eligibility. Reverse mortgages come in all shapes and sizes, so it's a good idea to shop around to find one that fits your elderly parent's needs, and check with a local area Agency on Aging or elder law specialist for the details before signing on the dotted line. Also, keep in mind that a reverse mortgage drains the equity in your home, which likely may be your biggest asset. Also, in order for a home to qualify, it must meet minimum FHA property requirements, and, as with any mortgage, up-front fees are incurred that generally can be financed as part of the reverse mortgage. Some of those fees include an appraisal fee, mortgage insurance premium, origination fee, servicing fee, and closing costs.

## Sale/Leaseback

Another option that generates cash for an elderly parent to help pay for long-term care expenses could be a sale/leaseback agreement with an adult child. The parent sells his home to their child, and then in turn leases the home back from that child. The parent gets the cash she needs, and the child gets the various tax benefits of a rental property and more. Of course, in order for this arrangement to qualify for tax deductions, the home must be sold for fair market value and the lease charge fair-market prices.

## Borrowing and Life Insurance

Another financial tool that many seniors may have but not realize the value of is a whole life insurance policy. Unlike a term life policy which pays a set amount only on the policyholder's death, cash value policies build up their value over time and earn modest interest at the same time. Depending on terms of the particular policy, an elderly parent may be able to borrow against the value of that policy to pay for living, medical, or other expenses. Although financial advisors usually suggest less expensive term life policies as a better approach, especially when general interest rates are high, cash value policies are a type of enforced savings for many older Americans.

Another financial tool related to life insurance that we touched on earlier and can generate immediate cash is a life or viatical settlement. With variations, typically both involve a life insurance policy owner selling, assigning, or transferring the death benefit of a life insurance policy in exchange for a single cash payment. The amount paid varies and can be more than the cash surrender value of the policy but less than the death benefit amount. The policy's buyer assumes ownership of the policy as well as picks up the cost of the remaining premiums. With a viatical settlement, the policy seller has a life-threatening illness or condition (such as AIDS), while with a life settlement they do not.

But before rushing out to sell your own or an elderly loved one's policy, think twice, experts caution. Even if you need the money, fees can be high, and such a move can have tax consequences. If you do decide to sell an unwanted or unneeded policy, make sure you're dealing with a reputable company as buyer. Compare fees and check them out thoroughly.

Will suffered from leukemia for many years. He had all kinds of treatment, including costly bone replacement and bone marrow transplant, and racked up what his family assumed were massive medical bills, especially because he hadn't worked much since the illness. But, to everyone's surprise, when he died the balance due on all his bills was zero, nada, nothing. It seems that Will, a confirmed bachelor who had been very successful in his working years, had several high-dollar whole life insurance policies ($500,000 each) that at one time had been paid in full. Over the years he systematically had borrowed against the policies' cash value to foot his living expenses and medical bills. After he died, the cash that remained in the policies then was disbursed to heirs.

# Long-Term Care Insurance

Long-term care insurance offers you and your loved ones a choice. It helps defray the costs of long-term care generally whether at home, in an assisted-living facility, or nursing home. Medicare and Medicaid are not enough! Medicare pays for occasional physician-prescribed skilled care visits and short nursing home stays up to 100 days with qualifications, copayments and limitations. Medicaid will cover long-term care costs with limitations and then only when one's assets are mostly depleted, and only after a grace period, and penalty period, if applicable. (More on that later.)

With the national average annual cost of a nursing home exceeding $74,000, Americans can't afford not to have long-term care insurance, experts agree, especially given the recent changes that tighten Medicaid eligibility requirements.

People must address ahead of time how they plan to pay for their long-term care. That's a financial essential for baby boomers and their aging parents, says Neal E. Cutler, PhD; vice president and dean of educational programs for the American Institute of Financial Gerontology *(www.aifg.org)*; a professor at Widener University, Chester, Pennsylvania; and recognized expert in lifelong wealth issues and aspirations of aging individuals and their families. He's also director of survey research for the National Council on the Aging and has been involved in studying money and health issues with the aging for several decades. With the cost and complexities involved, long-term care insurance becomes essential, Cutler says.

*People absolutely have to plan for end-of-life issues,
especially how to pay for long-term care.*

Long-term care is expensive, as is the cost of insurance to cover it, but it can be money well spent and far less money out of your pocket than if you had to foot the bill for care yourself. Policy costs vary widely by benefits, limitations, an individual's health, and geography.

In 2005, a policy with benefits that included $100/day ($3,000/month) long-term care lifetime benefit with a 90-day deductible, 5 percent annual inflation protection, and covering home care, assisted living, and nursing home care might have cost an average couple about $2,614/year at age 45, $3,072/year at age 55, $4,887/year at age 65, and $10,475/year at age 75, according to Claude Thau, president of Thau, Incorporated, Overland Park, Kansas–based consultants to the long-term care insurance industry. Put another way, in exchange for premiums, if a couple both need to use the coverage in the first year, the insurance company could pay out up to $73,000. That amount continues to increase, climbing to $118,909/year 10 years later, $193,691/year after 20 years, and $331,277/year 30 years later.

So, would you rather pay $100,000 or more a year out of pocket for care or a few thousand dollars a year in premiums? "What's your alternative? Everything around the end of life is expensive," adds care manager and consultant Joie.

*"The chances are one in four that if you're 65 today, you'll end up in a nursing home. We insure our houses. We insure our cars. We insure our mortgages. Why then don't we also insure ourselves with long-term care insurance?'*

—Jim Barry, CFP®, wealth manager, Barry Financial Group, host of *Talk About Money* (NBC TV)

When looking for a policy for yourself or an aging loved one, shop around. Choose wisely, too. Don't just search for "long-term care insurance" on the Internet and take the first or cheapest option that pops up. This is insurance for the future. An insurer needs to be around down the road when you or your loved one suddenly needs to collect on the policy. Look for major providers with long track records. Some of the majors include:

- MetLife *(www.metlife.com)*
- John Hancock *(www.johnhancock.com)*
- Genworth Financial, Inc. *(www.genworth.com)*

A few more issues to consider when you're shopping for long-term care insurance:

- Not all plans pay for all care in all places.
- Certain conditions must be met for various policies to kick in with coverage. What are those conditions? Do they make sense for a parent's situation? Read the fine print for your loved one and choose accordingly.
- Waiting periods before benefits begin vary from 0 to 180 days. The longer the time elapsed before they kick in, the lower the premium. But, keep in mind that if a policy has a 100-day waiting period before benefits kick in and your elderly parent requires nursing home care, you or your parent will have to foot the bill for those 100 days of care.
- Premiums also vary depending on the length of the benefit period and the amount of the daily benefit payment, ranging from $40 a day to more than $300 for nursing home coverage.
- How much daily benefit is acceptable, and is it adjusted for inflation? No policy covers all costs. Keep in mind that you are responsible for any costs incurred over the daily benefit amounts.
- Is there a guarantee that the policy can't be canceled? What about a clause on suspension of payments in the event the policyholder is hospitalized or becomes incapacitated?
- The longer someone waits—as in the older they are—to buy the policy, the higher the premiums. And by waiting, they run the risk that they may not medically qualify for coverage.

---

### ON LONG-TERM CARE INSURANCE

*The longer the time period before benefits kick in, the lower the insurance premium. What if, though, an elderly parent has to enter a nursing home and his long-term care policy has a 100-day deductible period? You or your parent will have to foot the nursing home bill for 100 days. Sometimes the lower premiums just aren't worth the "what if" factor.*

■ Buy the policy in advance because if you wait until you need it, you won't be able to get it.

*Broker World* magazine *(www.brokerworldmag.com),* an insurance industry publication, also does an annual survey on long-term care insurance that's available for purchase on its Web site.

Not everyone can get or afford long-term care insurance even if family members are willing to help with the cost. Certain preexisting conditions may preclude such insurance. Some of those conditions include mental

---

## A LONG-TERM CARE POLICY CHECKLIST

*From the nonprofit America's Health Insurance Plans (www.ahip.org)*

1. What services are covered?
   - ■ Nursing home care?
   - ■ Home-health care?
   - ■ Assisted-living facility?
   - ■ Adult day care?
   - ■ Respite care?
   - ■ Other?
2. How much does the policy pay per day for each of the above?
3. How long will benefits last in a nursing home, assisted living, or other facility?
4. Does the policy have a maximum lifetime benefit? If so, what is it for nursing home care, home-health care, assisted living, or other facility?
5. Does the policy have a maximum length of coverage for each period of confinement? If so, what is it for each living situation?
6. How long is the waiting period before pre-existing conditions are covered?
7. How long is the waiting period or "deductible" before benefits begin for nursing home care, home-health care, assisted-living facility, or other?

8. Are Alzheimer's disease and other organic mental and nervous disorders covered?
9. Does the policy require an assessment of activities of daily living, cognitive impairment, physician certification of need, or a prior hospital stay for nursing home care or home-health care? Also, is a prior nursing home stay required for home-health care coverage?
10. Is the policy guaranteed renewable?
11. What is the age range for enrollment?
12. Is there a waiver of premium provision for nursing home care or home-health care?
13. How long must the policyholder be confined before premiums are waived?
14. Does the policy have a nonforfeiture benefit?
15. Does the policy offer an inflation adjustment feature? If so what is the rate of increase, how often is it applied, for how long, and is there an added cost?
16. How much does the policy cost per month, per year, and with and without the inflation adjustment and nonforfeiture features?
17. Is there a 30-day free look or refund policy?

or nervous disorders other than Alzheimer's or dementia (which are covered), attempted suicide, or drug or alcohol addiction. Attorney Davidow's 82-year-old father who had heart issues was ineligible for it. However, even people with some preexisting conditions may be

## INSURANCE POLICIES YOU DON'T NEED!

*From Today's Seniors and Senior Solutions of America (www.TodaysSeniors.com), whose president and publisher, Mike Gamble, has spent more than 40 years specializing in issues important to seniors, including insurance:*

■ **Accidental death insurance.** *Accidents cause few deaths of people over 65, so spend your money on a term life insurance policy instead.*

■ **Cancer insurance.** *Most people don't get the types of cancer covered by these policies. Skin cancer is usually not covered. If you're under 65, buy a regular health insurance plan that covers all medical conditions. Those 65 or older can use the money to pay for Medicare's Part D prescription drug coverage.*

■ **Car rental collision damage waiver (CDW) insurance.** *Car rental companies like to sell it to you, but check your own auto insurance policy and credit card benefits. You're probably already covered for rental cars.*

■ **Credit and mortgage disability insurance.** *These policies pay the minimum installments on your loan or credit card, typically for up to 36 months, if you are disabled according to the terms of the policy. Instead, maximize the short-term and long-term disability coverage that's often available from an employer. It will pay other expenses as well and costs much less per dollar of benefit.*

■ **Credit and mortgage life insurance.** *If you want to protect your family, buy or add to your term life insurance protection. It's much more affordable.*

■ **Credit card fraud protection.** *You're already covered by law and have to repay only $50 if you tell them about the fraudulent charges, or about your lost or stolen credit card, as soon as possible.*

■ **Extended product warranties.** *Typically they pay out only 30 cents on the dollar.*

■ **Flight insurance.** *Airport life insurance is expensive, and given the extremely low probability of a crash, don't waste your money.*

■ **Hospital indemnity insurance.** *Sold under names like Hospital Cash, Hospital Money, HIP, Hospital Indemnity Plan, and more, it basically pays a fixed daily cash benefit for each day you are hospitalized—cash that you can spend any way you want. Unfortunately it doesn't pay out enough because you'll probably be discharged in a few days and the benefits, usually about $100 a day, won't go too far given the soaring cost of medical care.*

■ **Unemployment insurance.** *Credit card companies and other lenders sell this policy to make the minimum payment on your card or loan for 6 to 12 months if you lose your job. You don't need this coverage. Instead, use the money you set aside in your emergency fund to make the minimum payments.*

**Source:** ©2006 Senior Solutions of America. Reprinted with permission.

able to buy a long-term care policy *if* a specific length of time has elapsed since the medical incident and they're willing to pay higher premiums.

Additionally, every state has a waiver program under its Medicaid program that offers coverage of at-home health for qualified individuals. Some states also have similar coverage for long-term care in an assisted living facility.

We all need to do financial planning that addresses long-term care financing. Parents need to know about it, and so do their kids and grandchildren. Its primary purpose is not to provide money for inheritances, but to ensure having an array of options, getting good care, and not financially crippling all parties in the process. "People want choice," says Davidow. "They want to know that they can be cared for at home or in assisted-living facilities. Boomers want to know that a plan is in place to take care of their parents and not overburden them so they'll still have time and energy to be a good spouse, employee, partner, and parent."

## Kids Are Not Exempt

Talk to your children, young or old, about money and the generational sandwich too. The long-distance emotional, physical, and financial hardships you may experience in the care of your elderly parents affect your children, too.

Dakota, a new high school graduate headed to college, was devastated when his dad came home from work one day and announced they were moving out of town. With the cost of Dakota's college, his mom recently laid off from her job, and his grandmother in a costly assisted-living facility that his dad helped pay for, finances were tight. His dad had taken a new job in a town with a substantially lower cost of living, in part to ease the financial burden. It wasn't fair, Dakota thought. Where would he call home because he'd be spending nine months at school 700 miles away? How would he ever see his old friends? Where would he stay if he came back to town? Worse yet, his parents were downsizing to a smaller home that meant "his" room also would be the guest room. On holidays and during summer vacations, when he normally would think about coming home, his aging grandfather would be visiting, too. That meant Dakota would have no space of his own and would have to sleep downstairs on the couch or the floor.

And then there's the cost of his college. Already his parents had told him that he had to work during school if he wanted any spending money, and that after the first year, he would be on his own. They just couldn't afford the cost of his grandmother's long-term care and his college, too.

Perhaps if Dakota could have participated more in discussions, decisions, and planning for his grandparents as well as the move, he would have been more accepting and better understanding of the financial straits of his parents' generation sandwich.

But Dakota was better off than his best friend, Clay, whose parents had been charging him rent since he was 16 to offset the family's rising cost of living and care for his grandparents. Clay wouldn't be heading to college in the fall because he had to foot the entire bill himself, couldn't get a scholarship, and hadn't saved up enough money.

## Overcoming the College Cost Squeeze

We all know about the soaring cost of college. For the 2005–2006 school year, the average cost of tuition and fees at a four-year private college or university was $21,235/year, up from $17,377 just five years earlier. At a four-year public university, the cost was $5,491 in 2005, up from $3,766, according to The College Board. Those figures don't include the cost of room and board, transportation, books, and other expenses, which add substantially to the overall bill.

Even if you're not yet completely sandwiched like Dakota's family, the cost of college for your child may be the most expensive purchase you'll ever make, next to buying a house. That, of course, excludes having to pay out of pocket for prolonged nursing home care for a loved one. If parents are caught having to pay for both at the same time, they face a challenge, to say the least.

*Sacrificing saving for your retirement to foot the bill*
*for your child's college may not be the right approach.*
*After all, plenty of other ways exist to finance college.*
*That's not the case with retirement.*

The piece of the Sandwich Generation's financial puzzle that tends to be squeezed out of the picture usually is the retirement nest egg. That's a mistake. There are other ways beyond savings and investments to pay for college but no other way to fund your retirement.

For the college bound, scholarships and grants abound, as do loans, work study programs, and various payment options and tax-advantaged savings programs. You can even save for college when you buy groceries or eat out. Don't overlook possible scholarships or assistance available for your kids through your employer, credit union, professional association, or other group. Even organizations like the Intermountain Rural Electric Association, which provides electrical service in parts of Colorado, offers scholarships via drawings in its regions. Talk to your company's human resources or benefits department. The key to all of these options, however, is to get started early at saving, signing up, and applying. Tons of interactive tools are available online to ease the job of finding and funding an education.

Also, talk to your college-bound young adult about money—yours and theirs. Talk about ways they can save and ease the financial burden on you. A few suggestions:

- Put them on a budget and make sure they stick to it. We all easily can fritter away money, especially a child on her own for the first time.
- Instead of sending checks, try a cash card. The cash card looks like a credit card but acts more like a checking account with a built-in spending limit. It's basically a gift card "loaded" with a set amount of money that then can be used like a credit card until the money runs out. It can be reloaded, too, as necessary.

- Consider a low-limit credit card as an optional spending tool. It's not only a lid on the spending, but it enables you to see where your college student's money is going.
- If a child gets a part-time or summer job, help them set up a plan to save a portion of their earnings for college costs. The savings even could be in the form of automatic withdrawal, from a savings or checking account.

Let's look at a few of those funding options.

---

## COLLEGE INFORMATION AND TOOLS

- *College Money* (www.collegemoney.com). *From a New Jersey–based college financial planning firm, the site has strategy and saving suggestions for boomers and their loved ones.*
- *College Savings Plan Network* (www.collegesavings.org). *An affiliate of the National Association of State Treasurers, this is a clearinghouse for information among existing college savings programs. Click on "Site Locator" to find your state's programs.*
- *FastWeb* (www.fastweb.com). *This is an online free scholarship search service from The Monster Network* (www.monster.com).
- *FinAid* (www.finaid.org). *This nonprofit offers a comprehensive annotated collection of information about student financial aid and has calculators, aid applications, and more. It also includes valuable information for student aid and the military.*
- *The College Board* (www.collegeboard.org): *More than 100 years old, this nonprofit offers all kinds of college information for students, parents, and educators, including scholarship searches, financing and loan interactive tools, and online loan applications.*

- *Sallie Mae®* (www.salliemae.com). *Company primarily provides federal and private student loans, including consolidation loans, for undergraduate and graduate students and their parents. In addition, Sallie Mae offers comprehensive information and resources to assist students, parents, and guidance professionals with the financial aid process.*
- *SaveAndInvest.org* (www.saveandinvest.org). *From the NASA Investor Education Foundation, click on "Save for College" to access information on strategies, calculators, and more.*
- *Saving For College* (www.savingforcollege.com). *A great source of accurate college financing information. Click on "529 Plans" for an easy-to-use plan locator.*
- *Scholarship Experts* (www.scholarshipexperts.com). *Plenty of free material on finding and paying for higher education.*
- *U.S. Department of Education* (www.ed.gov). *Click on "Students" and then "Find & Pay for College" for information on choosing colleges, financing, and more.*

**529 PLAN.** This includes the popular tax-advantaged education savings program set up by the federal government. It gets its name from the portion of the Internal Revenue Service code, Section 529, that established it. It's funded with after-tax dollars and is treated like a gift, thus subject to federal gifting laws that set a maximum for annual contributions without triggering gift-tax consequences (for 2006, the maximum is $12,000 per recipient for an individual or $24,000 per recipient for a couple; lump sum exemptions and state exceptions are also available), but earnings grow free of federal and state taxes if used for qualified higher education expenses, including tuition and fees, books and supplies, and room and board. Some states exempt earnings and/or allow at least part of contributions to be state-tax free. (Check with your state to be sure.) Individuals also can contribute a lump sum (up to $60,000 in 2006) that amounts to up to five years of funding for a 529 plan.

Nonqualified withdrawals are subject to your federal income tax plus a 10 percent withdrawal fee. Additionally, the tax status of these plans is set to expire in 2011 unless Congress extends it.

*Upromise and BabyMint are two different programs that rebate cash back to a designated education savings plans.*

529 plans are available through a variety of sources. An unusual twist on the 529 plan is from Needham, Massachusetts–based Upromise, Inc. *(www.upromise .com)*. After you sign up online and register your credit cards, a portion of your cards' purchases from any of thousands of companies, restaurants, hotels, and online retailers goes into your designated 529 plan, which can be managed by a variety of professional investment teams. Another organization with a "rebate-to-education" formula is BabyMint *(www.babymint.com)* from Collegiate Funding Services. Sign up and get a BabyMint College Savings Credit Card from MBNA and then earn a 1 percent rebate back to a designated 529 or Coverdell savings plan on every purchase, no matter where you shop. Additional rebates are available from hun-

dreds of participating businesses. For purposes of financial aid, 529 plans are considered a parental asset as opposed to a student asset.

**QUALIFIED STATE TUITION PLANS.** These are another twist on the 529 plans. The prepaid option allows anyone to pay for future tuition at state colleges or universities or qualified out-of-state institutions. There are limitations in that private universities may not be included. The advantage is that you're paying for school at today's rates instead of tomorrow's and are guaranteed you won't have to pay any higher rates. Payment may be in a lump sum or over time. The money also can be used out of state with limitations. (Visit the College Savings Network, *www.collegesaavings.org,* for more information.) One big tax advantage of these qualified state plans is that you can contribute up to $100,000 in a lump sum (it's viewed as $20,000 over the five years) without incurring the gift tax penalty.

**COVERDELL EDUCATION SAVINGS ACCOUNTS (ESA).** Formerly these were known as Education IRAs. Earnings on cash in these accounts are federal income tax–free as long as they're withdrawn for qualified education expenses, in this case including expenses incurred for grades K through12. That's a plus over 529 plans. But the maximum annual contribution limit on an ESA is $2,000, and they have certain eligibility requirements, including age, to qualify. No funding is allowed after the beneficiary reaches age 18, and all funds must be withdrawn by age 30.

You can have both a 529 plan and an ESA in the same person's name. You can have multiple ESAs, but be careful that the total amount put aside for one individual doesn't exceed the $2,000 maximum contribution a year.

**ROTH IRAS.** Funded with after-tax dollars, a Roth IRA's earnings are tax-free if certain conditions are met, and not subject to penalty for early distribution if the money is withdrawn for qualified education expenses. In

2006, annual contributions are limited to $4,000 ($5,000 for those age 50 or over).

**GRANTS AND SCHOLARSHIPS.** This is free money from various organizations, people, and schools. Recipients must qualify based on a variety of factors, from academics to athletics to need and more. Don't let your kids be dissuaded from looking and applying for scholarship or grant monies. Just because a student doesn't have a 4.0 grade average doesn't mean he can't qualify for some free monies. Check out the myriad Web sites out there and talk to guidance counselors and potential schools to determine if your child might qualify for free money.

Some states also offer various scholarships for the college bound. Of course, the catch with many of these scholarships is that the student must achieve a minimal grade point average to continue receiving the money. Other savings programs are available, too. The state of Colorado, for instance, has the College Opportunity Fund. Because of increased tuition at state colleges and universities, the state's legislature set aside about $2,500 per year per student for those attending in-state public schools. Students register online, the school sends in a list of its students, and the COF sends a $2,500 check made out jointly to the student and the school, to be applied to the student's tuition.

**FEDERAL STUDENT LOANS.** The details for each of these types of loans vary, as do the qualifications and payback periods. For more information, check out many of the Web sites we mentioned or visit Sallie Mae® (*www.salliemae.com*). Some of the loan options include:

- PLUS loans, low variable-interest rate parent loans not based on income or assets.
- Stafford loans, loans with a low variable-interest rate; available subsidized (need-based) where the government pays the interest while student is in school and immediately following; or unsubsidized (not need-based) where the borrower pays the interest from the beginning.

- Perkins loans, low-interest student loans based on need.

**MORE OPTIONS.** Beyond these options are various Treasury bonds and notes (available through Treasury Direct, *www.savingsbonds.gov*) and investments such as mutual funds, stocks, bonds, and more. Determining what works for your situation is up to you and your investment advisor and depends on your time frame, "acceptable" levels of risk, need, and, of course, the demands of your generational sandwich.

# Remember:

- Talk about money with your elderly loved one before it becomes a time of crisis.
- Before you determine a care plan for someone, first figure out where you are financially and where your loved one is financially so that you can realistically evaluate the options.
- Consider buying long-term care insurance for your elderly loved one if she is eligible, and for yourself and your own future, too.
- Possible sources of income for an elderly loved one could include reverse mortgages, whole life insurance policies, or life settlements.
- Include your children in discussions and decisions about your elderly parents. If not, they may not fully understand the emotions and hardships that can be associated with the role of caregiver.
- Plenty of options exist to fund college expenses. Saving for retirement, on the other hand, is up to you.
- Among options to fund colleges are 529 plans, student loans, scholarships, education savings accounts, Roth IRAs, and more.

# Living Arrangements

## Chapter 8

**A**s members of the Sandwich Generation, you, along with your parents, face many choices with varying financial ramifications as you age. The decisions you both make subsequently have a far-reaching effect on your lives as well as the lives of future generations. Make the right decision, and an aging parent enjoys the last years of his life in financial comfort, peace, and tranquility while you and your family look forward to your future with confidence. Choose incorrectly, and the financial and emotional upheaval can cross all generations and leave you with few or no retirement options.

What's the best living situation for Mom and/or Dad? What can they afford? What do they want to do? What's best for their health? How will their choice of living environs affect the lives of you and your kids? What works best for you? All are questions that you, family members, and aging loved ones must ask, address, analyze, and answer to ensure financial as well as physical and emotional satisfaction with these weighty decisions.

Beyond maintaining the status quo or simply going to a nursing home, aging seniors have myriad living options—some costly and others not so. A few of those include modifying an existing home to make it senior-friendly; in-home companionship, assistance, or home-health care, full- or part-time; moving in with you or one of your siblings; downsizing to an apartment, condominium, or smaller, one-floor home; moving to a co-housing community; moving to a retirement community; moving to a continuing care (step-down) retirement community; or moving to an assisted-living facility.

Each option comes with its pros and cons, and is of course influenced by an individual's health and overall well-being as well as her finances and those of the adult children. Some options, especially those where care or camaraderie is readily available, may make better sense than others for an elderly parent, especially if you are a long-distance caregiver to your aging parent. With the soaring costs of elder care, money always will be a consideration.

How much a living setting for a senior costs depends on what, if any, care is provided; how much care; where it is located; his eligibility for assistance and entitlements; and any financial planning or lack thereof. But don't be dissuaded from exploring the various living options for your aging loved one just because you or your parent thinks it's not affordable. It may be quite manageable if you tap into all the available revenue sources. We discussed a few such resources in the Chapter 7, and more are available. Of course, as we emphasized, the affordable options are much more abundant for those with long-term care insurance. If your parent doesn't have that insurance and has done no advance planning—as in investments, savings, and more—then you may want to consider working with experts in finance and accounting as well as elder care to determine the best use of existing funding sources.

The real issue, though, is how an aging loved one can best deploy her financial and emotional resources to provide the best possible quality of life, says geriatric care manager Joie. That issue becomes more problematic when adult children live at a distance from their aging parents and perhaps lack the resources—of finances or time—to thoroughly research the answers.

Elder law expert Sabatino suggests that before making any decisions that involve paying large sums of money to an assisted-living or other facility, talk to an elder law expert who knows the law and your options and can be your advocate. A place may have fancy brochures and great food before you move in, but what about once you're there? What services and quality does a facility promise? What's the five-year track record of its fees?

## Statistics and Expectations

Making the right choices starts with knowing and understanding all the options, then addressing them *before* a living situation for an elderly parent develops into a crisis. Talk with your parents about current and future living options as they age, while they're still competent and aging well. Don't wait until a parent is hospitalized and faced with little or no choice except a move to whatever nursing home will take him. Keep in mind, too, that many retirement and assisted-living communities, as well as nursing homes, often have waiting lists. Nursing homes, especially, limit the number of Medicaid beds. Plus, with the new eligibility requirements, qualifying for Medicaid is *not* a last-minute option. (More on that in Chapter 10.)

*Talk to aging parents about long-term housing options while they're still vibrant and sharp. If you wait until a crisis occurs, you may find yourself scrambling to find anything that works.*

Waiting until a crisis to have "the talk" is in fact the biggest mistake that baby boomers and their elderly parents make, says financial gerontologist Cutler.

To approach the issue of living and care options with an aging loved one, Cutler suggests the "kitchen table talk" or even a discussion at Thanksgiving dinner. The death of an actor, an elderly friend's illness, a tough financial situation, or even politics could segue into a conversation about an aging parent's preferences in future living situation and care and how that could be financed when the time comes. If the approach to the subject doesn't work the first time, don't give up. Approach the topic again later. "Some of the talk isn't financial in nature, but it has important financial ramifications," says Cutler.

Even if parents aren't ready to move to a smaller home, condo, or retirement community, discuss ways to make their lives easier. Can their existing home be made more comfortable or easier for an aging parent to navigate? Some of those modifications could include installing handrails near steps, fixing that buckled walkway out front, installing an air purifier or humidifier, and more. Don't overlook simple, inexpensive purchases that can go a long way toward making a senior more comfortable in his surroundings and thus, often, able to remain independent longer. That includes assistive devices like ergonomic can or bottle openers, large-handled utensils, shower or bath seats, telephones with oversize keypads or amplifiers, and pill box organizers. Even if a parent doesn't need any of these devices right now, what if she becomes ill or weakened? Wouldn't a few of those items help?

If a parent is living in a multistory home, what about installing an elevator or creating a self-sufficient environment on one floor? Better yet, would that parent consider selling the larger home, putting the proceeds in a low-risk investment like an annuity for future needs, and then moving to a single-floor ranch or patio home? Talk with your parents about other living options, too. Instead of hanging on to that obviously too-big house with its attendant worries, high maintenance, and isolation, why not consider a cohousing community (more on that later) with a group of friends or a multigenerational group, a condominium with great living spaces and amenities, or even a patio home or apartment community with maintenance provided? If your or a sibling's home is conducive to it and the psychological and emotional fit is right, what about remodeling a detached garage or extra area in the home to create an apartment for an elderly parent?

Retirement communities with multiple types of living situations are also worth considering. Sometimes called step-down or continuing-care retirement communities, they offer a senior the option of moving into an apartment or even a single-family home while he is still vibrant and independent, and then—as the need arises—stepping down to assisted living and then to skilled care, or vice versa, depending on the situation. Be aware, however, that many of these multilevel retirement communities require significant buy-ins or cash commitments up front.

## SOURCES OF INFORMATION AND HELP

- *AARP (www.aarp.org). Site has extensive suggestions on living options as well as advice on how to modify an existing home to make it elderly accessible.*
- *American Health Care Association (www .ahca.org). This is a nonprofit federation of affiliated state health organizations of all kinds. Be sure to check out its Families 4 Care (http://longtermcareliving.com) for lots of very helpful information and resources.*
- *Assisted Living Foundation of America (www .alfa.org). Includes loads of free, helpful information, including guidelines to help with decision making, facility locator tool, and consumer checklists.*
- *Consumer Consortium on Assisted Living (http://ccal.org). Nonprofit consumer-based, nationwide organization focuses on the needs, rights, and protection of assisted-living consumers, their caregivers, and loved ones.*
- *H2U (www.h2u.com). Affiliated with community hospitals and health facilities, local programs offer events, health screenings, classes, information, hospital upgrades, and more.*
- *Hospice Foundation of America (www .hospicefoundation.org). Nonprofit that offers helpful explanations and information on hospice.*

- *National Association of Professional Geriatric Care Managers (www.caremanager.org). For more information and to locate a professional geriatric care manager in your area, click on "Find a Care Manager."*
- *National Hospice and Palliative Care Organization (www.nhpco.org). A wealth of helpful information as well as local links to hospice sources.*
- *NCB Development Corporation (www .ncbdc.org). Affiliate of National Cooperative Bank, a national nonprofit organization that empowers underserved communities. Check its "Coming Home Program," about assisted living for low-income, frail elderly living in rural areas (www.ncbdc.org/ta_hs_ ComingHomeProgram.aspx).*
- *SeniorHousingNet (www.seniorhousing .net). From Move, Inc., formerly Homestore, Inc., this site offers helpful information on senior housing and health issues and options.*
- *U.S. Administration on Aging (www.aoa.gov). Click on "Elders & Families" and then "Housing."*
- *U.S. Department of Medicare and Medicaid Services (www.mms.gov). The government's official site for these two programs.*

Remember Liza from earlier in the book? Her vibrant mom, Marie, fell, hit her head, and wound up dependent on Liza, living under her roof, and making them both miserable until she moved into a continuing-care retirement community. Although Liza's mom started out in assisted living, she ended up in her own independent apartment.

At the other end of the spectrum are Kathy and Ray, also from earlier in the book. Ray, who had written a living will, had a massive heart attack and was rushed to the hospital. Because he didn't have the document with him and his doctor didn't have a copy, Ray was put on life support and remained in a vegetative state for a year while Kathy fought in court to have him removed from the machines. Luckily, several months before the attack, both had realized that Ray's health was failing so

---

## TIPS FROM REAL LIFE

*Do you have an elderly parent who needs to move out of a large, cumbersome home but refuses to do so?*

- *Talk to him or her about the three Ss—safety, social life, and security—and the one big F—finances—of downsizing to a senior-centered retirement community or even a condo or apartment and whether it meets their needs.*

- *No matter how competent a senior is, research his options from a financial and care standpoint. That includes talking to community managers about financing options, then comparing costs with your parent's finances as well as your own and that of your siblings. Seniors often aren't aware of the true cost of a living option.*

- *Visit potential places first without your elderly loved one but with her attitudes, beliefs, and ideas in mind so that you can eliminate those situations that you know won't be a good fit for your parent.*

- *Then choose several places and take your parent to visit them so he can make his or her own choice. This isn't about taking away their independence; it's about giving it back to them. If your parent's choice is out of her price range, look at ways you and/or siblings can help.*

- *When the big move does occur, make sure your parent takes some familiar belongings to the new home.*

- *If a parent gives up her car, make sure there are other personal mobility options that suit your parent's tastes and needs. It could be an on-call chauffeur/limousine service; nearby on-call friends or family; a driving maid or caregiver for one, two, or more days a week; local government-sponsored senior transportation service such as Access-a-Ride at reduced rates; or even the regular bus or shuttle service provided by many retirement communities.*

they moved into a patio home in a continuing-care retirement community. After Ray had his heart attack, Kathy at least didn't have to worry about taking care of the big house they had sold just months earlier.

Unfortunately many Americans aren't as knowledgeable about living options as Kathy and Ray were. Let's look at a few statistics from an October 2004 MetLife Mature Market Institute survey of 40- to 70-year-olds, "The MetLife Long-term Care IQ Test." Incidentally, only slightly more than one in three (37 percent) of Americans passed this IQ test!

- 45 percent underestimated the average annual cost of receiving long-term care in a private room in a nursing home; 27 percent overestimated the cost, and 27 percent estimated correctly.

- Fewer than four in ten (39 percent) recognized that a 65-year-old has a 50 percent likelihood of living another 18 years. Only slightly more than one in four (28 percent) of these same people understood that once someone reaches 85, it's even odds that they'll eventually need help with activities of daily living—or ADL, in the jargon.

- 55 percent of respondents thought that most people who receive long-term care do so in a nursing home. Only 18 percent correctly recognized that the most likely place for long-term care is in their homes.

- Only 37 percent recognized that the cost of long-term care insurance is three times more expensive if you buy the policy at age 65 rather than age 45.

- 41 percent believed long-term care is an entitlement that all Americans are eligible for when they retire. The same number cited Medicare, Medicare supplement (Medigap), or disability insurance as forms of insurance that pay for the care. (In reality, long-term care insurance is the primary form of insurance that pays for extended care at home, in assisted-living facilities, or in a nursing home.)

*72 percent of Americans are unaware of the real cost of receiving care in a private room in a nursing home.*

—"The MetLife Long-term Care IQ Test"

On a more positive note, however, the same survey showed that 86 percent of respondents do know that long-term care involves ongoing assistance with day-to-day activities and that it can be necessitated by many conditions, including Alzheimer's, dementia, accidents, or chronic illness.

Nonetheless, as the MetLife survey shows, the majority of the Sandwich Generation is ill-prepared to make the long-term care choices that inevitably we must make for ourselves and, most likely, our aging loved ones.

This could be a situation in which bringing in an outside professional geriatric care manager or other expert might make sense to help you analyze all aspects of a parent's situation. As we've talked about, these professionals are familiar with the finances, options, and ramifications of long-term care and know what it takes to create a successful living environment for an elderly individual as well as his family members—whether at a distance or nearby. The cost of such expertise varies dramatically across the country and can be priced per situation analysis, or what's referred to as "intervention" (generally well under $1,000) or per hour for simple consultation ($80 to $200 an hour). A full intervention generally buys a comprehensive assessment that involves going into an elderly person's home; meeting with that person, their children, and other family members; considering all the areas of her life (finances, assets, income, medications, diagnoses, home safety, social network, religious affiliations if applicable, location of children, doctors, medical history); and then analyzing or assessing all those elements to design a care plan and action plan that include short- and long-term goals.

A full intervention is a snapshot of where the senior and her family are now and what needs to be done in the future, says Joie. Her firm's fee for this kind of help is approximately $700 to $850.

Some attorneys specializing in elder law, such as New York–based Davidow, for example, also may have geriatric care specialists on staff to help.

If bringing in professional help is out of the question, then you'll need to consider all of the above on your own, just as the geriatric care manager does, in order to accurately assess the current situation and determine what's best for everyone long term. Your assessment should consider:

- The elderly person's personality, preferences, health, lifestyle choices, and finances
- The location, lifestyles, preferences, and finances of you, your family, your siblings, and their families
- Your elderly loved one's health and well-being currently, as well as projected into the future based on diagnoses, medical history, and more
- Medications involved
- Home safety, accessibility, and maintenance
- Social network
- Religious concerns and affiliations
- Short-term goals as well as long-range ones

Try to be objective in your assessment. That's probably the toughest part, but it's essential. Joie says that where her own mother is concerned, even she brings in an outside, completely objective individual to oversee the choices she makes.

# The Relocation Dilemma

Just as the status quo isn't always the best option when it comes to a suitable living situation for an elderly parent, neither is an automatic move to where the grown kids and grandkids are. Among the issues involved are:

- Uprooting of a senior accustomed to his routine in a familiar locale with an already established social network in place
- Leaving a medical network already in place. This is especially significant if a senior has a doctor she trusts and who is familiar with preferences, care, history, and conditions.
- Loss of a senior's independence as a result of a move to unfamiliar territory

- Cost of the move—not only the dollar amount for the moving company, but also in terms of your time. If, for example, you, the adult child, work, can you afford to take time off work to oversee the move? The Medical and Family Leave Act mandates the time off if your employer qualifies, but without pay. Can you and your own family afford your lost wages to help elderly Mom or Dad clean out the family home, pack up, move across country, and get resettled in their new home?
- The ongoing commitment to caregiving. Are you willing emotionally and financially to accept the job?

Johnny, his wife, and three children lived in New York for the time being—they have moved twice coast to coast over the past five years. Johnny worried about his 82-year-old mother, Betsy, who lived in suburban Chicago, and he constantly prodded her to move to New York, where he and his family could be there to help her if something happened. But Betsy refused to budge. Although none of her family was nearby, she had a stable social and medical network, and she liked it. Money wasn't a concern because Betsy had several million dollars socked away in various retirement and savings vehicles. And, as she kept saying to Johnny, "What happens if you move again? Then where will that leave me? I'll have to move yet again."

Then Betsy had a massive heart attack. Fortunately, Johnny had been footing the bill for Betsy's personal emergency alarm around her neck for several years, and that alarm saved her life. Johnny spent the next three months commuting between New York and Chicago two days every week—a commitment sandwiched between his responsibilities as a doctor, a husband, and a father to three kids, ages 8 to 17. Luckily Johnny's partner in his practice was able to cover for him in his absence. But the commuting was a financial, physical, and emotional strain, especially with his oldest nearing college age. The hassles and headaches could have been avoided had Betsy been willing to move while she still could. Unfortunately, when she recognized the need to move after the heart attack, it was too late. Her health was too frail and she simply couldn't handle the upheaval of a move. Johnny then contracted lung cancer and had to scale back his commutes. "At some point, I just had to accept my mom's decision and let go," he says matter-of-factly. "My own family has to come first."

Let's look more closely at some of the living options available to seniors and the financial ramifications and considerations of each.

# Independent Living

## INDEPENDENT IN-HOME LIVING/CARE

*Care Options:* Range from unassisted, to homemaker or home-health aide, to skilled nursing and more, depending on situation, finances, facilities, and other factors.

*Cost:* Varies dramatically depending on service provided, frequency, and care required—from a few dollars to more than $100,000 a year; the national average 2005 hourly rate for home-health aides is $19, for homemaker/companion, $17, according to the MetLife Mature Market Institute®.

*Payment Options:* Long-term care insurance generally will pay for in-home medical care if a senior qualifies (check the policy for details); financial assistance may be available for certain home modifications (check with local Agency on Aging); Medicare pays cost of periodic doctor-prescribed skilled nursing visits; in some cases Medicaid will cover the cost of in-home care through its waiver programs.

*Special Considerations:*
- Are the costs of home modifications and/or home upkeep prohibitive?
- What are the health and safety issues associated with remaining in a too-large and/or multistory home?

- Is assistance close by and readily available if necessary? What's the cost of that assistance? Can you or an elderly parent afford it?
- What is the possibility of isolation and lack of social interaction, and their effect on an aging parent's mental and physical health?
- What are the transportation issues and cost of that transportation?

*More Information:*
- AARP (www.aarp.org)
- National Reverse Mortgage Lenders Association (www.reversemortgage.org)
- Senior HousingNet® (www.seniorhousingnet .com)
- Helpguide® (www.helpguide.org; click on "Aging Issues")
- SeniorOutlook.com (www.senioroutlook .com)
- Senior Resource (www.seniorresource .com; click on "Housing Choices")
- U.S. Administration on Aging (www.aoa.gov; click on "Elders and Families")
- U.S. Department of Housing and Urban Development (www.hud.gov)

**KEEP THE HOUSE AND STAY PUT.** That's a popular, fast answer for many aging Americans who worry about the finances of a move or don't like the idea of moving to unfamiliar surroundings. But it's not necessarily the preferred choice from the point of view of the Sandwich Generation, who often sees the bigger picture.

For some seniors, though, the familiarity and comfort of a longtime home works well with the help of ingenuity, home modifications, and in-home assistance or care. Keeping the big family home also can be a viable option if an adult child opts to move back in as caregiver for an aging parent. An adult child might welcome the opportunity to move back home for financial reasons—perhaps after a layoff or divorce—or to enable him to save money to buy a house or condo.

For other seniors, though, remaining in the too-big, too-costly-to-maintain, too-remote home can be an intense and lonely struggle. Every sneeze ignites the fear of falling ill in isolation as well as worries about routine matters such as getting out to mail bills or buy groceries, even though the nearest neighbor is 12 feet away next door.

Remaining in their home may not be what's best for the health and welfare of your loved ones or the best use of financial resources. Contrary to what a senior might think, staying in the home isn't always a cheap solution. How high are those monthly utility bills on the big (and drafty) old house? They are probably a lot higher than those of an energy-efficient, smaller home. And what happens if a parent becomes ill? The old homestead could be the least flexible or most expensive option of the lot. If a parent requires round-the-clock care, is the house conducive to in-home care? Are there extra living quarters? Can the electrical wiring handle the sophisticated machinery that might be necessary? By staying put, a senior might actually be minimizing her options.

*Remaining in their home may not be what's best for your loved ones' health and welfare, and may not be the best use of financial resources.*

## INEXPENSIVE OPTIONS TO MAKE LIFE EASIER

*Don't overlook investing a few dollars in assistive devices (if prescribed by a doctor, some may be covered by health insurance policies) and utensils that can make life easier for an aging parent. A few items to consider and their approximate costs include:*

- *Shower seat or chair, $30 and up*
- *Detachable handheld flexible shower head, $32 and up*
- *Nonslip grips in tub, $7 and up*
- *Handrails for toilet and tub, $31 and up*
- *Movable and/or extendable magnifying mirror, $30 and up*
- *Zipper puller, $8.50 to $10.50*

- *Nonslip footwear, $10 and up*
- *Waterproof/rubber mattress pad, $35*
- *Reacher/grabber, a few dollars to $55*
- *Air purifier/antibacterial humidifier, $100 and up*
- *Large-handled kitchen utensil, $4 to $8 each*
- *Easy-to-grip cups and mugs, $6*
- *Pill organizers, $2 and up*
- *Hot/cold packs, $5 and up*
- *Long-handled shoe horn, $6*
- *Glasses' chain, $5 to $10 and up*
- *Cane, $60*
- *Lift chairs, $470 and up*
- *Door knob gripper, $5 and up*

Deciding what works for your elderly loved ones takes frank discussions with them about their money, mobility, and care; careful analysis of their home's condition and maneuverability from a safety standpoint; and a hard look at the financial ramifications of their choices. Keep in mind that if a parent decides to tap the equity in his home through a reverse mortgage, as we mentioned in Chapter 7, the home must pass inspection and meet certain building standards in order to qualify. It's possible that if a parent's home is older, the cost to make the necessary corrections negates any significant cash gain from a reverse mortgage.

*Does an elderly parent's home offer flexibility or can it be retrofitted for flexibility in the event of a serious and debilitating illness?*

At 96, Ella has outlived three husbands. She's still vibrant, but a fall last year has slowed her to the point that she now needs a 24-hour home-health aide. The annual tab for the assistance is $156,000 a year. Luckily Ella is wealthy, has a large home, and can afford the in-home care she needs. Could you or your elderly loved one afford this care? The average person obviously can't without proper planning.

Ed, 79, was single and owned a large, old, rambling home. Years ago he had it converted into four one-bedroom apartments, one of which he lived in. Rent from the extra apartments added to his already substantial income from investments, his pension, and monthly Social Security. When Ed suffered his massive and debilitating heart attack, his net worth was approximately $3.5 million, not including the house. That was certainly enough to enable him to have in-home care for years to come. Yet he was forced to go to a nursing home (which he never left) because his small apartment didn't have room for a live-in home-health aide or similar caregiver.

Remember Sarah, the 97-year-old with the arthritic knees who has lived in her home for 72 years? She's at the other end of the spectrum. Sarah's home was modified to make it more elderly friendly. She has a motorized chair elevator so she doesn't have to negotiate the stairs. She had grab bars installed in the bathrooms and along the walls in the hallways. She has sturdy fur-

---

## COST OF SARAH AT HOME

**In-home help**

| | |
|---|---|
| 25 hours a week at $15/hour: | $375 a week |
| **Total:** | **$19,500/year*** |

**Home modifications**

| | |
|---|---|
| ■ Installation of grab bars: | $30 |
| ■ Bathroom modifications (including shower seat, detachable handheld flexible showerhead, handrails for tub and toilet, nonslip grips): | $100 |
| ■ Chair elevator: | $9,800 |
| **Total:** | **$9,930*** |

*Not including domestic worker/nanny tax obligations (FICA, Medicare, and unemployment taxes, estimated at 7.65% of wages; payable if wages are $1,400 or more in 2005 and $1,500 or more in 2006.)

niture strategically placed throughout the home to help her maneuver, and she has affordable private help that she pays $15 an hour for five hours a day, five days a week. She also has an active social life and plenty of interaction with her family, so she's not alone and aging. Additionally, Sarah and her recently deceased husband planned ahead financially. A professor at a local university, he actively participated in pensions and savings programs. They had more than adequate health insurance and were early participants in long-term care insurance.

---

## TYPICAL REPAIR COSTS:

*Following are estimated typical costs for possible repairs/maintenance that could be associated with an elderly parent remaining in an existing home. Prices, of course, vary dramatically by geography and project, including size of job, contractor, and more.*

- *New roof: $4,000 to $6,000 for asphalt, three-tab, 30-year roof that is 2,151 square feet/two-story.*
- *Replace/repair plumbing: $6,000 to remodel four-piece bathroom; $1,500 to $3,500 to replace a water line into the home.*
- *Replace/repair wiring: $60 an hour and up.*
- *Exterior painting: $3,400 to repaint 50-foot by 30-foot two-story with 16-foot by 12-foot garage, 15 windows, and one door in average condition.*
- *Interior painting: several hundred dollars to several thousand depending on how many rooms are painted.*
- *New heater/air-conditioning unit: $2,500 to $3,500 to install new high-efficiency, forced-air furnace; independent central air conditioner installation, $8,000 to $15,000.*
- *Add insulation: a few hundred dollars and up.*
- *New windows: several hundred dollars and up.*
- *New concrete walkway or driveway: $2,200 for 30-foot by 12-foot driveway, including tear out of existing driveway.*
- *Removal/repair of buried fuel tank/environmental cleanup: $7,000 to $20,000 and up.*
- *Lawn and garden maintenance: $30 to $50 and up per visit.*
- *New kitchen stove or refrigerator: several hundred dollars and up.*

The fruits of all that preparation enable Sarah to deal with the financial ramifications of anything she might need to make her life easier.

Unfortunately, Art, 87, wasn't as lucky. Although he was devastated after his wife of 37 years died, he refused to move to a retirement community. Instead he just sat in the empty house, shuffling through old photographs and papers. "The house is paid off," was his response whenever the discussion of a move came up. Money wasn't an issue, either, because Art still received residual commissions from his longtime sales job as a manufacturer's representative as well as $3,000 a month in Social Security. (He worked and continued to pay into the system until age 82.) He did give in to his long-distance adult children's demands that he have grab bars installed in the hallway and outside the front door, non-slip grips and a flexible handheld shower head installed in the tub, and a handrail along the back steps. He also had a housekeeper who came in five days a week for several hours a day at $15 an hour to help with the cooking, cleaning, grocery shopping, and other day-to-day matters (his daughter had found her by networking with friends in the community). He talked daily to his children and grandchildren, and they visited regularly. But no one, not even his physician, could persuade him to move to a retirement community where he could live a vibrant, socially interactive life.

Although Art knew his kids and physician were right, he refused to budge until he became seriously ill. After he recovered, his children were adamant that he absolutely had to move, and they helped ease him into the decision. They researched the various retirement communities, visiting them first, and then taking Art to visit. Instead of an "old folks' home" or nursing home, Art was surprised to find that the small religious-affiliated retirement community was a normal apartment complex filled with his peers, where he could have meals served to him in a beautiful dining room if he liked.

"You're right," was Art's response to his kids. He moved in along with his favorite furniture and photographs, which gave a familiar feel to his new, smaller

## ART'S FINANCES*

**Income**

- Social Security: $ 3,200/month
- Sales commission residuals: $ 400/month
- Investment dividends and income: $ 800/month
- Mandatory IRA withdrawal
  ($8,897/year from $250,000): $ 741/month

**Total monthly income:** **$ 5,141**

**Monthly Retirement Home Cost**

| | |
|---|---|
| Room/board: | $ 4,320 |
| Phone: | $ 20 |
| Housekeeper ($15/hr, 3 hrs/day, 5 days/wk): | $ 900 |

**Total expenses:** **$ 5,240**

**Shortfall:\*\*** **$ 99**

**Monthly at-home cost**

| | |
|---|---|
| Maintenance/upkeep* | |
| Yard ($50 × 4), etc.:* | $ 275 |
| Repair/replace items as needed (annual cost/12):* | $ 850 |
| Food/supplies:* | $ 800 |
| Other: | $ 320 |

**Total:** **$ 2,445**

**Car**

| | |
|---|---|
| Insurance:* | $ 200 |
| Gas:* | $ 75 |
| Maintenance:* | $ 50 |

**Total:** **$ 325**

**Utilities**

| | |
|---|---|
| Electrical/gas:* | $ 500 |
| Phone:* | $ 150 |
| Cable:* | $ 65 |
| Other:* | $ 180 |

**Total:** **$ 895**

**Total at-home cost (including car):** **$ 3,465**

*\* Tax liabilities not included in totals.*
*\*\* Shortfall made up by increasing IRA withdrawal.*

home. His caregiver kept up her visits, too, which provided him the mobility and freedom he might otherwise have lacked. Art spent his twilight years without fretting about the house, enjoyed a large circle of friends, and had an active social life. The cost of renting the apartment—$3,200 a month—was a nonissue, too. His Social Security check covered most of it. The rest of the monthly expenses were manageable, especially because he no longer had to pay for upkeep of the large home he had sold (utilities alone amounted to more than $500 a month). Because he was over age 70½, he also had a required minimum distribution on his IRA retirement savings, and because he no longer had the expense of his car, he found himself quite comfortable. He didn't have to touch the proceeds from the home's sale (it sold for $200,000, substantially under the $250,000 exclusion of gains on the sale of a house that would have incurred taxes) and was able to invest in an annuity for his grandchildren. Not all seniors adapt as well as Art, however.

Sam, 83, was frail but healthy. A widower, he had lived alone in their home since his wife died 12 years earlier. Finally, though, his kids decided he just couldn't handle the big house any longer. They held a big estate sale and sold the family home of 50 years and much of its contents. The rest they put in storage. They then used the sale proceeds to pay for Sam's care in a senior assisted-living facility. Sam was so overwhelmed and overcome with the emotion of the move that he doesn't even know what possessions he has left—no familiar belongings made the move with him. After 12 years alone, he's also very shy and is having a tough time socially in his new living situation.

**COHOUSING.** From Asheville, North Carolina, to Nevada City, California, and cities in between, cohousing is taking hold as an intergenerational and seniors-only neighborhood living alternative for thousands of people.

In cohousing, which began in Denmark in the early 1990s, people own private homes in a neighborhood-designed environment that includes common supplemental community spaces. Those spaces generally include a community house with kitchen, dining area, laundry facilities, work rooms, playrooms, and other areas along with outdoor spaces. The spaces are inviting and conducive to social interaction, which can be vital for the elderly.

Residents do not share a community economy. Cohousing generally is structured as a condominium association or planned unit developments. Each resident owns her own home and is responsible for her own bills and living expenses. But residents do share responsibility for ongoing management and decisions about the community.

Residents may be integrally involved in the planning and details of cohousing developments, or they can buy into existing communities.

---

## COHOUSING

*Care Options: From homemaker to home-health, skilled nursing, and more, depending on situation, finances, facilities, and other factors*

*Cost: Home purchase and common-area fees, which vary by community and location*

*Payment Options: Private pay; rental generally not an option; home purchase involved*

*Special Considerations:*
- *Can be a great way for an aging person with long-distance family to become part of and a participant in a community.*
- *Cost may be high depending on location.*
- *Some cohousing developments are designed as senior living.*

*More Information:*
- *Abraham Paiss and Associates (www.eldercohousing.org)*
- *The Cohousing Association of the United States (www .cohousing.org)*
- *The Cohousing Company (www.cohousingco.com)*
- *ElderSpirit (www.elderspirit.net)*
- *Wonderland Hill Development Company (www.whdc.com)*

# Retirement Community

With retirement communities that require deposits or expensive buy-ins, what's the refund policy if later you or your aging parents decide against staying there? Make certain of that policy up front or you could be sorry later. If a community has no written policy or won't refund at least part of your funds, look elsewhere.

## RETIREMENT COMMUNITY

*Care Options:* Independent living to nursing home care, depending on the community; some offer step-down or extended care/continuing care options including assisted-living and nursing home care.

*Cost:* Varies dramatically depending on the facility, options available, and whether it is a home-ownership or rental community. Continuous-care facilities often require buy-ins or commitment of assets up front.

*Payment Options:* Private pay for unassisted living in retirement community; long-term care insurance generally covers cost of assisted living for qualified individuals (check your policy for limitations) or nursing home; Medicare will pick up partial cost of occasional skilled nursing visits; Medicaid will cover the cost of in-home care with what's known as waivers (though Medicaid is for the poor, and retirement communities likely will be too expensive); Medicare does not pay for long-term care.

*Special Considerations:*
■ Most, generally including continuous-care facilities, require that an individual be truly independent and able to walk in on his own to move in.
■ Unless your parent is moving into a continuing-care community, moving in may actually limit the options for a person who isn't truly independent and requires assistance, because another move could be a last-minute crisis move instead of thoroughly planned out.
■ If an expensive buy-in or asset commitment is required, consult with your attorney first to review the contract. Is there a refund or recourse if you or an elderly parent has a change of heart and decides not to go or to leave once they're there?
■ What happens if one parent requires more skilled care than the other? Will the healthy spouse remain in independent living while the one needing assistance moves to assisted living, or will assistance be provided so the couple doesn't have to split up, or will some other arrangement be made?

*More Information:*
■ Del Webb, a division of Pulte Homes (www .delwebb.com)
■ Helpguide (www.helpguide.org; click on "Aging Issues")
■ RetirementHomes.com (www .retirementhomes.com)
■ SeniorOutlook.com (www.senioroutlook .com)
■ Senior Resource (www.seniorresource .com; click on "Housing Choices")

Paul and Jane, both elderly and in relatively good health, and their son, an only child, decided their best option was a religious-affiliated continuous-care community near their home in Fort Lauderdale, Florida. The buy-in required the couple to commit their entire estate—worth approximately $5 million—but they and their well-off son thought the price worth the peace of mind for all of them. Plus, the money was for their church, so Paul and Jane made the commitment and moved in.

From the beginning it was a nightmare for the couple. Accustomed to fine food, upscale lifestyle, and enjoying their freedoms, the couple was shocked by the regimen and felt terribly uncomfortable and out of place. When they decided to leave and wanted their money back, they were told they could leave but couldn't have the money. Their son ended up suing the community for the refund. Just before the case was slated to go to court, the parties settled. But it was a costly lesson financially, emotionally, and physically. *Read the fine print* of any contract and consult with a qualified legal advisor *before* you or your elderly parents sign any agreement.

# Moving In with Adult Child (or Vice Versa)

Sharing your home with an elderly loved one can be the ultimate in shared family time for you, your children, and your parent. Or it can be a tremendous sacrifice and source of friction and worry depending on many things ranging from relationship dynamics to space considerations and, of course, money. Even if you have the best intentions in bringing Mom or Dad to live with you, it may not always work out. Liza found that out the hard way when she and her mother ended up at each other's throat.

On the other hand, if a parent wants to or has to move in, if you or your parent can afford it, remodeling the house with a separate apartment or even adding on a separate living area can be a win-win situation for everyone. Before you automatically say that's an unaffordable solution, compare it to the cost if a parent must move to a retirement apartment, assisted living, or a nursing home. The cost of those options starts at tens of thousands of dollars a year! That money could go a

---

## MOVING IN WITH ADULT CHILD

*Living Options:* Family setting.

*Care Options:* Varies depending on need, finances, and more; ranges from simple homemaker assistance to adult day care to skilled in-home nursing care.

*Cost:* Includes the cost of your time as caregiver and lost wages; the average rate for home-health aide is $19/hour, homemaker/companion, $17/hour; some employers provide reduced-cost adult day care for family of their employees; don't overlook tax breaks (more on that in Chapter 9).

*Payment Options:* Private pay; long-term care insurance may cover cost for qualified caregiver expenses (check your policy for qualifications); not covered by Medicaid unless a parent or adult child who claims parent as dependent meets low-income requirements; Medicare does not pay for custodial care per se unless the care is associated with treatment of an illness and then only for a limited duration and as prescribed by a physician; Medicare will pick up partial cost of occasional skilled nursing visits.

*Special Considerations:*
- Is the adult child willing to commit to caregiving responsibilities, or will additional caregiving assistance be required?
- How will the additional cost of the added member in a household be covered?
- What are the potential effects of the move on adult children and their children as well as the elderly person?
- If an adult child is moving into his parent's home, will that child have any household responsibilities other than caregiving?

*More Information:*
- Eldercare Locator (www.eldercare.gov)
- Family Caregivers Alliance (www.caregiver.org)
- National Family Caregivers Association (www.nfcacares.org)

---

---

**COMPARE YOUR OPTIONS**

*Retirement Apartment (monthly)*

| | |
|---|---|
| Room/board | $ 3,000 |
| Utilities (phone, cell phone): | $ 100 |
| Entertainment/other: | $ 100 |
| Transportation | $ 50 |
| Caregiver/companion | |
| ($12/hr, 6 hrs/day, 5 days/wk): | $ 1,440 |
| **Total cost per month/per year:** | **$ 4,690/$56,280** |
| **Home remodel w/bath:** | **$ 32,000** |

---

long way toward a home remodel or addition; plus you, your family, and your elderly parent would have the enjoyment and satisfaction of sharing your lives with each other. And when Mom or Dad is gone, the accessory apartment could be rented for extra income.

# Assisted Living

Assisted living combines residential housing with personal care and minimal health care. Assisted-living facilities do provide 24-hour staffing with basic services for activities of daily living, as well as, generally, housekeeping, three meals a day, transportation, medication management, and social and recreational activities. They do not, however, provide skilled nursing services. That's an important distinction. If an elderly loved one requires ongoing skilled nursing services, consider a nursing home or in-home health care instead. The national average rate for the latter is about $19 an hour, according to MetLife Mature Market Institute® numbers, although it's possible to find private skilled care for less by networking and talking with medical professionals in the community.

More than one million Americans live in about 20,000 assisted-living facilities nationwide, according to the Assisted Living Foundation of America. No federal guidelines exist on care or quality, and state regulations and guidelines differ, so always thoroughly check out

---

## ASSISTED LIVING

*Living Options:* Private, semiprivate, and congregate living areas.

*Care Options:* Custodial care for activities of daily living (ADL) like bathing, washing, dressing, toileting, help with medications and meals; skilled nursing not provided.

*Cost:* Varies by facility, accommodations, and services needed. Nationwide, daily basic fees range from approximately $150 to $200, according to the Assisted Living Federation of America.

*Payment Options:* Private pay; long-term care insurance will cover cost as long as conditions for coverage—as stipulated in insurance contract—are met; generally not covered by Medicaid although exemptions and limited programs in some states offer waivers to pick up the cost; the February 2006 changes to Medicaid now allow states to offer more Medicaid-funded home and community-based services (basically in-home health and personal care services); Medicare does not pay for custodial care; Medicare will pick up cost of occasional skilled nursing visits as prescribed by a physician and for limited duration.

*Special Considerations:*
- Care and costs vary widely, so thoroughly check out any facility up front and on an ongoing basis
- Verify what is and is not included in the basic services package

*More Information:*
- Assisted Living Foundation of America (www.alfa.org)
- Consumer Consortium on Assisted Living (http://ccal.org)

---

any facility up front and on an ongoing basis. That includes drop-in, unscheduled visits.

The cost of care in an assisted-living facility, generally paid for with personal funds, nationally averages about $96 a day, $2,900 a month, or $35,000 a year for basic services in a private room with private bath. That's up about 15 percent from $2,500 a month or about $30,000 a year in 2004, according to MetLife Mature Market Institute® figures. Base rates generally cover room and board, housekeeping, and personal-care assistance. Anything else adds to the daily, monthly, and annual cost. Some facilities also have up-front charges and/or security deposits that may or may not be refundable. When comparing costs of various facilities, ask questions. For example:

- Does the basic rate include two meals a day or three? And what about between-meal snacks?
- Is phone service included in the price? What about long-distance calls?

- Where are meals served? Is it possible to get them in your room? Is there additional cost for that?
- Is laundry service included in the basic rate, or is it added to the cost?

---

## CHECKLIST FOR CHOOSING AN ASSISTED LIVING FACILITY

*The Assisted Living Federation of America (www.alfa.org) has a thorough checklist available online to help you and/or a loved in choosing the appropriate facility. Here is a small excerpt:*

- *Do you and your elderly loved one like the location, outward appearance, atmosphere, and interior décor?*
- *Is the staff friendly? How about the residents? Are they happy?*
- *Is the community designed to fit your parent's needs with an easy floor plan and doorways, halls, and rooms accessible via walkers or wheelchairs?*
- *Does a physician or nurse visit residents regularly to provide medical checkups?*
- *To what extent are medical services available and how are they provided? Does the facility provide a list?*
- *Is staff available to provide 24-hour assistance with activities of daily living (ADLs) if needed?*
- *Does the residence provide housekeeping services in residents' units?*
- *Is transportation available, and on short notice?*
- *Are pharmacy, barber/beautician, and/or physical therapy services offered on site?*
- *Are additional services available if the resident's needs change?*
- *Is there a procedure to pay for additional services like nursing care when the services are needed on a temporary basis, and are billing, payment, and credit policies fair?*
- *Are there different costs for various levels or categories of services?*

- *Is there an appeals process for dissatisfied residents?*
- *Does the residence have specific policies regarding storage of medication, assistance with medications, training and supervision of staff, and recordkeeping?*
- *Is self-administration of medication allowed?*
- *Is there a staff person to coordinate home-health care visits from a nurse, physical therapist, occupational therapist, etc., if needed?*
- *Is staff available to assist residents who experience memory, orientation, or judgment losses?*
- *Does the residence have a clearly stated procedure for responding to a resident's medical emergency?*
- *Are residents' pets allowed in the residence? Who is responsible for their care?*
- *Do volunteers, including family members, come into the residence to help with or to conduct programs?*
- *Does the residence create a sense of community by encouraging residents to participate in activities?*
- *Are different sizes and types of units available?*
- *Do residents have their own lockable doors?*
- *Is a 24-hour emergency response system available from the unit?*
- *Are bathrooms private and designed to accommodate wheelchairs and walkers?*
- *Are residents able to bring their own furnishings for their unit? What may they bring?*
- *Do all units have a telephone and cable or satellite TV? How is billing handled?*

As with a move to a retirement facility, it's essential to ask questions so that you and your elderly parent know what is and isn't included in the cost and what services are and are not provided, so you're not surprised by unexpected additional costs.

Of note with assisted living: It may not be covered by a long-term care insurance policy if an elderly person's condition is such that it doesn't trigger the coverage. Triggers could include the level or type of care needed, the type of facility, or a deduction in the form of a waiting period before benefits begin.

## Nursing Home

The nursing home option has become a dominant image of aging in America today, and one of the out-of-control health care expenses as well. The average cost of a private room in a nursing home today is $203, or $74,095 a year. The average cost of a semi-private room is $176 a day, or $64,240 a year, according to MetLife Mature Market Institute® numbers.

The nursing home image also conjures up fear among many elderly and not-so-elderly among us. Unfortunately, though, the fear generally hasn't been enough to force us to buy long-term care insurance or to save more. Part of the reason for that is misinformation. Remember, most Americans failed MetLife's "Long-term Care IQ Test" discussed earlier in this chapter. Many people mistakenly still believe that the state (Medicaid) or federal government (Medicare) will pick up the tab for nursing home care. Unfortunately, that's generally not the case unless someone has virtually no assets. And with recent changes to Medicaid qualifications, an elderly parent or his adult children will have to pay hefty out-of-pocket expenses long before that parent ever qualifies for the government to pick up the tab. (More on the details of Medicaid qualifications in Chapter 10.)

---

## NURSING HOME

*Care Options:* Skilled and custodial long-term care; some have hospice care available.

*Cost:* National average daily rate for a private room in a nursing home is $203, or $74,095 a year; and $176, or $64,240 a year for a semiprivate room, according to the MetLife Mature Market Institute®

*Payment Options:* Long-term care insurance or private pay. Medicare will pick up the cost for a limited period, up to 100 days (days 21–100 copay required) after a minimum 3-night hospital stay. If individual is covered by both Medicare and Medicaid (dual eligibility), Medicaid will pick up the copay.

*More Information:*

■ *Centers for Medicare and Medicaid Services (www.cms.gov)*

■ *Hospice Foundation of America (www.hospicefoundation .org). Nonprofit that offers helpful explanations and information on hospice.*

■ *LongTermCareLiving.com (www.longtermcareliving.com). From the American Health Care Association and the National Center for Assisted Living, site offers valuable tools to help with locating, evaluating, and deciding on the best living choice for an elderly patient.*

■ *National Hospice and Palliative Care Organization (www .nhpco.org). Much helpful information as well as local links to hospice sources.*

---

# Remember:

■ Talk to aging parents about future living options while they're vibrant and before they ever need to move

■ Involve the entire family in decisions and discussions about what works in the individual situation

■ Make life a little bit easier for an elderly loved one with easy-to-find-and-use assistive devices

■ Sometimes slight modifications to an existing home go a long way toward enabling a senior to keep her independence longer

- Work with an elderly loved one to figure out what degree of independence works for his situation. It's different for everyone
- Don't assume Mom or Dad wants to move in with you. In many cases, they don't
- Thoroughly research all the options and then discuss them with the elderly parent. The cheapest or first solution may not be the best use of available money or the best solution to the living needs of all involved
- Medicare does not pick up the cost of custodial care or long-term nursing home care

# Coping with Continuing Caregiving

## Chapter 9

No one, least of all an elderly parent accustomed to financial and physical independence, wants to become a burden to anyone else. Parents, especially, are averse to relying financially, emotionally, and physically on an adult child with his own familial responsibilities. Neither do many seniors want to deal with the emotional or psychological family baggage that often accompanies turning to a child for help.

Nonetheless, with today's ever-increasing cost of living, soaring health care costs, and longer life spans, many in the Sandwich Generation end up parenting their parents in some way, whether financially, physically, or emotionally. Along with those responsibilities to your parents are the financial, physical, and emotional commitments to your own children and yourself. Organizing your finances and financial future, as well as your children's, is just as important as making sure your aging parents' finances are in order. You also must find a way to satisfy the time and physical commitments to your children and yourself, as well as to your aging parent or grandparent. Experts across the board agree that your financial and emotional security—and that of your family—requires your attention to all three generations, not just one.

"The most important thing for any caregiver to remember is that they must first take care of themselves, and that if they don't take care of themselves, they won't be available to take care of anyone else," says psychiatrist Swantek. "For any person who is the primary caregiver of an older adult—whether they live with them or not—it's stressful. . . . Probably the hardest job they'll ever do is to take care of an ailing older family member. It means constantly negotiating your needs and your family's needs versus the older adult's needs. The fantasy has been that we can do it all. The reality is that, unless we have a lot of cooperation and support, we can't. That's why some families eventually place a loved one in a nursing home. It's not that they don't care—they simply can't do everything," adds Swantek.

Let's look at a few facts and figures. As a caregiver, you're far from alone. According to Pew Research's "Baby Boomers: From the Age of Aquarius to the Age of Responsibility," 71 percent of today's baby boomers have at least one living parent. That same study revealed that three in ten boomers provide financial assistance to that parent, while two in ten boomers actually receive it.

More numbers to consider: An estimated 33.9 million adults in the United States provide unpaid care to someone age 50 and older. That's 16 percent of the U.S. adult population, according to "Caregiving in the U.S.," the National Alliance for Caregiving/AARP study funded by the MetLife Foundation.

Who are these caregivers? What care do they provide? What does it cost, and who pays for it? What are the ramifications, financial and otherwise, of their caregiving? How can you as a caregiver get financial relief and make the job easier for you, your family, and loved ones? Let's take a closer look at some of the answers.

## Caregiver Profile

You may be surprised by the profile of the average caregiver. According to the AARP study:

- 61 percent are women; 39 percent are men.
- 46 is the average age.
- 62 percent are married or living with a partner.
- 18 percent are single.
- 14 percent are divorced or separated.
- 6 percent are widowed.
- 35 percent say they experience emotional stress as a result of their caregiving responsibilities.

## SOURCES FOR MORE INFORMATION

- *AARP (www.aarp.org). Helpful information, studies on caregiving, and tips for caregivers.*
- *Alzheimer's Association (www.alz.org). Nonprofit that offers research, resources, information, help, direction, and care consultation to those affected by Alzheimer's and related diseases.*
- *Area Agencies on Aging (www .eldercarelocator.gov). Helps locate local organizations and services for seniors across the United States.*
- *BenefitsCheckUp® (www.benefitscheckup .org). From the National Council on Aging, this free service helps screen for a senior's entitlements through local, state, federal, and some private programs.*
- *Children of Aging Parents (www .caps4caregivers.org). A nonprofit with support groups in a number of states that offers information and links to caregivers.*
- *Family Caregiver Alliance® National Center on Caregiving (www.caregiver.org). Caregiving and health information; includes a database of local resources.*
- *healthfinder®/U.S. Department of Health and Human Services (www.healthfinder .gov). Excellent, easy-to-navigate source of tons of medical, health and wellness, fitness, and drug-related (including alternative medicines) information.*
- *Medicare (www.medicare.gov). The home page for the nation's medical program for seniors.*
- *MedlinePlus (www.medlineplus.gov). From the U.S. Library of Medicine and National Institutes of Health, includes links to directories of health care providers, doctors, dentists, hospitals, clinics, and physicians that are Medicare providers nationwide.*
- *National Association of Professional Geriatric Care Managers (www.caremanager.org). A resource of geriatric care manager professionals who work privately with older adults and their families.*
- *National Family Caregivers Association (www .nfcacares.org or www.thefamilycaregiver .org). Provides education, direction, information, and resources for caregivers.*
- *National Institutes of Health SeniorHealth (www.nihseniorhealth.gov). Developed for older adults by the National Institute on Aging and National Library of Medicine, both part of the National Institutes of Health, site contains a wealth of health and medical information. Also check out NIH's Web site (www.nih.gov).*
- *Seniors Resource Guide (www .seniorsresourceguide.com). Provides information on services in communities in 22 markets across the United States.*
- *U.S. Administration on Aging (www.aoa.gov). An excellent online resource and link to services, organizations, and information on everything from Alzheimer's to housing, money matters, elder rights, volunteer opportunities, and more.*

- Caregivers provide an average of 21 hours of care per week; 48 percent provide 8 hours or less of care a week; and 17 percent provide more than 40 hours of care a week.

- The average length of care is 4.3 years.
- 66 percent of male caregivers work full time; 55 percent of female caregivers work full time.

The majority of baby boomers, 56 percent, also consider it their responsibility to open their homes to an elderly parent if the parent wants to move in, according to the Pew study. Incomes of caregiving families may be lower than those of families who provide no caregiving, according to the National Family Caregivers Association. Forty-three percent of caregiving households have annual incomes less than $30,000. That compares with a national average of 35 percent.

As we mentioned earlier, these caregivers provide all kinds of assistance—from transportation and grocery shopping to housework, managing finances, preparing meals, helping with medications, and more. Every situation is different, as are the ramifications for all involved.

## Footing the Bill

As we've discussed, the tab for all this caregiving reaches into the hundreds of billions of dollars in direct out-of-pocket expenses and billions more dollars in indirect costs. Consider a few numbers from another MetLife Mature Market Institute–funded study, "The MetLife Juggling Act Study: Balancing Caregiving with Work and the Costs Involved," done by the National Alliance for Caregiving and the National Center on Women and Aging at Brandeis University. The study looked at—among other things—the financial impact of informal caregiving on 55 caregivers:

- Eight years is the average time spent providing care.
- Total loss in terms of wage wealth for each caregiver (family involved in the caregiving) averaged more than $566,000.
- Caregivers' retirement savings dropped by an average $25,500 in lost Social Security benefits alone.
- Among caregivers eligible for pensions, average annual pension benefits fell by more than $5,300 annually or about $67,200 over their retirement years.

- Caregivers on average had out-of-pocket caregiving expenses that averaged $19,525 over anywhere from two to six years.
- The average loss in total wealth for a caregiver was an astounding almost $660,000 over his lifetime. And these are just direct dollar losses.

Employers also report billions of dollars in losses indirectly as a result of their employees' caregiving responsibilities. Work-related issues add to stress and strain for caregivers, too. Almost 60 percent of caregivers have worked at some time while actively providing care. For those workers, six in ten report having to work late, leave early, or take time off during the day to provide care.

And what about the cost in terms of time caregivers don't spend with their own children or grandchildren because they're taking care of their elderly parents? Yes, they learn important lessons on the value of time, money, and planning as well as how to juggle multiple responsibilities. But watching your children grow up and spending time with them is essential, too.

Remember Liza from earlier in the book, whose vibrant, 70-year-old Mom fell, suffered brain damage, and ended up dependent on her and temporarily living in her home? After several instances of coming home from work to find her mother disoriented and confused, Liza discovered that her mother had mixed up her drugs. So Liza decided it would be in her mother's best interests if she, Liza, spent more time at home. Liza gave up working full-time in order to care for her mother. However, that meant lost income for the family and increased costs for ordinary living expenses.

| **LIZA'S LOST INCOME** | |
|---|---|
| **Lost wages** (20 hours week@ $15/hour): | $15,600/year |
| **Additional income** from mother (Social Security, $800/month): | $9,600/year |
| **Deficit:** | **$6,000** |

Estimates are that the nation's businesses lose between $11 billion and $29 billion annually related to employees caring for people age 50 and older, according to the National Alliance for Caregiving/Met Life Study, "Employer Costs for Working Caregivers."

Workplace statistics from the same study show:

- 57 percent of working caregivers say they have to go in to work late, leave early, or take time off during the day to provide care.
- 17 percent report having to take a leave of absence.
- 10 percent go from full-time to part-time work.
- 6 percent quit work entirely.
- 5 percent lose job benefits.
- 4 percent turn down a promotion.
- 3 percent choose early retirement.

*"Once the kids are in high school, more days are lost to the working public for elder care than child care. So taking care of one's parents supplants the out-of-work days of taking care of one's children."*

—Gary J. Kennedy, MD, geriatric psychiatrist

## The Compromise Approach

As the numbers show, caregiving is expensive for everyone involved. But you as a caregiver can lessen its financial impact across the generations both currently and long term. As with most other aspects of coping with aging, planning and the right approach are paramount. Even if you or your elderly loved ones failed to plan ahead, as a caregiver you can take steps today to at least improve your own financial future as well as that of your kids, and often even your elderly parents.

*Even if you spend only $100 a week on caregiving for an elderly parent, that's $5,200 a year. Don't forget to factor in the cost of lost wages associated with caregiving as well. That's why it makes sense for your future and that of your children to help a parent take advantage of available financial assistance.*

The caregiving compromise, as with most aspects of handling the generational sandwich, starts with organizing your finances and those of your loved ones. Pinpoint where you are now so that you can look at the options for what lies ahead. As we discussed in Chapter 7, talk with your elderly parents about your role as a caregiver and its financial impact on you, your family, and them. If it means taking off an unpaid half-day of work every week to run errands for them, an elderly parent needs to recognize the financial impact. That $100 a week, or $5,200 a year, can have a significant impact on your own retirement savings. Consider the rule of 72. That's the time it takes to double your investment at various rates of return compounded annually. Divide the number 72 by the total return on the investment. For example, 72 divided by 10 percent is 7.2 years. That means at a 10 percent return, the lost $5,200 would have become $10,400 in 7.2 years, $20,800 in 14.4 years, and so on.

Make it clear to your parents that you do want to help, but that you also need to look at the long-term financial ramifications for everyone involved. Taking the right approach today can help everyone come out ahead—whether or not you or your elderly loved ones have prepared ahead of time. Caregiving is not about helping another at the expense of your own retirement or well-being. Your elderly parents will be the first to tell you that.

## Easing the Financial Impact

Caring for an elderly person adds to household expenses, including higher utility, food, and transportation costs and, possibly, home remodeling. In 1999, research by public policy and health economics expert Langa from the University of Michigan found that the average cost of informal care to stroke victims ranged from $3,500 to $8,200 a year. Informal caregiving for dementia patients was somewhat higher, $3,630 in cases of mild dementia to $27,700 for severe dementia. The cost obviously is much higher when the value of wages and retirement savings, lost as a result of caregiving, is included.

Even if the financial impact on a caregiver is minimal for the moment—perhaps the cost of roundtrip airfare to visit a distant parent several times a year—what will that impact be two, five, or ten years down the road? Chances are high that expenses will only mount. A parent, if she can afford it, may insist on reimbursing you in some way for caregiving or, at the very least, perhaps pay for those roundtrip airline tickets or a few tanks of gas, or invest a little money in a retirement account for you. To an elderly parent, paying part of his way is rarely about the money. It's about asserting some bit of independence and the fact that they don't *need* anyone.

"Of course I'm going to pay for it. I wouldn't hear of you spending that kind of money just to come see me," a frail but indignant and obviously proud Martin, 79,

---

## TIPS FROM REAL LIFE

*Do you help an elderly loved one but "wouldn't dream" of asking for money in return? There are ways they can help defray your costs, and enjoy doing it.*

- Is the money you spend on caregiving at the expense of your own retirement savings? Why not suggest a parent donate to your retirement account? Even a small amount helps.
- Is it tough saving for junior's education? If you're caregiving for Mom or Dad, perhaps suggest that they contribute to your child's 529 plan for college.
- Another option: let an elderly parent pay for (and help prepare in some way, even if it's simply setting the table) one family meal a week or even a month. Sunday evening, perhaps?
- Are you an at-a-distance caregiver? If they can afford it, let Mom or Dad pick up the cost of airfare to visit them.
- If you need a major home repair, perhaps a major appliance replaced or even a large piece of furniture, it could be an ideal way for an elderly loved one to contribute. Often they don't think to offer because they figure you'll ask if you want or need their help.
- In the really big-ticket department, perhaps an elderly loved one can help with the down payment on their caregiver's home or a new car.

told Luanne, his adult at-a-distance daughter, when she mentioned that the cost of airfare had risen yet again. "Take the money and put it in Holly's college fund," he added with satisfaction, referring to his 12-year-old granddaughter.

Jill and her husband desperately needed a new dresser, but everything they looked at was so expensive and seemingly beyond their means. Meanwhile, Jill's mother had died two years earlier, leaving her dad in a house with empty drawers in plenty of dressers. Yet he never offered the couple any of his unused furniture. Finally exasperated, Jill outright asked her dad why he wouldn't let them have one dresser. Surprised, he immediately told her to take whichever one she wanted. "Why didn't you ask before?" he asked. "Of course you can have it." It never had occurred to him that his beloved daughter wouldn't ask for something she needed or wanted.

> *Often an elderly parent or even her adult children*
> *don't realize the actual financial cost of caregiving.*

Even with an aging parent who, unlike Martin or Jill's dad, doesn't have discretionary money to spend or unused household items to share, it's crucial that the conversation about finances be frank and open. How much can elderly parents realistically afford to contribute to their caregiving expenses? Should they do so if they live with you—or even if they don't? If you're averse to asking a parent to help with expenses and don't want to call it the "cost of caregiving," call it something like "the pot" or "the kitty," whatever makes sense in your family. But the reality is that caregiving at any level and its financial ramifications can be costly for everyone. Talk about it now and together so that whether young, middle-aged, or old, no one ends up shortchanged financially.

Even if you think your elderly parents have no income other than Social Security, chances are they have some other entitlements, whether they know it or not. Even capitalizing on available state and federal tax breaks may make enough financial difference to ease the money crunch for the senior or an extended family strapped by Sandwich Generation responsibilities. For example, this year Grandma realized that because she files her taxes as a single head of household, is over 65, and is legally blind, she's eligible for a personal exemption ($3,300 in 2006 due to inflation adjustment), an additional $1,250 standard deduction for her age, *and* a $1,000 deduction because of her blindness. (Check out the IRS's Web site *(www.irs.gov)* for more details.) The savings on her taxes was just enough to allow her granddaughter Jeannie to take that trip to New York with the marching band. Without Grandma's help, the family couldn't have afforded it and Jeannie would have done without, a typical scenario among sandwiched families.

If an elderly parent regularly can pitch in even a small amount of cash—whether directly or indirectly—toward the expense of his care, not only can it help you the caregiver and your family, but it also provides the senior with an important sense that he is contributing in some way, too. Jeannie and her family adored Grandma and thoroughly enjoyed the family time, stories, and love they all could share. But for Grandma, the dependency on the family was a constant source of concern. Typically she could offer nothing but her love and gratitude in exchange for their hours of caregiving. The ability to help finance Jeannie's special trip was a source of tremendous satisfaction.

Tilly's daughter Marie took a half-day off work every week and spent every Saturday morning helping her mom, 77, with her grocery shopping, errands, trips to the doctor, and more. Marie never really thought about the financial cost or long-term ramifications of her role as caregiver. It was, after all, for her mom, and she gladly did it all, enjoying their one-on-one time together—something she rarely had with her as a child. Marie refused any financial reimbursement from Tilly except an occasional lunch. Then one evening Marie and her husband, both 50-somethings, attended a free financial seminar from a local brokerage on the actual cost of caregiving.

| TILLY'S FINANCES | |
|---|---|
| **Monthly income** | |
| Social Security: | $  860 |
| Alimony: | $1,000 |
| Investment income (annual amount divided by 12): | $   50 |
| **Total income:** | **$1,910** |
| **Monthly expenses** | |
| Household, including mortgage, utilities: | $1,100 |
| Medical, including insurance, Medicare, medicines: | $  350 |
| Food and entertainment: | $  300 |
| Miscellaneous: | $  100 |
| **Total expenses:** | **$1,850** |
| **Discretionary income:** | **$60/month** |

They were shocked by the realization of the silent impact on their finances, especially because they had virtually no retirement savings after helping put all three of their children through college.

Nonetheless, to Marie and many others like her who gladly help an aging parent, the finances of caregiving are a catch-22. Tilly is on a small fixed income, just more than $1,900 a month, with almost that much in expenses—$1,850. Whereas Marie and her husband both work and bring in three times that amount monthly, admittedly they have far greater expenses than Tilly. It's a tough situation that needs to be addressed so that, somewhere down the road, today's caregivers don't find themselves in worse situations than their elderly parents ever faced. We'll talk more about saving for your retirement and juggling caregiving responsibilities in Chapter 11.

# Finding Financial Options

However, looking more closely at Tilly's finances, Marie and her husband discovered that Tilly wasn't taking advantage of a number of local, federal, state, and private programs and entitlements that could save her money every month on her prescription medications as well as home utilities, taxes, and various support services. The savings are enough that Tilly easily could afford to pitch in a little cash each month to offset the cost to Marie and her family of caregiving. Instead of cash exchanging hands, Tilly might want to consider investing the cash regularly in a mutual fund or other retirement savings vehicle as a starting point, albeit a late one, for Marie and her husband's retirement future.

One way you can try to ensure that your elderly parent doesn't overlook benefits and entitlements like Tilly did is to tap into free services that help locate a parent's entitlements. BenefitsCheckUp® *(www.benefitscheckup .org)* from the nonprofit National Council on Aging, for example, is a good place to start. It's a comprehensive online service that screens for federal, state, local, and some private and public benefits for those ages 55 and up. It provides details of the programs along with local contacts and more. To access a parent's benefits and entitlements, you'll need their zip code, month and date of birth, official military status if applicable, details of monthly household income and expenses, insurance coverage, and names of medications, to name just a few things. Filling out the form then takes about 10 or 15 minutes.

*Government organizations such as a local Agency on Aging*
(www.aoa.gov) *in the city or vicinity of your loved one
or Eldercare Locator* (www.eldercare.gov) *can help
you discover what services are available for seniors
and their caregivers and where to find them.*

Another option to help Tilly foot her bills and assist her daughter and her family would be a reverse mortgage. Remember Diane and Jay from Chapter 1? They have two young children and help support Diane's mom as well as Jay's son from a previous marriage who's in graduate school. They're talking to Diane's mom about taking out a reverse mortgage, which would use the equity in her home to help pay her expenses and ease the financial pressures on the family. They've also enrolled in state-sponsored 529 plans to provide tax-advantaged college savings for their kids and are talking to a financial advisor about how to gift Grandma a few investments without exceeding the $12,000 ($24,000 if both give) annual gift tax exclusion amount that would trigger additional taxes. After all, she's in a lower tax bracket and therefore would pay lower taxes. There is one caution with that approach, however. If Medicaid is a concern, gifting assets to her could affect her ability to qualify for the federal or state low-income medical assistance program. Plus, simply by asking the ombudsman at their mom's Medicare Advantage HMO, they learned that Diane's mom could be eligible for additional prescription drug assistance through a special program.

> *Whatever the issue with senior care, financing, and health, don't be afraid to ask questions. The answers may pleasantly surprise you and save you and your elderly loved one money.*

Joe, the single dad with the 15-year-old son in New York and the elderly mom and grandmother in South Dakota, also found help for his situation merely by asking. Working with the Agency on Aging in his elderly loved ones' town, he located a dependable and empathetic caregiver to regularly check on his mother and grandmother for a nominal cost—$20 per visit. As a result, he no longer must make the time-consuming and costly biweekly trips from New York to Deadwood, South Dakota, to check on them. Now he makes the trip only once a month, and sometimes even less.

## Tips and Tricks

**DEVISE A CAREGIVING BUDGET.** Consider setting up a caregiving budget. Whether an elderly parent lives with you or not, include the expenses of caregiving (don't forget lost wages incurred by you, your spouse, or children due to caregiving) as well as the recipient's income and entitlements. Keep in mind this is not intended to measure what is gladly performed assistance for an elderly loved one. Instead, it's a way to help you provide a better perspective on caregiving's effects on your own family's finances. Are your retirement savings nonexistent or falling behind as a result of caregiving?

*Financial options dwindle when you're forced to react at times of crisis. Plan ahead!*

Does the picture for funding your child's college look like you'll need help and/or that he must work toward certain scholarships? Whether you will need a little or a lot of financial help, get started early by filling out the Free Application for Federal Student Aid (FAFSA) form *(www.fafsa.ed.gov)* that's required for virtually all financial aid and scholarships. As with many other issues you as the Sandwiched Generation face, don't assume everything will be OK or take care of itself. If you do, you'll often end up even more sandwiched and forced to react in crisis, when you'll generally have far fewer choices. Instead, plan ahead and plan often.

Share the budget and its numbers with your siblings, too, so that they understand the real costs and financial effects. Writing down the budget also may help alleviate money squabbles or sibling rivalries that might be rekindled if, for example, Mom moves in with you.

If a parent does move in, allow her to share household expenses. If, for example, they become the fifth person in the household, divide the expenses by five, and that portion then becomes their cost of living. If a parent can't afford to contribute, look to your siblings for assistance. If they can't or are unwilling to help, keep accurate records. You may be able to claim your parents as a dependent for tax purposes, or if you and your siblings share the cost of a parent's care, you can file a Form 2120 Multiple Support Agreement permitting one of you to claim the personal exemption for your parent. You also may be able to recoup expenses from the parent's estate before it's divided among the heirs, according to the Financial Planning Association (*www.fpanet.org*), a nonprofit membership organization of financial industry professionals.

Review the budget periodically to make sure it's up to date and reflects the real expenses of caregiving—everything from transportation and living costs to lost wages and performing medical or home-health tasks.

**PAYBACK TIME II.** If a parent's income, or lack thereof, precludes his contributing to the cost of care, sometimes a parent may structure his will in such a way that a caregiving heir receives more than noncaregiving ones as "repayment" for the time and expense of care. As mentioned earlier, however, sometimes dividing an estate unevenly can cause more headaches than not. Conversely, a parent may choose to ignore a caregiver's efforts.

Joey's elderly mother lived with him for almost 15 years, during which he and his wife provided her primary care. Yet when she died at age 92, her will left everything to Joey's two siblings, specifying that Joey was to get nothing because he was too irresponsible. Horrified, the siblings gave Joey an equal share from their inheritance.

"I never told Joey about the will before Mom died because I was afraid he might turn her out," explained one brother, who was the estate's executor. "But we really felt that Joey deserved at least a fair share" after voluntarily taking in his mother.

**TAKE ADVANTAGE OF TAX BREAKS.** We've already talked about a few breaks, such as extra personal exemptions for age 65 or older and legal blindness. There's also a tax credit for the elderly or permanently and totally disabled that varies by filing status. If your elderly loved one qualifies for any of these, be sure to take advantage. The savings can be worth it. For more information, check out any of the many online information sources such as CCH Financial Planning Toolkit (*www.finance.cch.com*), or talk to your tax professional.

**HEALTH SAVINGS ACCOUNTS (HSA), MEDICAL SAVINGS ACCOUNTS (MSA), AND FLEXIBLE SPENDING ACCOUNTS.** All of these, with varying limitations, restrictions, and qualifications, are tax-favored accounts that allow you or an eligible individual to set aside dollars earmarked for medical and, in some cases, dependent care expenses. For example, with a flexible spending account through an employer, an employee can set aside pretax dollars to pay for qualified health and dependent care expenses. That means if you're in the 28 percent tax bracket, you're getting a 28 percent discount on the cost of qualified health or dependent care paid from the amount you set aside. If you claim an elderly parent as a dependent, you get the same savings on qualified medical or dependent care expenses for her, too.

An aging parent with income also can set up such an account as long as he is under age 65 and receives his own "cost" savings on qualified expenses. (You cannot set up or contribute to an account after you turn 65, but you can withdraw from an already established one.) MSAs and HSAs generally work in conjunction with a qualified high-deductible health plan. Of note: MSAs and HSAs allow the funds to be rolled over year to year. A flexible spending account, on the other hand, comes with a use-it-or-lose-it provision. Spend it in the calendar year, or else it's history.

**SAVINGS FOR EDUCATION.** As we talked about in Chapter 7, these include:

- *529 plan.* A tax-advantaged program funded with after-tax dollars that grow tax-free, then may be withdrawn tax-free for qualified higher education expenses; some states allow deduction for initial contributions.
- *Coverdell Education Savings Accounts.* Also federal income tax-free as long as they're withdrawn for qualified education expenses, including those incurred for grades K through 12.
- *Roth IRAs.* Funded with after-tax dollars, earnings are tax-deferred and are not subject to income tax or penalty if the money has been held for five years, you're at least 59½ at time of withdrawal, and the money is

used for qualified withdrawals, including education expenses and certain first-time homebuyer expenses. Roth contribution limits mirror those for traditional IRAs: $4,000 ($5,000 for age 50 and up in 2006).

**GET HELP.** Whether Mom or Dad lives with you or just needs your occasional help, don't wait until you're overtaxed, stressed out, and strung out from your caregiving duties. Consider bringing in people or reaching out to siblings or organizations for help. That's especially important if an elderly parent suffers from dementia, Alzheimer's, or some other disease that affects their mental capacity. In many cases, caregivers may take personally outbursts directed at them when actually the disease is causing the outpouring. Nonetheless, such outbursts add to the stress of caregiving. Says geriatric psychiatrist Gary Kennedy, "Recognize your limits. Share the care earlier rather than later." Get the senior accustomed to receiving the help she needs and deserves, whether it's provided by family or someone else, Kennedy adds.

**IDENTIFYING HELP THAT'S AVAILABLE.** The Family Caregiver Alliance *(www.caregiver.org)* suggests that to identify the available help and support to best fit your and your elderly loved one's needs, start by asking yourself a number of questions. Write down the answers on paper, too, so you'll have a better handle on needs, costs, and logistics. Their suggested questions include:

- What type of help does my elderly loved one need to live as independently as possible? (For example, transportation, meals, health care.)
- How much money is and could be available to pay for outside resources? (Refer to your notes on your and your parent's net worth and budgets.)
- Will the insurance of my elderly loved one or even myself cover any of the necessary services? (Medicare, for example, will pick up the cost of doctor-prescribed periodic skilled nursing visits.)
- What specific days and times does my elderly loved one need help, and when do I need help?

- What assistance or care can I provide my elderly loved one myself (transportation, meals, minimal medical assistance, or assistance with activities of daily living)?
- What types of help can my elderly loved one's friends or my friends and family members provide willingly?

Of course, if you've chosen to work with outside professionals such as a professional geriatric care manager, elder law attorney with on-staff case managers, or some other specialist in devising care and action plans, they can assist in much of the effort. However, if you're going it on your own, once you recognize your and your elderly loved one's needs and options available, you'll then have to do the legwork to get the caregiving system in place. It may take several frustrating hours to get it all done, but be direct, persistent, and don't give up. Chances are that organizations are out there to make it easier on you, save you and/or your loved one money, and lead to a better quality of life for all.

Available programs and services vary. The Family Caregiver Alliance suggests a few of the types of services and how to capitalize on them:

- *Adult day care.* This provides the elderly opportunities for social interaction, peer support, and health and social services in a familiar environment. It also provides a break for caregivers responsible for someone who can't be left alone but doesn't require 24-hour nursing care in a residential facility. Adult day care can include individual and group activities; meals; transportation; case management; recreation and exercise; nursing care; family counseling; assistance with activities of daily living; and occupational, speech, and physical therapies. Talk to your local Agency on Aging, or visit the National Adult Day Services Association *(www.nadsa.org)* and click on "Consumers" for a guide to selecting an adult day center.
- *Case management services.* These professionals can locate and provide hands-on management of services for a loved one. They're trained to assess situations, implement and monitor care plans, and work with everyone involved. Free or low-cost case management

may be found through hospitals, mental health programs, home-health agencies, social service agencies (such as Catholic Charities, Jewish Family Services, and Adult Protective Services), and other health care–related programs. Or consider hiring a private case manager such as a professional geriatric care manager.

■ *Employee assistance programs.* Employers may offer free or low-cost special counseling and/or assistance for personal issues that include elder care and child care resources. Some employers also may offer paid time off for caregiving duties. Check with your employer's benefits specialist or human resources department.

■ *Home care.* For the homebound sick or those with disabilities who want to live at home as independently as possible, these caregivers provide varying degrees of health care and support services, depending on the need. Physician approval may be needed for insurance coverage. Medicare, Medicaid, and some private insurers pay for limited home-health care with restrictions. Some sources to help locate the right provider include personal referrals, private home care agencies, hospitals, social service agencies, public health departments, nursing schools, local Agency on Aging, or other community organizations.

■ *Hospice care.* Hospice may be in a special facility or at home. It's a concept of care that provides services and therapies for the terminally ill and their families. Hospice emphasizes improving the quality of life for the patient by controlling the symptoms of the illness and restoring dignity for the person until death. Insurance coverage is available through Medicare, Medicaid, and some private insurance plans. For information, contact the Hospice Foundation of America *(www .hospicefoundation.org)* or National Hospice and Palliative Care Organization *(www.nhpco.org)*.

■ *Informal care.* Informal support network may involve friends, family, and community and/or religious volunteers. Make a list of these helpers with their phone numbers for easy access.

■ *Information and referral.* These are agencies, organizations, and people that can help you identify local resources. Some possibilities include national Area Agencies on Aging, senior centers, community mental health centers, and religious-affiliated family services groups.

- *Legal and financial counseling.* When it comes to an elderly loved one, areas of concern to family caregivers include future health care decisions, management of assets, public benefits planning, and even litigation. Legal referrals and advice may be available for seniors through senior legal services provided by local Area Agencies on Aging, or local and online attorney locator and referral services such as a local bar association, the American Bar Association *(www.abanet.org)*, the National Academy of Elder law Attorneys *(www.naela.org)*, or lawyers.com from Lexis Nexis/Martindale Hubbell. Don't overlook asking if other nonprofit organizations like your credit union, for example, provide free or low-cost services either.

- *Nutrition programs.* These generally low-cost meals programs can involve a group setting or be delivered to the homebound. They include programs like local Meals on Wheels or work through religious groups, housing projects, senior centers, community centers, and more.

- *Respite care.* Designed to provide family, partners, friends, or caregivers a relief or respite from the stress and demands of caregiving, it can include adult day care or home care services, or even overnight stays. For more information contact your local Agency on Aging.

- *Transportation services.* The Americans with Disabilities Act requires transit agencies to provide curb-to-curb service to those unable to use regular public transportation, and generally includes wheelchair-accessible vans or taxis. To find out more, contact your local Agencies on Aging or search Project Action's national database *(www.projectaction.org;* click on "Free Resources" and then "Travelers Database").

- *Support groups.* Friends and/or family members can meet regularly to share information and resources and discuss practical solutions to problems. The interaction with others with similar issues also helps to reduce stress. To find a support group, contact hospitals or mental health programs, as well as support organizations such as your local Caregiver Resource Center or Alzheimer's Association chapter.

*(Adapted with permission from the Family Caregiver Alliance/National Center on Caregiving; visit* www.caregiver.org *for more information.)*

# The Role of Choice

As caregivers or potential caregivers, we all face choices that—although they may not be financial in nature—have broad financial ramifications for young and old. Those choices include whether to provide care, at what level, in what setting, and how it will be financed. A senior who's still cognizant has those choices, too. That's important for you, your spouse, children, and your elderly relative or parent to recognize—and to recognize prior to crisis time. Those people who do have a choice are less likely to look at their caregiving role as a financial burden or to suffer emotional stress related to it, according to "Caregiving in the U.S.," the AARP and The National Alliance for Caregiving study.

*"When people are so busy with their own parents from that part of their life, they're neglecting their current life—and that's a very big thing. If it's temporary and you know there's an end in sight, that's one thing. But if it's a situation that goes on and on, it can take a tremendous toll on the family."*

—Beverly Bernstein Joie, professional geriatric care manager

Almost four in ten caregivers (39 percent) of those in the survey say they had no choice in becoming a caregiver, and half those people say their situation is emotionally stressful. However, among those caregivers who felt they had a choice, only 25 percent experience the highest levels of emotional stress.

In another study, "Caregiving Across the Life Cycle, 1998," from the National Family Caregivers Association, 51 percent of those family caregivers who provided high levels of care experienced sleeplessness, and 41 percent suffered back pain.

## Caring for the Caregiver

Don't overlook the importance of caring for the caregiver. As a caregiver, no matter your age, be sure to take time for your own mental, physical, and, of course, financial health, or else you could end up needing more help than the aging parent for whom you're caring.

*"It's important to recognize that the caregiver has to take care of themselves. It's OK to ask for help."*

—Sandra S. Swantek, MD, Clinical Practice Committee, American Association for Geriatric Psychiatry

Consider what other caregivers point to as their most often unmet needs, according to The National Alliance for Caregiving/AARP MetLife-funded study:

- 35 percent say finding time for oneself
- 29 percent say managing emotional and physical stress
- 29 percent say balancing work and family responsibilities

Not surprisingly, a vast majority of caregivers—seven out of ten—say praying helps them cope with their stress. Talking helps, too. Sixty-one percent say they talk with or seek advice from friends and relatives.

Having access to a professional caregiver coach such as a social worker, psychologist, psychiatrist, or other expert also can help a caregiver sort out the trials, tribulations, and sadness that often affect caregivers. It's especially helpful in the case of dementia or Alzheimer's patients, says Kennedy.

Caregivers in general, not just those who provide full-time care, also need activities of their own to succeed at, even simple pastimes done at home like scrapbooking, needlepoint, lifting weights, or writing.

---

### HOW DO YOU COPE WITH DEMANDS OF CAREGIVING?

- *Praying, 73%*
- *Talking with or seeking advice from friends or relatives, 61%*
- *Reading about caregiving, 44%*
- *Exercising or working out, 41%*
- *Searching the Internet for information, 33%*
- *Talking to a professional or spiritual counselor, 27%*
- *Taking medication, 12%*

**Source:** Caregiving in the U.S., National Alliance for Caregiving and AARP, 2004

# Remember:

- As a caregiver you must satisfy the time and commitments to your children, your elderly parents, and yourself.
- "Free" caregiving is an expensive proposition, at the expense of many caregivers' pocketbooks as well as their employers' bottom lines.
- Caregiving is *not* about helping a loved one at the expense of your own retirement or well-being. Your elderly parent will be the first to tell you that.
- Allow and encourage an elderly loved one to contribute monetarily in some way, whether directly or indirectly. It's not just about money. It's about independence and self-esteem, too.
- Get help in your caregiving responsibilities, and do it sooner rather than later.
- Take advantage of tax breaks and all the programs, entitlements, and assistance available to you as a caregiver or your elderly loved one.
- Take care of yourself, too!

# Medical Issues

**Chapter 10**

**H**ealth and money dominate concerns about aging in America these days, no matter your age, health, or financial well-being.

More than nine out of ten adults (92 percent) see health as a serious problem for those over 65 today, while nearly the same number (88 percent) point to running out of money as a serious issue as well. When it comes to living to age 75, six in ten adults (60 percent) are very or somewhat worried about memory loss, nearly half (49 percent) about suffering uncontrollable pain, and 45 percent the cost of long-term care. Three in ten (30 percent) worry about outliving their pensions. These are among the latest findings from "American Perceptions of Aging in the 21st Century," the National Council on the Aging's 2002 continuing study of the Myths and Realities of Aging™.

Despite these worries, just more than four in ten (43 percent) of those surveyed feel it's important to have long-term care insurance! As we've discussed, a cavalier attitude toward long-term care insurance could be a very big mistake.

Just how big are the dollars and cents of aging, health, and health care? Consider some statistics:

- The cost of providing health care for someone 65 or older is three to five times greater than the cost for someone under 65. (Centers for Disease Control and Prevention, "Public Health and Aging: Trends in Aging—United States and Worldwide," MMWR 2003, 52 (06): 101–106)
- By 2030, the cost of health care will climb 25 percent because the population will be older—and that's

without taking into account inflation or new technologies. (Agency for Healthcare Research and Quality, Centers for Disease Control and Prevention, "Physical Activity and Older Americans: Benefits and Strategies," June 2002)

■ Medicare spending has grown more than sevenfold in the past two decades, from $33.9 billion in 1980 to $252.2 billion in 2002, and is projected to double again by 2012. (Medicare Payment Advisory Commission, "A Data Book: Healthcare Spending and the Medicare Program, June 2003," Sections 5: National Health Care and Medicare spending)

Still more numbers add to the picture:

■ Chronic disease accounted for more than three out of four deaths among U.S. adults over age 65 in 2002. (Centers for Disease Control and Prevention, National Center for Health Statistics, National Vital Statistics Report, 2002)

■ Unintentional falls are the leading cause of nonfatal injuries among those age 65 and older. (2004, CDC, Web-based Injury Statistics Query and Reporting System; *http://webappa.cdc.gov/cgi-bin/broker.exe*)

■ In 2000, those over age 65 accounted for nearly 2.6 million nonfatal falls with resulting medical costs of $19.3 billion. ("Injury and Violence in America: Meeting Challenges and Sharing Solutions," a conference report from Department of Health and Human Services, CDC)

■ The cost to friends and family caring for older Americans with dementia exceeds $18 billion annually. (University of Michigan Health and Retirement Study, 2001, funded by the National Institute on Aging)

Misinformation and confusion only add to the health and monetary concerns of the Sandwich Generation and the older Americans for whom they care. Knowing what care and services are available and where to get them—as well as understanding who pays for what, and how—before a crisis strikes is key to successful aging for all parties involved.

## SOURCES FOR MORE INFORMATION

- *AARP's Public Benefits Outreach Program (www.aarp.org/pbo). This nonprofit's site is a good place to start to learn what it takes to qualify for Medicaid.*
- *Alzheimer's Association (www.alz.org). Nonprofit offers reliable and up-to-date information and care consultation on Alzheimer's and more as well as support services for families, resource links, and guidance. Check out its Maintain Your Brain® workshops to help baby boomers maintain a brain-healthy lifestyle.*
- *Alzheimer's Disease Education and Referral (ADEAR) Center (www.nia.nih.gov/ alzheimers). From the National Institute on Aging, ADEAR helps provide current, comprehensive Alzheimer's disease (AD) information and resources.*
- *American College Student Association (www .acsa.com). A nationwide association that provides educational services and benefits, including health insurance, to domestic and international students.*
- *American Health Care Association (www .ahca.org). A nonprofit federation of affiliated state health organizations that together represent assisted-living, nursing facility, developmentally disabled, and subacute care providers. Check out its LongTermCareLiving .com (www.longtermcareliving.com).*
- *BenefitsCheckUp® (www.benefitscheckup .org). A free service from the National Council on Aging. This online service is an easy way to find out the federal, state, and some local private and public benefits for older adults (ages 55 and over).*
- *Centers for Medicare and Medicaid Services (www.cms.gov or www.medicare.gov). Your official Medicare/Medicaid information*

*source, although navigating this site can be time consuming, cumbersome, and confusing; www.medicare.gov/NHCompare/home .asp provides detailed information about the past performance of nursing homes.*
- *Eldercare Locator (www.eldercare.gov). A free service of the U.S. Administration on Aging, the locator connects older Americans and their caregivers with sources of information on senior services.*
- *Healthfinder.gov (www.healthfinder.gov). The government's guide to generally reliable health-related information.*
- *Insure.com (www.insure.com). A comprehensive online consumer insurance information service, Insure.com is a wholly owned subsidiary of Quotesmith.com, Inc. Be sure to check out its helpful Consumer Insurance Guide for all kinds of valuable information, including details of mandated health treatments and procedures coverage by state.*
- *National Alliance for Hispanic Health (www .hispanichealth.org). A nonprofit aimed at improving the health and well-being of Hispanics. Visit Su Familia (from its home page), its national helpline with free reliable and confidential health information in Spanish and English.*
- *National Council on Patient Information and Education (www.talkaboutrx.org). Nonprofit coalition of more than 100 organizations with helpful information on prescription and over-the-counter drugs and their use; click on "For Medicine Users" to access helpful information on prescriptions and more.*

(continued)

---

## SOURCES FOR MORE INFORMATION, continued

■ *National Mental Health Association (www .nmha.org). Nonprofit organization addressing all aspects of mental health and mental illness; includes easy-to-understand information on mental illness, related financial issues, and more.*

■ *The National Council on the Aging (www .ncoa.org). A national network of organizations and individuals dedicated to improving the health and independence of older persons and increasing their contributions to communities, society, and future generations. Check out the Seniors' Corner BenefitsCheckUp® and Health Tips from the home page.*

■ *National Institute of Neurological Disorders and Stroke (www.ninds.nih.gov). From the National Institutes of Health, NINDS conducts and supports research on brain and nervous system disorders. Check out its disor-*

*ders dictionary for basic information on hundreds of disorders. Also offers free pamphlets by mail.*

■ *Nolo (www.nolo.com). Publisher and source of reliable do-it-yourself legal and business tools. Click on "Family Law & Immigration" to find helpful articles, forms, and explanations.*

■ *Partnership for Prescription Assistance (www .pparx.org). Private-sector program to help patients in need who lack prescription coverage get the medicines they require—some even free; also helps educate Medicare beneficiaries to learn about the new drug benefit.*

■ *RxAssist (www.rxassist.org). From Volunteers in Health Care, a national resource center for safety net organizations, this is a pharmaceutical access information center that can help with locating free prescription drugs for those who need them.*

## Preventive Maintenance

An elderly parent is much more likely to age successfully—financially and physically—if she can forestall or prevent major medical expenses by remaining active, healthy, and in her own home. Exercise pays huge dividends in that regard, as we've mentioned earlier. Getting a parent to join a health club or seniors exercise group such as Silver Sneakers is well worth the free enrollment or nominal cost. The cost is covered by some health insurance plans, but even if it's not and a parent is reluctant to spend the money, you or your siblings might seriously consider paying their dues. The peace of mind from knowing that your parent is doing all he can to stay healthy—as well as getting great interaction with peers—is well worth the cost.

You might also explore seniors clubs associated with area hospitals or local Agencies on Aging. H2U, as mentioned earlier, is affiliated with hospitals across the country and helps members save money and manage their health. It offers free online health assessments in conjunction with hospital affiliates as well as special VIP hospital benefits that vary by hospital, but may include meal discounts, free parking, and free upgrades from semiprivate to private room in case of a hospital stay at participating hospitals. The latter is well worth the $15 annual cost of membership. Hospitals and medical centers also may offer low-cost—as little as a few dollars—exercise programs for seniors.

While considering the importance of exercise for your parents, don't ignore the other end of the spectrum. Get your children started early so they can get the full benefit of a lifelong healthy lifestyle that will pay dividends for them when they become seniors. Better still, let Grandpa and Junior work out together!

Let's look at some other aspects of the health and medical issues and decisions that you as part of the Sandwich Generation and your elderly parents may face, and how to better cope with them.

## Health Financial Literacy

Health financial literacy is essential for baby boomers as well as their aging parents, says financial gerontologist and senior money expert Neal Cutler, the author of several books, including *Advising Mature Clients: The New Science of Wealth Span Planning* (Wiley, 2002).

Unfortunately, many Americans come up short in health financial literacy. Studies show that Americans are confused about what aspects of medical and aging care are covered by private insurance, Medicare, or Medicaid, and what areas are not; what the various qualifications are for coverage; and even the difference between Medicare and Medicaid.

Such confusion is "a major disaster from the vantage point of financial planning," says Cutler. "Parents and their adult children need to know the laws and know their finances, and then they can act accordingly."

*About 46 million Americans are uninsured!*

Literally tons of free information and advice are available, along with services from trained professionals such as geriatric care managers, social workers, and attorneys specializing in elder law. To increase your health financial literacy and that of an elderly loved one, start with almost any of the vast array of resources we've mentioned throughout this book.

## The Health Insurance Dilemma

Almost 46 million Americans, nearly 16 percent of the total population, don't have health insurance, according to Census Bureau numbers (2004). Could one of these people be your elderly loved one or even you or your child? Don't automatically figure that the answer to that question is, "No one I know." You could be surprised to the tune of big medical bills.

Even if you were raised and, in turn, brought up your own children to the mantra of "be sure to always have health insurance," don't assume that your parents or your kids are covered. One hospital stay, after all, could end up costing them and—directly or indirectly—you thousands of dollars; a catastrophic injury or illness could cost tens of thousands more.

If your kids are younger and you still claim them as dependents on your taxes, read the fine print on your own health insurance policy, then talk to your insurance professional. Follow up with your agent to make sure of your kids' coverage. Some policies may exclude college-age children or require additional premiums, paperwork, or an individual policy to ensure young adult coverage. With the latter, it could be that health insurance through your child's college makes more financial sense than an individual policy.

If your kids are adults and out on their own, talk to them to make sure they're covered. Even if you have to help foot the bill of a high-deductible, catastrophic-care-only policy, such coverage is well worth the protection. Prices will vary dramatically, so shop around.

(Insure.com, *www.insure.com,* is a good place to start.) If you're self-employed, be prepared to pay more, a lot more, for coverage unless you can find a group policy. If you belong to a professional association or group, often they'll offer group health insurance that can be—but definitely is not always—cheaper and have fewer hassles than going in on your own. AARP, for example, is just one organization that offers health insurance at a group rate to its members.

Don't assume elderly Mom or Dad have coverage, either. Dad may have forgotten to pay the premium this month—on top of last month's oversight, when he was in the hospital. Or widowed Mom may have overlooked the issue altogether after Dad died because she assumed she still was covered under his pension plan. (Don't assume!)

Sid, 84, widowed, lived in a retirement apartment alone. At the beginning of January, he fell ill and was hospitalized. After about a month of tests, doctors thought they had resolved the problem, but Sid was too weak to go home alone. He moved temporarily into a

---

### TIPS FROM REAL LIFE

*Are you sure your adult kids or elderly parents are covered by an in-force health insurance policy?*

■ *Many family insurance policies stop coverage of family members at age 18. Check your policy, and then check with your insurance representative to be sure your children are covered.*

■ *If a college-age child isn't covered by your policy, look into student coverage through the college or university he attends or student health insurance organizations such as the American College Student Association (www.acsa.com). That could be less costly than an individual policy through your insurer.*

■ *Have your elderly parents properly filed for Medicare benefits within required time limits? What about Medigap or supplemental insurance?*

■ *Are your parents' premium payments up to date? Consider suggesting automatic withdrawal or even Internet pay if a parent is computer savvy or you have financial power of attorney.*

skilled nursing facility connected to the hospital, with the plan that he remain there until he regained his strength. But after another month or so, Sid's condition suddenly worsened and he died unexpectedly.

As his children went through his apartment after the funeral, they discovered that their father, who always had handled his finances punctually and without fail, hadn't paid the premiums on his Medigap, or supplemental insurance, for almost three months—long past the grace period allowed by the insurer. If the insurance were canceled, that would mean sizable out-of-pocket expenses not covered by Medicare for Sid's doctors, hospitalization, surgery, and continuing care.

Fortunately, though, after an initial panic, Sid's daughter was able to talk to and work with the insurer so that the family had to pay only a very small amount. It seemed that a similar series of missed payments occurred when Sid had been hospitalized several years earlier. Taking the time to work with the insurer and get through the bureaucracy and red tape paid off.

## Medicare Maze

Medicare is the federal health insurance program for all seniors, age 65 and older, and certain qualified individuals with disabilities. Mandated by the Social Security Act, it covers qualified medical, doctor, hospital, and now drug expenses with limitations. Like private insurance, Medicare also includes deductibles and often copays for services as well as some premiums that must be paid. The parts of Medicare include:

- *Part A.* What's covered (in general): Hospital insurance that covers in-patient hospital care (semiprivate room) and services; limited and qualified care in a skilled nursing facility (up to 100 days for qualified stays with copayments); home-health care; hospice care.
- *Part B.* What's covered (in general): Physician insurance that includes some nonphysician services such as diagnostic, laboratory tests, and some therapy services.

- *Medicare Advantage.* What's covered (in general): These are private Medicare programs like health maintenance organizations (HMOs) that provide Part A, B, and D benefits. Coverage and costs vary by provider and individual plan.
- *Part D.* What's covered (in general): New in 2006, this is Medicare's first attempt at prescription drug coverage; dozens of optional plans with varied costs, coverage, and reimbursements.

What does all this cost you or your elderly loved one? That depends on several factors ranging from the Medicare option chosen (Medicare Advantage—typically an HMO/PPO-type plan—or traditional Medicare); whether it's Part A, B, or D; the service involved; who's providing it; the duration and circumstances surrounding the service; and plenty more.

According to the Center for Medicare and Medicaid Services, which administers the federal program, a few of the basics include:

- *Deductibles (2006).* Part A, $952 (paid by beneficiary on admittance to hospital as inpatient); only cost for up to 60 days of Medicare-covered inpatient hospital care in a benefit period (limits on frequency of benefit period), after that co-insurance amounts required for up to 150-day maximum; Part B, $124; Part D, varies by plans but no more than $250 in 2006.
- *Copays (the patient's share of cost) for services.* Part A, deductible for hospital stays of 1 to 60 days, then $238/day for 61 to 90 days, $476/day for 91 to 150 days, all costs after that; Part A, skilled nursing facility, the deductible, then nothing for first 20 days then $119/day for 21 to 100 days each benefit period; Part B, usually 20 percent of cost of services, but can be higher (50 percent for mental health services), and no copay for approved home-health services.
- *Premiums (2006).* Part A, none if beneficiary has at least 40 quarters of Medicare-covered employment, otherwise $216 to $393/month; Part B, $88.50 a month in 2006, up more than $10 from 2005 monthly premiums; Part D, annual cost varies but 2006 maximum, $250

deductible plus set copayments that vary by plan and drug (estimated average $32/month), then plan covers 75 percent of the next $2,000 of drug costs, you pay the next $2,850, and after that the plan pays 95 percent.

*Medicare coverage, inclusions, exclusions, deductibles, copays, and options can be confusing to anyone of any age. Work with elderly parents to help them—and you!— understand it all.*

What Medicare does and doesn't cover fills pages and volumes with a galaxy of exceptions, exemptions, qualifications, and limitations, so it's best to check with Medicare (*www.medicare.gov*; check out its Personal Plan Finder, and Prescription Drug Plan Finder) to find out what fits your situation. And be forewarned: Medicare can be confusing to anyone, any age, so no matter how cognizant or competent an elderly loved one, work with her so both of you understand the details. Involve your kids, too, if, for example, they're the ones who take Grandma to the pharmacy or the doctor, where she may run into complications or confusion about payment. It also will help your children better prepare financially for their own future. Financial health literacy is a family proposition.

---

## WHAT MEDICARE DOESN'T COVER

*A few of the things that Medicare doesn't cover include:*
- *Deductibles, premiums, and copays*
- *Vision, hearing, and dental services in general, including dentures, hearing aids, eyeglasses, and exams*
- *Mental health care support groups in nonmedical settings*
- *Private-duty nursing, if, for example, someone receives inpatient mental health care*
- *Routine foot care*
- *Cosmetic surgery, except when associated with injury and disfigurement*

Most seniors also need supplemental health insurance, or Medigap coverage, through a private insurer to cover some of what Medicare doesn't. As NBC money guru Jim Barry pointed out earlier, that difference can be substantial, about $200,000 during retirement if someone doesn't have an employer-funded retirement health insurance plan—which is fast becoming an endangered species.

Don't expect an easy time navigating this Medicare maze, either. It's always been time consuming, and it's even more so with the addition of Part D and its many options. As an example of the choices on Part D alone, there are 34 "prescription drug plan regions" with anywhere from a dozen or so to two dozen organizations offering stand-alone prescription drug plans in each region, with some organizations offering plans in multiple regions. Plans offer varying levels of copays and cover various drugs listed in what's known as formularies. Before signing up for a plan, always check its formulary to be sure that the drugs you or an elderly parent take or

## MEDICARE HELP AND INFORMATION:

■ The Access to Benefits Coalition™ (www .accesstobenefits.org). With 55 coalitions nationwide, this nonprofit is working to educate consumers on available prescription drug savings, including Medicare Part D. Includes tons of helpful resources, analysis, and comparisons as well as interactive tools and contact information to its various coalitions.

■ Henry J. Kaiser Family Foundation (www.kff.org). Nonprofit, private operating foundation focusing on the major health care issues facing the nation. Click on Medicare to access solid, easy-to-understand information; click on Medicaid/SCHIP for Medicaid and long-term care coverage information.

■ Medicare.gov (www.medicare.gov). The official U.S. Web site for the Medicare program.

Be sure to check out its Medicare Plan Finder and Prescription Drug Plan Finder tools.

■ MyMedicareMatters (www .mymedicarematters.org). From the National Council on the Aging and the Access to Benefits Coalition, with support from AstraZeneca Pharmaceuticals LP, this national education program helps Medicare beneficiaries and their families understand and assess the new prescription drug program options.

■ National Consumer Protection Technical Resource Center (www.smpresource.org). Funded by the U.S. Administration on Aging (AoA), the center provides a number of key services to health care consumers and AoA's 57 Senior Medicare Patrol (SMP) programs located throughout the country.

## MEDICARE: TIPS AND TOPICS

- *An individual becomes eligible for Medicare at age 65.*
- *Open enrollment. Keep in mind that a senior has six months after her initial filing for Medicare to enroll in a Medigap or supplemental insurance program of her choice. Federal law prohibits companies from denying eligibility during that time.*
- *If a senior doesn't sign up for Part B when he becomes eligible for it at age 65, he could face higher premiums later. Ditto with Part D.*
- *Don't lose your patience when trying to resolve a Medicare payment issue for an elderly parent. The situation could be just as confusing to the customer service person on the other end of the phone.*
- *Medicare Part A (and most supplemental policies) generally pays for a semiprivate room only. If a parent insists on privacy, she will have to make arrangements to pick up the cost of the difference between a private and semiprivate room in a hospital or other covered facility unless she is affiliated with a group or organization that has some other arrangement. As we mentioned earlier, some hospitals affiliated with the group H2U offer room upgrades as part of membership.*
- *MyMedicareMatters (www.mymedicarematters.org) has a helpful step-by-step tool, "7 Simple Steps," to help individuals make decisions on Part D coverage.*
- *Some seniors may qualify for extra help with their drug costs, according to Medicare.*
- *Don't wait until the last minute to file for coverage. The government, after all, is a bureaucracy with reams of red tape.*
- *The cost of some Medicare services may be tax deductible to the extent they and all other medical-related expenses exceed 7.5 percent of a taxpayer's adjusted gross income. Out-of-pocket expenses associated with Part A hospital coverage do not count toward the deductibility threshold because participation in the programs is mandatory. Costs associated with Parts B and D are deductible because participation is voluntary, according to the tax experts at CCH Incorporated.*

acceptable substitutes are covered. Medicare provides plenty of online tools it claims will help you navigate the maze *(www.medicare.gov)*.

## The Medicaid Option/Myth

True or false: The government will pay for Mom or Dad's nursing home stay when the time comes, no problem, no strings attached.

*False.* Medicare, as indicated above, does not cover the cost of long-term care. Medicaid, the state-administered welfare program under the auspices of the federal government that pays for nursing home care for the poor, is *not* available to all seniors. Plus, qualifying for Medicaid coverage just got more difficult for the average American, thanks to the Deficit Reduction Act of 2005 that went into effect February 8, 2006.

If an elderly loved one needs to enter a nursing home and you're expecting Medicaid to pick up the tab, realize that you'll have to spend a big chunk out of pocket before the welfare program kicks in—and it will kick in only if your elderly loved one qualifies. Keep in mind too that an elderly loved one can't file "in advance" for Medicaid before he needs it.

Typically some elderly "spend down" their assets or transfer them out of their name—to a spouse, for example—in order to meet the low-income qualifications for Medicaid. The income qualifications vary by state. Exempt from those qualifications, with limitations, is an

---

### MORE INFORMATION ON MEDICAID AND SENIORS

- *AARP (www.aarp.org). Plenty of helpful information and articles.*
- *Centers for Medicare and Medicaid Services (www.cms.hhs .gov/home/medicaid). The official government site for Medicaid.*
- *Henry J. Kaiser Family Foundation (www.kff.org). This nonprofit provides valuable resource and explanations on Medicare and Medicaid basics of coverage for seniors.*

individual's house if the equity is under $500,000 (some states may increase that to $750,000), one car, and personal possessions. Don't get your hopes up, however, that Medicaid is the answer to your loved one's needs.

Just how much will it cost you or your elderly loved one out of pocket today if you take the spend-down route? That of course depends on the state where you live. However, elder law attorney and expert Lawrence Davidow offers a general explanation for the state of New York, where nursing home costs can run $120,000 to $150,000 a year.

Medicaid has what's known as a "look-back rule" that sets a time limit on when someone can give away assets in order to meet its minimal assets eligibility requirement. The rule, revised by the Deficit Reduction Act, is designed to prevent someone who needs nursing home care from suddenly giving away all her assets so they become poverty-stricken and the state then will have to pick up the cost of care. The new look-back rule now extends to five years from the date of *filing* for Medicaid eligibility for anyone who filed for Medicaid eligibility after February 8, 2006. It used to be only three years from the date the assets were divested. But today, if an elderly parent needs nursing home care and has given away any assets within the past five years from the day he filed for Medicaid eligibility (even if the divesture was four years and 360 days ago), he is subject to the penalty period.

For instance, says Davidow, for every specified amount of money given away—the base amount varies by state—that person is ineligible to receive Medicaid for a one-month penalty period. In New York, the dollar amount is approximately $10,000. So for every $10,000 an elderly person transfers out of her name, she is then ineligible for Medicaid for a one-month period, and is responsible for any medical bills—that is, nursing home costs—incurred during that penalty period. For instance, a middle-class person in New York state who transferred away $100,000 in assets within the past five years would not be eligible for Medicaid to pick up his nursing-home tab for ten months—one month for every $10,000—from the *date of filing for Medicaid eligibility*. Even if he gave away the $100,000 four years ago and applies for Medicaid today, he technically would not be eligible for another ten months. (Of note: Because the new rules didn't go into effect until February 8, 2006, subject to individual state approval—check with your local Medicaid office—any assets transferred prior to that time still fall under the old transfer rules, a three-year look-back period beginning on the date of the asset transfer.)

Consider the following scenario as it might apply to the new rules: The average monthly cost of a semi-private room in a nursing home in New York is $308/day, according to MetLife numbers. Assuming that person who transferred away her assets in hopes of qualifying for Medicaid enters the nursing home today, she will have to come up with more than $90,000 out of

---

## SAVVY MEDICAID MOVES

*Some options that may help an elder qualify for Medicaid, from Lawrence Davidow, president of the National Academy of Elder Law Attorneys (www .naela.org):*

- Look at the exceptions of Medicaid's look-back rules to see if an elderly loved one can qualify for any of them:
  - The law allows transfer of assets to a spouse without penalty depending on an individual's situation. There is no set dollar amount.
  - If you have a child with disabilities, consider planning tools to transfer assets from a senior to that child. That could include a special needs trust (more on that in Chapter 11).
  - Some states (New York, for example) may allow instances where property can be transferred to a caretaker adult child in much the same way you can transfer assets to a spouse in order to qualify for Medicaid.
- Prepay funeral expenses
- Set up a formal lifetime personal care contract between an elderly loved one and family member, and fund it in full up front

---

pocket to pay for care before Medicaid will begin to pick up the tab. If she doesn't have $90,000, that's too bad. She will have to rely on adult children or other means of caregiving until becoming eligible to receive Medicaid.

Adds elder law attorney Sabatino, "I think the changes are so unworkable that it's very likely we will see things continue to change for the better or for the worse over the next few years as far as Medicaid is concerned."

As an illustration, Sabatino adds, consider that many of the seniors who go on Medicaid are already in a nursing home. Under the new law what will happen to them? For example, "You've been in a nursing home and spent down your assets and apply for Medicaid. Medicaid tells you, 'No, this transfer you made fours years ago is going to disqualify you for the next ten months, starting today.' You don't have the money to pay the nursing home. You can't live in the community. The nursing home doesn't have anybody to collect their money from. . . . (They) can't turn you out on the street because, under federal regulations, they have to have an appropriate discharge plan to meet a person's needs, so there's no way that is going to happen. My fear is that the very next time you get a temperature of 99.9°, they'll ship you off to the hospital, and then it will become the hospital's problem. And, of course, then Medicaid and probably Medicare will be paying five times the rate they would have had to pay the nursing home to pay for your hospital care, and you'll be stuck there until there's a (nursing home) bed that will accept you."

Nursing homes limit their number of Medicaid beds so that often they have long waiting lists. One way around those lists may be for an elderly person to enter a particular nursing home as private pay and then transfer to a Medicaid bed when he becomes eligible and the bed becomes available. Technically, nursing homes are not allowed to discriminate against Medicaid patients, but it comes down to dollars and cents. Facilities often receive less money for Medicaid patients than they do for private-pay ones.

---

**WHAT'S COVERED AND WHAT'S NOT?**

*What nursing home services does the hefty price tag provide an elderly loved one?*
- *24-hour nursing and trained medical care*
- *Room and board*
- *Personal supervision (although nursing home staffs can be rather lean)*
- *Some types of therapy; other services may require additional payment*
- *Housekeeping and linen service (although theft of belongings frequently occurs)*

*In no way, however, is the price all-inclusive. Not included is the cost:*
- *Physicians*
- *Medications*
- *Certain therapists and therapies*
- *Personal care items*
- *Laundry services*
- *Hospice care*

---

Something else to keep in mind regarding Medicaid: if possible, don't wait to file until you're in crisis mode. It's that government bureaucracy again, so if you wait until the last minute, chances are you'll end up with complications, delays, and gaps in coverage.

It's confusing, but the last word on these new Medicaid rules hasn't been heard. As of press time, they face lawsuit challenges.

# Already in Crisis Mode?

If your elderly loved one can't afford or can't get long-term care insurance, hasn't planned ahead for long-term care costs, and you're concerned about their finances, health coverage, or care, you can take steps to alleviate some of your concerns and the crippling costs.
- As we discussed previously, be sure your parent takes advantage of all available services and entitlements.

Visit BenefitsCheckup.org *(www.benefitscheckup.org)* from the nonprofit National Council on Aging.

- Talk to health care providers about possible programs, organizations, or private caregivers who can help
- If a parent seems to be skimping on necessary medical care because it's unaffordable, consider looking into Medicare Advantage—health maintenance organization or preferred provider organization-type options—as opposed to traditional Medicare and Medigap health insurance. Signing up for one of these plans may mean that a parent has to give up a favorite physician to gain necessary access to medical care, often at significant savings.
- Allow a senior to prepay her funeral expenses
- If a senior isn't going into a nursing home immediately, contract with a family member to take care of that elderly person and fund the contract up front and in full. It should be a formal personal care agreement based on the realistic life expectancy of that senior. The National Center for Health Statistics reports the average life expectancy of a male is just over age 74. If your father, for example, is 72, perhaps a three-year contract would make sense. The contract should include an itemizing of the annual costs associated with caregiving multiplied by the number of years of projected life/care. Pay the total caregiving amount in full, and you've removed that money from a senior's assets. It's not a gift, either; it's payment for services rendered, says Davidow, who has been successful in helping seniors with this strategy. The strategy may sound far-fetched, but why not pay the money to a family member instead of a stranger? The concept has been challenged and won on appeal before the Department of Social Services, says Davidow.

The bottom line, though, is that unless you and your elderly loved ones preplan financially for elder care, the expense will be painful.

However, with the right financial planning and the right approach, you can help a loved one without worrying that she will lose it all if faced with the burden of long-term care. When Michael's elderly mother finally became too ill to remain in her home and needed the full-time care provided by a nursing home, she easily qualified for Medicaid. She had no assets—although for years she lived very comfortably in a middle-class neighborhood, drove late-model cars, and was always well-dressed. Why was it all so easy? It seems that her son, who supported her, had done his homework and planned ahead. A successful businessman, he purchased the condo for his mom but kept it in his name, and instead of gifting her money and investments, he kept all of the money and assets earmarked for her in a separate account in his own name. He paid taxes on the income and property, but that cost was negligible when compared with the monthly charges for nursing home care.

## The Dental Dilemma

When money is tight, many families and their young, old, and in-between often forgo dental care as just too costly an option. They also ignore dental insurance options, some of which are offered as low-cost additions to other health insurance policies (one example is from PacifiCare Health Systems *(www.pacificare.com)*. Those all-important regular checkups and teeth cleaning just aren't in the budget for anyone but the children.

Many elderly especially are reluctant to spend money on their teeth until a cavity has turned into an abscess and they have trouble eating. When they finally do visit the dentist, they usually want the tooth pulled, not saved. "It's just too much money. I can't afford anything else," says Nan, 76, with an obviously swollen right cheek, when asked why she waited so long. "It's not covered, so I don't need it."

Paul, 58, won't fix his chipped tooth, either. "If I spring for the $1,200 for the tooth, there goes my son Pete's spending money at college for the next three months. Besides, it hasn't started to bother me (yet)."

Unfortunately, neither adult's approach to dental health may be the best approach to healthy aging, which includes eating (and chewing) properly. Dental infections, too, if not treated can worsen and lead to other serious problems.

The American Dental Association *(www.ada.org)* and its local chapters may have various programs that can help provide financial relief when it comes to dental care. An individual dentist, too, if he is aware of the financial hardships, may be willing to work with you or an elderly loved one on payment.

## Choosing the Right Medical Professionals

The quality of health and medical care varies vastly, as do providers' skills in various areas, their willingness to treat certain conditions, and health care plans' willingness to refer patients to usually more costly specialists.

It's important that you as caregiver take an active role in your elderly parents' health care—when they're healthy and when they're not. That means helping them choose the right providers who understand their special needs, strengths, and weaknesses, and then taking the time and making the effort to explain your parents' situation thoroughly. Try at least to meet the provider so that, in an emergency, you and she feel comfortable discussing the issues. That's especially important if you live a long distance from elderly parents.

If your parents balk at what they consider an intrusion into their privacy, try to explain that it's not about interfering in their lives. It's about helping them maintain their independence as long as possible. If you know the situation, you can better help them understand it and handle it. It will help save you and your parents time, money, and trouble in the long run when they do have to depend on you.

Unfortunately, many seniors today too quickly accept any diagnosis and any tests ordered, and they are afraid to question something even if it doesn't seem right. That expensive MRI or complete blood-count test really might not be necessary. Or a medical provider might not take the time to thoroughly explain a complicated diagnosis or could just be flat-out wrong.

Empower your aging parents to understand their patient rights. Check with the providers and any hospitals they use for a copy of their specific patients rights.

When trying to find the right providers for an elderly parent, ask yourself:

- Do they have the proper credentials? What about the right training and expertise to meet a parent's needs?
- Have they received high marks for their quality of care?
- Are they approved as a Medicare provider? Medline-Plus *(www.medlineplus.gov)* from the National Institutes of Health and National Library of Medicine has a wealth of useful free information as well as provider finders.
- What about your parent's preference as far as gender, age, race, or religion? This is, after all, a provider for your parent, not you.
- Is the provider's office easily accessible and nearby?
- Ask other medical professionals for possible referrals or suggestions of providers
- Ask any potential provider for references, and talk to those references

# Alternative and Complementary Medicine

People, especially those with chronic or life-threatening diseases, no matter their age, often look to alternative or complementary therapies and treatments for answers. The National Institutes of Health's National Center for Complementary and Alternative Medicine *(nccam.nih.gov)* has helpful information as well as tips and questions to ask to assist in locating the right practitioner for an individual's situation. Another source of information is the National Library of Medicine *(www.nlm.nih.gov)*.

Don't overlook talking to a parent's primary health provider, either. He may be aware of reputable alternative therapy providers. Check with a parent's insurer, too. Some will cover at least a portion of the cost, especially if the therapy or treatment is given by a licensed medical provider such as a physician, advanced practice nurse, nurse practitioner, physician's assistant, or physical therapist.

## The Silent Disease of Seniors

Depression is a very real threat to those ages 65 and older. It affects more than 2 million of the nation's 34 million seniors, according to the National Institutes of Mental Health ("Older Adults: Depression and Suicide Fact Sheet"). It also co-occurs with other serious diseases, including heart disease, stroke, diabetes, cancer, and Parkinson's disease, and, if left untreated, can have adverse affects on other illnesses. Depression is not normal, and as a caregiver you need to pay attention to it.

Depression among the elderly carries a huge price tag, too—about $9 billion a year in terms of the extra time and assistance that informal (unpaid) caregivers provide, says the University of Michigan's Langa, lead author on a 2004 study into the huge unrecognized costs of depression. The study showed that people with depressive symptoms had significantly higher likelihood of needing help with basic tasks like dressing, bathing, eating, grocery shopping, medication management, paying bills, and even using the telephone. Specifically, they needed more than twice as much care a week as those seniors with no symptoms.

Some symptoms of depression, according to the National Institutes of Mental Health, include:
- Persistent sad, anxious, or "empty" mood
- Feelings of hopelessness or pessimism
- Feelings of guilt, worthlessness, or helplessness
- Loss of interest or pleasure in hobbies and activities that were once enjoyed, including sex
- Decreased energy, fatigue, or feeling "slowed down"

- Difficulty concentrating, remembering, or making decisions
- Insomnia, early-morning awakening, or oversleeping
- Appetite and/or weight loss or overeating and weight gain
- Thoughts of death or suicide; suicide attempts
- Restlessness, irritability
- Persistent physical symptoms that do not respond to treatment, such as headaches, digestive disorders, and chronic pain

Pay attention to forgetfulness in an elderly loved one, too. It's normal that we all forget things occasionally, and forgetting becomes a bit more prevalent as we age. But if it becomes something more that interferes with daily living, it could signal something more serious. The American Geriatrics Society's Foundation for Health in Aging *(www.healthinaging.org)* suggests some things to keep in mind:

- Be alert for signs of short-term memory loss
- Be aware that memory changes often evidence themselves as changes in daily functioning such as planning, organizing, and making decisions
- Make sure that memory changes are thoroughly evaluated by a doctor and that all appropriate treatments have been considere.
- Keep a detailed record of all medications that an older person is taking, including prescription, over-the-counter, and any herbal remedies. This will help the doctor to decide whether they could be contributing to the problem.
- Understand that delirium might occur in someone with dementia. (Other causes could include urinary infection, pneumonia, dehydration, or heart attack.)
- Learn techniques for helping reduce the stress and burden of memory loss

## A Note on Online Information

Be careful of the sources of information you use, especially with medical information. Just as you would thoroughly check out any individual provider or organization *before* hiring them or availing yourself of their help or information, likewise assess Internet sites. Also, as with any product you're considering buying, consider the source of the information or advice. If someone is trying to sell you a product or service, bear that in mind.

Generally reliable sources of medical information include:

- Government sites, those identified by a ".gov" in their URL. That includes healthfinder.gov and Medicare .gov.
- Nonprofit organizations dedicated to a particular disease or cause, usually identified by a ".org" in their URL. Most of these organizations can be extremely valuable to caregivers and the aging alike.
- Medical facilities such as hospitals, medical centers, and clinics. Often these sites have pages of helpful consumer information.
- Health insurance plans and HMOs. These sites may offer health and wellness information and directions. Blue Cross Blue Shield Association *(www.bcbs.com/ resources/)* is just one example.

Some other tips:

- Look for testimonials to a product and read them. They're a great source of information *if* the people making them haven't been paid for their glowing words.
- What's the site's reputation? Search the Internet and read what others say about the site.
- Is a product or service endorsed by a reputable organization or individual you trust?
- Is a site open about what it is and how it makes its money? If you can't easily click on something to find out who's funding the information, tread carefully.

■ Does a site make it easy to contact them for anything other than buying their product?

Organizations like AARP are a wealth of knowledge for young and old alike. It's almost always a good starting point. If you or a loved one is looking at the possibility of nursing home care now or in the future, check out its state-by-state guide.

# Remember:

■ Preventive health is the best approach to managing health care costs for all generations.
■ Financial health illiteracy is a major problem in America today. You can't plan financially if you don't understand what's available and what's not, the qualifications required to obtain it, who pays for it, and who doesn't.
■ Medicare does not pay for long-term care for seniors. Medicaid, the state-administered federal health care program for the poor, doesn't pay for it either unless an individual meets stringent qualifications, and then generally only after significant out-of-pocket expenses.
■ Medicare does *not* cover all the health care expenses of the aging.
■ The new Medicare drug benefit program offers many options, not all of which cost the same or cover the same medications. Before an elderly person signs up for a plan, be sure to check the plan's formulary for whether the prescription drugs she needs are reimbursable under the plan.
■ Don't wait until it's a medical/financial crisis to apply for medical-related financial entitlements or benefits
■ Pay attention to depression as a serious disease that affects millions of seniors to the tune of billions of dollars of related cost

# Your Retirement Picture, Taxes, and Estate Planning

**Chapter 11**

How do you envision the perfect retirement? It's a pretty good bet that, ideally, your later years would be free of worries and financial hardships.

More realistically, though, what kind of retirement will you be able to afford? Do you have the *funded* retirement savings and pension vehicles in place to achieve your dream, or will your children end up having to take care of you? Have your children learned from watching the dynamics of you and your aging parents so that they're already on the right track for their own retirement future?

Chances are if you're like many of the Sandwich Generation, you've funded today's needs for you, your children, and your aging parents at the expense of your own tomorrow. The new car you needed came from your end-of-quarter bonus at work; you paid your kid's college expenses this year rather than contribute to your 401(k) last year; you made all those trips back east to help an aging Mom instead of contributing to your 401(k) this year, and those higher health-insurance premiums meant putting off yet again purchasing that disability insurance everyone's talking about.

Let's look at a few sobering statistics from the Pew Research Center's "Baby Boomers/Age of Aquarius" study:

- 17 percent of boomers say they won't have enough money for the basics when it comes to their own retirement.
- Another 24 percent say they'll be able to "just meet basic living expenses."
- 40 percent earn $75,000 a year or more.
- 21 percent earn less than $30,000 a year.

■ 38 percent have been divorced, which often adds to financial responsibilities with extended families.

Whatever the level of caregiving you provide an elderly parent or the degree of support you give your own children, neither need be at the expense of your own future. Let's look more closely at some things you can do to ensure your own healthy retirement.

## Your Share

We've all heard it dozens of times from all kinds of financial advice-givers: "Pay yourself first." For the Sandwich Generation, that's not only good advice, it's essential to avoid what can be harsh realities in your later years. If you don't take the right approach to funding your cross-generational responsibilities—including your retirement—today, you could end up far worse off financially than anyone you know or even can imagine when it comes time for your own retirement. The issue gains special urgency given the ongoing discussions on the future solvency of the nation's Social Security system, a key leg of what traditionally has been the three-legged stool on which Americans' have funded their retirements for decades. The other two legs are personal savings and retirement/pension plans, both of which also have become endangered species for many in the Sandwich Generation.

Consider a few more statistics from the annual Employee Benefit Research Institute® "Retirement Confidence Survey (2006)." The annual survey examines the attitudes and behavior of U.S. workers and retirees toward all aspects of saving, retirement planning, and long-term financial security. They continue to paint the unrealistic picture many Americans have of retirement.

■ Seven out of ten workers (70 percent) and/or their spouses have saved money for retirement, yet fewer than two in three (64 percent) of those workers currently save for their retirement.

■ Almost three in ten (28 percent) workers think they can afford a comfortable retirement with 70 percent to 85 percent of preretirement income. And, in fact, many planners do suggest that people plan to replace at least 70 percent of their income in retirement. However, 34 percent of current retirees say their retirement income is the same as preretirement, and 21 percent say that income is higher!

ChoosetoSave.org and the American Savings Education Council—both programs of EBRI, the Employee

---

## SOURCES FOR MORE INFORMATION

- *CCH Planning Toolkit (www.finance.cch.com). From CCH Incorporated, a longtime provider of business, tax, and legal information to the business community, this is a one-stop financial planning, retirement, and money site.*

- *Choose to Save (www.choosetosave.org/ asec). The American Savings Education Council, a program of the Employee Benefits Research Institute Education and Research Fund, is a national coalition of public- and private-sector institutions committed to making saving and retirement planning a priority for all Americans. Check out its Ballpark E$timate® to help you determine what you'll need to save for retirement.*

- *Employee Benefits Security Administration (www.dol.gov/ebsa). From the U.S. Department of Labor, the site has lots of free information.*

- *Financial Planning Association (www.fpanet .org, click on "Public/Find a Planner"). The membership organization for the financial planning community has plenty of helpful explanatory information for consumers.*

- *Garrett Planning Network (www .garrettplanningnetwork.com). This is a network of fee-only financial planners; includes an online tool to locate a planner near you.*

- *Internal Revenue Service (www.irs.gov). The "tax man" has plenty of information you'll need to know and then some, along with downloadable forms, contacts, questions, and answers. Its Taxpayer Advocate Service (www.irs.gov/advocate) helps taxpayers with disputes with the IRS, too.*

- *Kiplinger (www.kiplinger.com). Your trusted information source for everything involving money and personal finances, from auto and college funding to elder care, investing, Medicare, Medicaid, retirement, taxes, and more; helpful free interactive tools available; click on "Store" and check out the retirement and planning aids available.*

- *Mymoney.gov (www.mymoney.gov). A site from the federal government designed to help people understand how to save, invest, and manage their money. Free My Money Tool Kit also available.*

- *NASD (www.nasd.com). Primary private-sector regulator of America's securities industry offers information on investing, investments, and brokers.*

- *Nolo (www.nolo.com). Longtime provider of do-it-yourself and informative books, software, information, and more with a helpful Resource Center.*

Benefits Research Institute—offer a free online tool, Ballpark E$timate®, to help you estimate your overall retirement savings needs *(www.choosetosave.org/ballpark)*.

## Start Early or Start Now

Start your retirement savings early—or as early as you can—because the longer your money has to grow and compound, the better. It's the rule of 72. To determine how long it will take a particular investment to double your money, divide the number 72 by the investment's rate of return.

Over the long haul markets go up. But short term it can be a bumpy roller coaster ride. If you're already beyond the early years of saving for retirement, don't despair. It's never too late to start. You can take steps today, teach your children to take steps today, and help even your aging parents take steps today that will make a difference to your future, and, in turn, your children's future. After all, are you so different from your elderly parents who don't want to be a financial burden on anyone?

So stock up on antacid for your stomach and get going today.

## Documents and Decisions: Yours

We've talked about all those necessary documents and decisions for your elderly loved ones. To be prepared for the future and

---

**DOUBLE YOUR MONEY**

*The rule of 72 is an easy way to figure out how long it will take your money to double with a particular investment based on its expected rate of return: 72 divided by the investment's rate of return equals the time it takes your money to double.*

*Example: 72 divided 10 (as in 10 percent rate of return) equals*

*7.2 years*

*72 divided by 5 (as in 5 percent rate of return) equals*

*14.4 years*

lessen your own retirement worries, you'll need to put many of the same and then some in place for you and your spouse. They include (turn back to Chapter 6 for the details):

- **Will** to designate how your assets will be disbursed
- **Guardianship provision** as part of your will if you have minor children. This states who will assume the legal responsibility for these children.
- **Testamentary trust** (more on this later in this chapter), also as stipulated by your will, can, among other things, detail the future for your child and provide for his financial support if a minor.
- **Durable financial power of attorney** to designate who will make financial and legal decisions for you if you can't. It's wise to set one up. If you don't, the state will choose someone for you.
- **Health care proxy** that designates another individual to make health care and medical decisions for you if you can't.
- **Living will** that stipulates what you do or do not want regarding life support in the event something happens to you. And it can happen to you—at any age.
- **Long-term care insurance** in place for both you and your spouse. Whether your elderly loved ones have it and the accompanying choices, or if they don't and struggle, it's a lesson to learn and pay attention to.

## The Importance of Planning

With the help of this book, you began your approach to better cope with the cross-generational sandwich by first getting an overview of the situation, problems, and solutions, and then planning a course that fits the situation and needs of you and your elderly loved one. The same approach is essential when it comes to your own retirement.

It's a three-step process that starts with financial planning. The steps:

1. Where are you today?
2. Realistically, where do you want to be tomorrow?
3. What action plan will get you there?

By now you've already completed the first step. You know where you are financially—refer back to Chapter 7's assessment of your net worth, your cash flow, and what's needed today. Now it's time for the next step: figuring out what you'd like to do in retirement, setting your goals, and then laying out a plan of action to get there.

## Do It Yourself or Not?

*"I'm pretty good at numbers, but I would never do my own taxes anymore. They're just too complicated."*

—Neal E. Cutler, financial gerontology specialist, on whether to use planning professionals

Whether you devise a retirement plan on your own or with the help of professionals is up to you. Some people welcome the knowledge, direction, and impartiality of a professional financial planner. Others don't. If you decide to use a planner, pay attention to her credentials. As with geriatric care managers, anyone can hang out a shingle and say he is an expert. Look for legitimate professional credentials and training (including CFP® or CPA) as well as referrals, references, and more. Talk to the references and ask questions including whether they find the person helpful, knowledgeable, and up to date.

Also ask the potential advisor about her track record with return on client portfolios. Do you get along well with the person? Do you feel comfortable sharing your intimate financial details with her?

*The Financial Planning Association* (www.fpanet.org) *has a free online search tool to help you locate a Certified Financial Planner™ with areas of expertise pertinent to your situation.*

If you opt for the do-it-yourself route, it's important to make unemotional decisions about what it takes to achieve your financial goals. It's the same impartiality required to analyze the best living situation for an elderly loved one. If you're not sure whether you need or want help, talk to qualified planners anyway. You'll be surprised at just how much they can help you.

## The Goals

How do you really envision your retirement years? Where would you like to live? What would you like to be doing? How would you like—or not like—your own children to figure into that lifestyle? What would you like your children to be doing? What about your grandchildren? How important is it, or do you think it will be, to spend time with them? If an aging parent is still alive, what role, if any, will he play, and will it mean a financial commitment from you? These are important questions that help shape your goals.

At what age would you like to retire? Would you like to keep working part-time, change your lifestyle, volunteer, or all of the above? More Americans are putting off retirement and not only for financial reasons. They enjoy the social interaction of a work environment, or they may use retirement as an opportunity to start a new career, for example.

If the multigenerational sandwich has stretched your finances thin and you think these choices aren't yours to make because you have so little money put away, think again. They are pertinent because you can't possibly figure out how much money you will need for retirement if you don't have a clear idea of what you want to be doing where. Even if you simply want to move the rocker to the front porch for the next 20 years, that's going somewhere and has financial ramifications. Include your spouse and her ideas when it comes to setting retirement goals, too. Otherwise one of you could wake up one day in retirement absolutely miserable.

# The Plan and the Basics

O nce you know your retirement needs and goals, you're ready to look at ways to get there, then choose what works for you. That's your plan.

Retirement goals can be achieved in many different ways, even if you're financially strapped right now. We'll touch on just a few of them. Each comes with its own pros and cons, both as an investment vehicle in itself and, often, in terms of your and your loved ones' circumstances—financial and otherwise. If you're trying to bolster your nonexistent nest egg, what can be very risky commodity futures might not be a good place to invest your limited resources. On the other hand, you may have only ten years to build your savings, so you'll need more growth than provided by low interest rate certificates of deposit.

Retirement plans basically fall into two categories, defined benefit plans and defined contribution plans, although a number of other options exist that may be hybrids of each.

A *defined benefit plan* is one in which an employer agrees to pay an employee on retirement a set amount based on some kind of a formula that takes into account years of service and salary history. These are the "traditional" retirement plans.

A *defined contribution plan* is one to which an individual contributes, in many cases along with an employer. At retirement, the benefit consists of all the contributions from the employee as well as the employer plus income and gains, minus expenses, losses, etc. Its amount is not guaranteed.

Types of tax-advantaged defined contribution plans include:

■ *401(k) plan.* This savings plan has replaced the traditional defined benefit pension plan as the vehicle of choice for employers and employees alike. Employees contribute up to a certain percentage of their earnings pretax. Employers may match a limited amount of employee contributions, no strings attached. The account grows tax-deferred until it's withdrawn, at which time income taxes are due on the amount withdrawn. Strict tax laws limit contributions, withdrawals without penalties, and more, so talk to your employer's benefits specialist or tax/planning expert for more details.

- *Traditional IRA*. Anyone can set up a traditional IRA. Contributions to it, which are limited by tax laws, may be deductible on your taxes subject to limitations. Whether the money contributed is taxed or not, no taxes are due on the account's earnings until withdrawal. With exceptions, withdrawals before age 59½ face a 10 percent penalty plus taxes on that money. You must begin withdrawals by age 70½; strict minimums apply. IRAs are a great way to save. For example, if you put $3,000 a year into an IRA each year for the next five years, at the end of those five years your money would have grown to $17,252 at just a 7 percent annual rate of return, according to the U.S. Department of Labor Employee Benefits Security Administration. Annual contributions are limited to $4,000 ($5,000 for age 50 and over).

- *Roth IRA*. Roths are similar in some ways to traditional IRAs, but have several advantages. You can't deduct your contributions, but you can withdraw them at any time without penalty—and pay no taxes because you've already paid them. And all earnings are tax-free, not tax-deferred as with a traditional IRA. While contribution amounts are the same as for a traditional IRA, there's no age limit on contributions to Roth IRAs, although income restrictions and limitations apply. (Contribution limits phase out for single taxpayers with modified AGI between $95,000 and $110,000; joint filers between $150,000 and $160,000; and marrieds filing separately between $0 and $10,000. With rollovers to Roth IRAs, the AGI limit is $100,000 though it's slated disappear in 2010. Check out the online CCH Planning Toolkit; *www.finance.cch.com.*) And you don't have to begin withdrawals at age 70½ as you do with a traditional IRA.

- *Roth 401(k)*. A Roth 401(k) offers all the tax-free advantages of a Roth IRA but with the higher contribution limits of a 401(k)—$15,000 for most workers and $20,000 for those 50 and older in 2006. And, there are no income limits, so if you were shut out of the Roth IRA because you made too much money, this could be your chance to build up a stash of tax-free income for retirement. But Roth 401(k) plans are new and only a small number of companies are offering them. Like traditional 401(k)s, the Roth 401(k) option requires you to take distributions starting at age 70½. But, if you roll your Roth 401(k) into a Roth IRA at retirement, you won't have to touch a dime until you want to. The disadvantage of contributing to a Roth 401(k) is that you lose your up-front tax deduction, meaning your take-home pay will be reduced compared to the same contribution to a traditional 401(k). If you like, you can split your contributions between the two types of 401(k) plans, preserving some of your tax deductions and building future tax-free income.

■ *Self-employed and small business retirement plans.* These include Keoghs or HR10, SEP-IRA, and SIMPLE (Savings Incentive Match Plan for Employees) and, like other defined contribution plans, are tax-deferred qualified retirement plans but are designed for the self-employed or small businesses and their employees. They tend to have higher maximum contribution limits that are figured based on a percentage of income.

## Other Retirement Savings Options

**ANNUITIES.** Another type of tax-deferred savings for the future, annuities are basically a contract, usually with an insurance company, that involve a lump sum or over-time investment to be paid out at a later date. They can be fixed, in which the issuer agrees to pay a set rate of return with a set amount due at the end of the contract. Or they can be variable, in which the investment earnings depend on the investment option.

**LIFE INSURANCE.** Depending on the policy you choose, this can be a method of forced savings as well as protection for your loved ones through income replacement if something happens to you. It also is a way to generate wealth for future generations in the form of cash paid out without hassle after your death. (A beneficiary provides the death certificate, and that's about it.)

The two basic types of life insurance are term and cash value, also known as whole life. Term involves paying a straightforward annual premium in exchange for a lump-sum payment in the event of the policyholder's death. It does not involve savings or borrowing on the policy. With cash value, or whole life, on the other hand, you pay in premiums and over time build cash into an account that accrues interest. On the policyholder's death, the face value of the policy will be paid out. In the interim, after a certain length of time—which varies by policy but often is five years—you can borrow against that policy's accrued cash value (details vary). As we've talked about, it's a form of forced savings that can make sense if interest rates in general are low. But if rates are high, you'll likely get a better return on your money by investing it somewhere else.

Whole life also can be a source of ready cash if you need it as collateral for a loan or to borrow against the cash value of the policy. Note, however, that a cash value policy generally pays out only the face value of the policy on the policyholder's death. Nothing more. But if the cash value of the $50,000 policy is only $30,000 and the policyholder dies, the beneficiaries will receive the full $50,000.

If you're concerned about protecting your loved ones after you die, ask yourself if you have adequate coverage in the event something happens to you. If your spouse works, too, and/or contributes significantly to the household—either in cash or perhaps by caring for or transporting your children or providing care for an elderly loved one—ask yourself if she has adequate life insurance. If something were to happen to her, would the dollar value of her policy cover the costs of her contributions if you had to pay someone else for them?

## Easy Money!

One of the simplest ways to put aside money for your future is to maximize your contributions to tax-deferred and tax-advantaged retirement accounts whether through an employer or on your own. If an employer matches your contributions—even if only a small percentage of them—great. That's free money. If not, maximize your annual contributions anyway. If you're self-employed, maximize your contributions,

---

### RETIREMENT IN 15 YEARS?

*If you had invested $1,000 a month in American Funds' the Investment Company of America in 1970 with plans to retire in 1985 (15 years later), the value of your account would have exceeded $500,000. If you then withdrew 6 percent a year over the next 20 years, the account's value at the end of 2004 would have totaled more than $2 million even after withdrawing more than $1.66 million! No small change.*

| Year | Cumulative investment* | Value of Account | Total taken in cash | Year | Cumulative investment* | Value of Account | Total taken in cash |
|------|------|------|------|------|------|------|------|
| 1970 | $12,000 | $12,642 | | 1990 | | 916,491 | 58,117 |
| 1971 | 24,000 | 27,003 | | 1991 | | 1,100,932 | 54,989 |
| 1972 | 36,000 | 43,686 | | 1992 | | 1,111,072 | 66,056 |
| 1973 | 48,000 | 47,092 | | 1993 | | 1,172,429 | 66,664 |
| 1974 | 60,000 | 48,955 | | 1994 | | 1,103,440 | 70,346 |
| 1975 | 72,000 | 78,799 | | 1995 | | 1,374,872 | 66,206 |
| 1976 | 84,000 | 114,911 | | 1996 | | 1,557,293 | 82,492 |
| 1977 | 96,000 | 123,785 | | 1997 | | 1,926,965 | 93,438 |
| 1978 | 108,000 | 154,221 | | 1998 | | 2,247,016 | 115,618 |
| 1979 | 120,000 | 196,567 | | 1999 | | 2,477,759 | 134,821 |
| 1980 | 132,000 | 251,592 | | 2000 | | 2,421,217 | 148,666 |
| 1981 | 144,000 | 265,392 | | 2001 | | 2,162,219 | 145,273 |
| 1982 | 156,000 | 369,891 | | 2002 | | 1,719,738 | 129,733 |
| 1983 | 168,000 | 456,998 | | 2003 | | 2,064,814 | 103,184 |
| 1984 | 180,000 | 500,170 | | 2004 | | 2,142,191 | 123,889 |
| 1985 | | 636,781 | $ 30,010 | Total withdrawals | | | $1,663,023 |
| 1986 | | 737,392 | 38,207 | * Cumulative volume discount applied when | | | |
| 1987 | | 732,421 | 44,244 | appropriate | | | |
| 1988 | | 785,411 | 43,945 | **Source:** Courtesy The Capital Group | | | |
| 1989 | | 968,615 | 47,125 | Companies/American Funds | | | |

too. If your spouse has a plan and you truly can't afford to fund both plans to the maximum, determine which plan provides the best option in terms of investment and growth, then fund that one to the maximum and the other as much as possible.

If finances are tight and you *try* to save but there always seem to be other demands for your cash, consider an automatic payroll deduction. Alternatively, arrange with an investment brokerage or mutual fund for automatic, regular withdrawal of a set amount from a checking or savings account. Such programs generally are free and in essence allow you to create your own "payroll" deduction plan. Even if you think you don't have the excess cash, if it's automatically taken out of an account on a regular basis, you're less likely to miss it. Even $20 a week (four fewer lattes perhaps?) is $80 a month, or $960 a year, and is saving something. (Sock it away in a traditional IRA, get the tax deduction, and watch your earnings grow tax-deferred, too.) Plus, once you get started, it becomes a foundation on which to build. Add a little bit more here or there—such as when you work overtime, pick up an odd job, or get a small raise—and pretty soon you're on your way to a nest egg.

---

### TIPS FROM REAL LIFE

*Do you have trouble finding that extra money to save/invest for your future?*

- Consider payroll deductions or automatic withdrawal from a checking or savings account. If you don't see it, you'll miss it less.
- If you work overtime or get a small raise, put the extra into your retirement savings instead of frittering it away.
- As a caregiver, talk to your elderly loved ones about ways, monetarily and otherwise, they can help you save for your future, especially by taking advantage of community services already available to them.
- Cut back on a few of the little things. Three fewer $4 lattes or soft drinks a week add up to $600 a year. Cut back on just $10 a week in snacks and goodies for the family, and that's another $468 plus tax. That's more than $1,000 saved.

Beyond maximizing contributions to your retirement plan, pay attention to how the plan is invested. Make sure it's diversified so your savings aren't all in one basket in the event of the collapse of that company or one segment of the market.

"I just don't have the money," says Katy, 52, when it comes to saving for her retirement. She's a single mom with two kids nearing college age and an elderly mother who counts on her for what she calls the "little things." Those little things, however, add up. "It used to be that when I occasionally worked late one or two days, I ended up with extra cash every month, but not anymore. I guess it's because I no longer can work extra and get everything done for Mom and the kids. The only way I've been able to save anything at all is to have automatic payroll withdrawals into my 401(k). At least I set aside a little regularly that way. It's not much, but I suppose every bit helps."

Katy worries constantly that when the kids start going off to college in the next couple years, she'll lose her child support payments and will be strapped financially. She's considering talking to her mom about how her mom can use low-cost transportation for seniors and those with disabilities to help her with some of her errands. Their church has a free volunteer program that helps transport seniors, too. Either option would allow Katy to work a few more hours each week. The kids also are working toward getting college scholarships. Her employer even offers one. Additionally, Katy is thoroughly researching student loan options, and the 529 plans started several years ago by her mom and now-deceased dad will help, too.

Too bad there aren't as many funding options for retirement as there are for college. Your retirement, unfortunately, is up to you. Katy found ways to cut back merely by going over the family's expenses. To glean other easy ways to cut back for the benefit of your retirement, let's revisit the finances of Jay and Diane. Remember, they have two young children, help support Jay's 24-year-old son from a previous relationship, and provide support to Diane's elderly mom. Jay's solution

## JAY AND DIANE'S FINANCES 2005

| | |
|---|---:|
| **Income:** | **$170,000** |
| **Estimated annual basic expenses** | |
| **House** | |
| Mortgage @ $1,100/month: | $ 13,200 |
| Utilities @ $350/month: | $ 4,200 |
| Upkeep/expenses: | $ 2,400 |
| Health care | |
| (self-employed, including insurance): | $ 11,500 |
| **Transportation** | |
| (including two car payments): | $ 11,120 |
| **24-year-old son:** | $ 28,000 |
| **College savings:** ($100/month per child): | $ 2,400 |
| **Federal/state income tax liabilities** | $ 30,000 |
| **Share of Mom's care costs:** | $ 35,000 |
| **Food and entertainment** ($500/week): | $ 26,000 |
| **Total expenses:** | **$163,820** |
| **Income** | **$170,000** |
| **Minus general expenses** | **$163,820** |
| **Total left for other expenses, saving,** | |
| **investing, retirement, and emergencies:** | **$ 6,180** |

was to talk to his mother-in-law about getting a reverse mortgage and also finding a few extra entitlements here and there. But other, simple adjustments can make a big difference. Saving just $500 a month on expenses and then allocating that money to retirement savings could add up to $296,793 at the end of 20 years at just an 8 percent rate of return.

It's great that Jay and Diane put aside $100 per child ($200) monthly for future college expenses. But the costs of their vehicles are high. Instead of driving two big, gas-guzzling, top-of-the-line SUVs, perhaps they might consider trading one in (along with its car payments) on a smaller vehicle that gets better gas mileage. (If they opt for one of the new hybrid varieties, they'll get a credit on their federal income taxes, too, beginning in 2006. The amount depends on the weight class of the vehicle and its fuel efficiency.) Even two fewer

## WAYS JAY AND DIANE CAN SAVE

- *More fuel-efficient vehicles*
- *Lower car payments*
- *Home equity loan instead of traditional loan to finance car*
- *Graduate student fellowship and/or student loans*
- *Trading in current midrange deductible health insurance plan for a high-deductible policy combined with a health savings account*
- *Review and revamp cellular phone policy*

tanks of gas a month can easily save close to $100, and the lower car payment saves at least another $100. If they need to finance the new car, opting for a home equity line of credit instead of a traditional loan allows them to deduct the interest paid on their income taxes (because they itemize), saving more money.

The stipend to Jay's older son, too, could be cut easily if the son would apply for a graduate student fellowship and take out student loans. The couple could cut back on health care costs by swapping their existing policy with monthly premiums well over $1,000 to one that has a high deductible combined with a health savings account (HSA). Not only would that save on monthly costs (the amount varies dramatically depending on insurer and plan), but they'll save on their income taxes because the HSA, which may be used for qualified medical or health expenses, is funded with pretax dollars. Utilities could be lowered if Jay swapped his two separate cellphone plans for one with a two-phone option. If the couple could save just $500 a month and invest that at an 8 percent rate of return, at the end of 20 years they would have put aside almost $300,000 ($296,793.45).

Luke started a sales representative business not long after his dad retired as president of the local bank. His dad, Martin, was bored and looking for something to do, so he began helping his son with his business' bookkeeping one day a week. It was informal; Luke needed the help, and his dad enjoyed the work. His dad refused to take any payment for his work, and the arrangement continued for a couple of years. Then the business took off. Martin still refused to take money because he and his wife didn't need it. His pension with its great health insurance benefits took care of everything. Finally, though, he acquiesced with the understanding that he would put it aside in a solid mutual fund, ostensibly for the future needs of his grandkids.

Fast forward ten years. For much of that time, Martin still worked with his son. Meanwhile, Martin's company has canceled its "lifetime" health insurance benefits; he's had several operations, including one for cancer; and his wife has slowed down considerably. Luke's business, however, is doing great. He has socked away plenty for his and his wife's retirement, and their children's college expenses aren't an issue either. Their son attends college on a full, four-year football scholarship, and their daughter was awarded a more-than-adequate academic scholarship. Long-term financial planning and saving—no matter whom it ends up helping—is for tomorrow, not today.

## Beyond the Dollars: Risk

Pay attention also to the level of risk inherent in a retirement savings option. Talk to your professional investment or financial advisor about what's right for your situation. Although Mom or Dad may look to certificates of deposits because, they say, they're guaranteed by the "full faith and credit" of the U.S. Treasury, NBC talk show host and wealth planner Jim Barry provides another picture. "They're certificates of depreciation!" The amount you earn on them doesn't even keep pace with inflation over time.

## Tax Topics and Strategies

Taxes can get rather complicated for members of the Sandwich Generation, who often have extended families, multiple levels of responsibilities, and more. The tax situation can get especially snarled

---

## 2006 TAX NUMBERS

**Standard deduction (phase-out levels apply):**
- Single, $5,150
- Head of household, $7,300 ($7,550)
- Married filing jointly, $10,300 (surviving spouses eligible, too)
- Married filing separately, $5,150
- Dependent claimed on someone else's return, $850 (minimum standard deduction but can be higher, up to $5,150, depending on earned and unearned income)
- Age 65 or older, $1,250 for single or heads of household filers; $2,000 for married filers if both 65 or older ($1,000 if only one age 65 or older)
- Legal blindness, $1,250 for single or heads of household filers; $2,000 if married and both legally blind ($1,000 if only one legally blind).

**Exemptions:**
- Personal exemption, $3,200 ($3,300 in 2006)

**Tax Credits:**
- Child and dependent care, up to 35 percent of qualifying expenses up to $3,000 ($6,000 for two or more qualifying individuals)

---

if you're financially responsible for an elderly loved one who has his own tax issues. With so many exclusions, inclusions, phase-outs, and variables, including confusing and convoluted tax laws, it's a good idea to bring in a tax professional to help. Of course, it's to your advantage to be aware of the issues and strategies up front.

Here's a roundup of a few of the literally hundreds of issues that may affect you.

**INCOME TAX DEDUCTIONS, EXEMPTIONS, AND CREDITS.** If you choose not to itemize, you're eligible for the $5,150 standard deduction. Tax laws allow for a two-year grace period after the year of death of a spouse during which a surviving spouse can continue to file the joint return and therefore take the full $5,150 deduction.

If you itemize, you're entitled to claim a personal exemption (indexed for inflation). The exemption is $3,300 in 2006 for single filers and $5,000 for married couples.

For those age 65 and older, there's also a $1,250 deduction on top of the personal exemption or standard deduction. If you're legally blind, you're eligible for another $1,000 deduction.

Elderly or permanently or totally disabled individuals also may be eligible for a 15 percent tax credit, which varies by filing status.

Don't overlook the child or dependentcare credit either. If, during a calendar year, you pay someone for care of a dependent who is unable to care for herself— such as an elderly parent—or to take care of your child while you work, you're eligible to claim a credit on your taxes if you meet certain criteria. The dependency test can be confusing, so check with your tax professional. It may involve support, income (yours and theirs), relationship to you, and more. Social Security payments generally do not count for purposes of determining a parent's gross income.

You cannot, however, take the credit if you pay a family member who also is a dependent or under age 19 to care for your elderly incapacitated mother. The credit can be up to 35 percent of your qualifying expenses (up to $3,000 for one or $6,000 for two or more qualifying individuals), depending on your income. See IRS Publication 503, "Child and Dependent Care Expenses."

**CHARITABLE CONTRIBUTIONS.** If made to qualified charities, these contributions are deductible. The donations can be in the form of cash or goods. With household goods, the deduction is based on thrift shop value. (The Salvation Army offers a free online valuation guide, *www.satruck.com/ValueGuide.aspx*.) You also can donate money, often using a credit card. Consider making the donation in December, taking the deduction for that year, and then you won't have to pay the bill until January of the next year.

If your son in college plans to finally get rid of that beat-up old car, consider donating it to a qualified charity rather than selling it if its value is more than $500. Laws have changed so that your deduction is limited to the gross proceeds the charity derives from the vehicle's sale, but it's still a solid deduction.

**LONG-TERM CARE BENEFITS.** Benefits paid out under qualified long-term care policies, as with health care policies, generally are not taxable although there are caps. Premiums paid are treated as health insurance premiums and are deductible only if the taxpayer itemizes and to the extent that total medical expenses exceed 7.5 percent of the person's adjusted gross income. In 2006, the deduction is based on the taxpayer's age, ranging from $280 for those 40 or younger to $3,530 for age 71 or over.

**HEALTH INSURANCE PREMIUMS.** These are 100 percent deductible for self-employed individuals. For those employees who share financial responsibility for premiums with an employer, they're also deductible to the extent that total out-of-pocket medical expenses exceed 7.5 percent of your adjusted gross income.

**LIFE INSURANCE PREMIUMS.** These are taxable.

**MILEAGE.** Remember, you can deduct the mileage driven for medical reasons, to the extent total medical expenses exceed 7.5 percent of your adjusted gross income (phase-out applies), as well as transportation or services in conjunction with qualifying charitable organizations. For 2006, mileage deduction rates are 18 cents/mile for medical reasons; 14 cents/mile for charitable organizations other than for Hurricane Katrina relief (32 cents/mile).

**BEWARE BORROWING ON TAX REFUND.** If you're strapped for cash, avoid borrowing money from an organization based on your anticipated refund. Such advertised short-term loans generally add up to paying a hefty amount just to borrow on what essentially is your own money. Consider filing your taxes electronically, instead, to get faster refunds (visit *www.irs.gov* and click "e-file").

## Trusts: Inheritance and Estate Planning

As if the Sandwich Generation doesn't have enough demands on its limited resources, its members need to consider future generations.

While you're trying deal with today's problems as well as save for your own future, you're looking to the futures of your children and grandchildren, too. That's where estate planning—yes, more planning—can help. Without spending a bundle of cash today, it's possible to protect your affairs from prying eyes, protect your loved ones, shelter your money, lessen your tax liability while you're alive and after you're dead, pass money to your heirs with minimal tax ramifications, fund the future needs of a loved one, control how your money is spent after you're dead, and more. All it takes is the right documentation and planning today.

In addition to the necessary legal documents (wills, powers of attorney, and more) we've discussed in this chapter and elsewhere, one of the best ways to accomplish much, if not all, of the above, is by establishing various trusts. Trusts are legal entities that contain assets for the benefit of someone else. That someone could be you, a child or loved one with disabilities, your heirs, a favorite charity, or someone or something else entirely. Trusts also are a convenient way to avoid what can be the costly nightmare of probate, the legal process that settles your financial affairs after you die.

Let's look at a few of the trust basics.

A *living trust* is one that operates while you're alive. A *testamentary trust* goes into effect after you die. The trustor, grantor, or settler is the individual who transfers her property or title to a trust, which in turn is managed by the trustee. It's possible to have more than one trustee. Cotrustees may make sense, for example, in a case where possible inheritance disputes with siblings are involved. A sibling and an impartial third party could serve as cotrustees. The successor trustee is a person chosen to take over administration of the trust if something happens to the trustee. If, for example, you are the trustee and you die, a successor trustee would then administer your trust.

The beneficiary or beneficiaries of the trust are those who benefit from it. A contingent beneficiary could be someone named as the ultimate recipient of a trust that currently provides income to someone else.

A trust can be revocable. You set it up while you're alive and have full control over its assets as long as you're competent. Any earnings or losses on the trust are yours and appear on your tax return. A revocable living trust is an excellent way to pass assets on to your heirs while avoiding the drawn-out hassles of probate. Once you die, the trust disburses your assets as directed. Only those assets in the trust avoid probate, however. According to Charles Sabatino of the American Bar Association, if you have a revocable living trust, it's also a good idea to have a pour-over will to ensure that any assets left outside the trust at death will transfer to the trust. But if anything of substance is left out, it likely will have to go through probate to transfer that property into the trust even though the trust itself won't be subject to probate, he adds.

A revocable living trust also is a way to ensure that if you become unable to handle your affairs, the trustee can automatically take over to direct them.

A trust also can be irrevocable. Once it's established, it's an independent entity that carries out your designated wishes. Under the control of the designated trustee, it has its own tax ID and files its own tax return. A special needs trust set up to provide support for a loved one with disabilities, for example, would be an irrevocable trust.

Trusts can be complicated to set up and administer, so it's important to work with a qualified legal advisor with trust expertise if you plan to establish one.

Here's a brief look at several other trusts:

- *Charitable remainder trust.* These are irrevocable trusts set up while you're alive that pass to a qualified charity of your choosing after your death. While you're alive, you may receive income from that trust as well as avoid capital gains taxes associated with selling the assets in the trust. After death, your estate receives an estate tax deduction for the value of the trust.

- *Special needs trust.* As mentioned above, this is an irrevocable trust that can provide income for another—a young or old loved one, perhaps—while removing the assets from your control. That can reduce tax liabilities. It also can be a tool for the elderly that helps them spend down assets for the purpose of meeting Medicaid income/assets requirements. To qualify for Medicaid, assets must be transferred to a trust at least five years before applying for Medicaid. While the new law lengthens the look-back period for most transfers from three to five years, trusts always have had a five-year look-back period.

- *Bypass trust.* This can be a living or testamentary trust set up by a couple concerned with future estate taxes as well as the surviving partner's financial well-being after one partner dies. Typically when a spouse dies, his assets pass to the other spouse free of estate taxes and without using up the deceased's estate tax exemption ($2 million in 2006). However, on the death of the second spouse, the total estate then faces estate taxes on any amount exceeding the single estate tax exemption. With a bypass trust, when the first spouse dies, her half of the couple's assets pass into an irrevocable trust. The surviving spouse can benefit from income from the trust, but its assets remain outside of his remaining assets and are controlled by a trustee. On the death of the second spouse, the final beneficiaries get the trust.

## Final Words

If you're helping an elderly parent today, don't count on a future inheritance to fund your retirement needs tomorrow. There are simply too many variables, ranging from personalities to health, long-term care costs, and more. Only you can fund your retirement. If you do get an inheritance at some point, great—that's more insurance for your future.

Also, where inheritances are concerned, whether you have the right documentation executed properly or not, be prepared for contingencies, especially when money, families, and personalities are involved. "Anybody can sue anybody for anything, regardless of what's been documented or signed," cautions California-based financial planner Cook. "Protect yourself (and your loved ones)."

"Protect yourself and your loved ones" could be the new mantra of the Sandwich Generation. These one-time flower children have become the power children of millions of families. They're squeezed, yet they've rallied to hold the family sandwich together. They bear their responsibilities with a diligence and grace few might have expected from the free spirits whose credo of sex, drugs, and rock 'n' roll set the world on fire not so very long ago.

We hope this book helps ease the burden for members of this unique generation. As their children might say, "Sandwich Generation, you rock!"

**adjusted gross income** The amount of your income (before itemized deductions) used to compute income taxes.

**advance directives** Legal documents that stipulate an individual's wishes if he becomes incapacitated and can't convey them.

**annuity** A contract, usually with an insurance company, to invest a lump sum or payments over time in an account for a certain length of time; can be fixed with a set interest rate and amount due at end of term, or variable which allows for various investments and various rates of return. With a deferred annuity, used as an investment vehicle; at the end of the set time period the account, including its tax-deferred earnings, will be paid out either in a lump sum or over time. With an immediate payment annuity, used to create an income stream; a lump sum is invested with payout beginning almost immediately.

**baby boomers** The 76 million Americans born post–World War II, from 1946 through 1964.

**coinsurance/copayments** With health insurance, the costs you must pay out of pocket as part of goods or services received.

**conservator** Someone appointed by the court to handle an individual's financial affairs if she is no longer able to do so on her own.

**copay** The money an individual must pay for medical care that's not covered by insurance.

**Coverdell Education Savings Account** Formerly known as education IRAs, these accounts earn interest tax free if withdrawn for qualified education expenses; contribution limits, withdrawal restrictions, and eligibility qualifications apply; may be used for grades K through 12 as well as higher education expense.

**deductible** An individual's share of the cost of goods and services, a portion of which is paid for by his health insurance.

**defined benefit plan** A retirement plan in which an employer agrees to pay an employee on retirement a set amount based on a formula that takes into account years of service and salary history; a "traditional" retirement plan.

**defined contribution plan** A retirement plan to which an individual contributes, in many cases along with an employer. At retirement, the benefit includes all contributions from the employee and employer plus income and gains and minus expenses, losses, etc.; the amount is not guaranteed.

**durable power of attorney for health** Also known as a health care proxy, this legal document names someone to make health decisions for a person in the event she becomes incapacitated.

**executor** An individual(s) named by a will to carry out the provisions of the will.

**Family and Medical Leave Act (FMLA)** Federal law that mandates eligible workers may take up to 12 weeks a year of unpaid leave for a variety of reasons, including the care of an immediate family member (spouse, child, or parent) with a serious health condition; eligibility restrictions include size of employer and length of employment.

**financial power of attorney** Designates an individual who will make financial and legal decisions for someone unable to make them for himself.

**529 plan** A tax-advantaged higher education savings plan that's funded with pretax dollars (some states allow a deduction); earnings grow tax free if withdrawn for qualified education expenses.

**401(k) plan** Defined contribution retirement plan in which employees contribute up to a certain percentage of their earnings pretax (employers may contribute, too); account grows tax-deferred until it's withdrawn, at which time income taxes are due.

**funeral directive** A document that stipulates the details of what should be done following that person's death as far as recognizing the life and handling the body.

**geriatric care manager** A private practice professional trained in the issues, answers, objectives, and concerns of elderly individuals in a community and their families; provides comprehensive assessment of a senior's situation, including her health, finances, family, social network, safety, and more, then analyzes and proposes an individualized care plan and action plan.

**geriatrics** A branch of medicine that deals with the study and treatment of the elderly.

**grantor** Also known as a settler, the individual who originates a trust and transfers his property or assets into it.

**guardianship provision** A part of an individual's will that stipulates who legally will be responsible for that person's minor children.

**health care proxy** A legal document that designates another individual to make health care and medical decisions for someone if she is unable to make them.

**home-health aide** A provider of medical support and care in someone's home, either short- or long-term.

**hospice** Type of care that provides services and therapies for the terminally ill and their families; intended to improve the quality of life for the patient by controlling the symptoms of the illness and restoring dignity for the person until death.

**individual retirement account (IRA)** A retirement plan set up by an individual in which earnings grow tax-deferred; contribution and withdrawal limitations and restrictions apply.

**intestate** The term applied if someone dies without a will.

**life settlement** When the holder of a life insurance policy sells, assigns, or transfers the death benefit of that policy in exchange for a single cash payment. The policy's new buyer assumes payment of the premiums and, on the original policy owner's death, receives the benefit payout.

**living will** A legal document that stipulates what a person does or does not want with regards to life support in the event he becomes incapacitated.

**long-distance caregiver** An individual who lives at a distance from and provides some form of care, whether emotional, physical, or financial, for an elderly individual.

**long-term care insurance** A type of insurance that will pick up the cost of care (or a portion of the cost) in the event an individual requires extended living assistance as in home-health care, assisted living, or a nursing home. Coverage varies by policy.

**look-back rule** A rule that enables Medicaid to go back five years (effective February 8, 2006, pending state implementation; previous time period was three years) in reviewing a potential applicant's finances to ensure that applicant hasn't transferred assets to others just to meet its low-income standards.

**Medicaid** The federal/state-administered welfare program that pays for health care for certain low-income individuals; also pays for nursing home coverage for qualified low-income individuals (with restrictions).

**Medicare** The federal health care plan for those age 65 and over.

**Medigap** Supplemental health insurance policy designed to pick up many of the costs not covered by Medicare.

**payable on death (POD)** An asset transfer in which the named beneficiary receives a particular asset on its owner's death.

**pet directive** A document that stipulates what will happen to a pet in the event its owner no longer can care for the animal or dies.

**reverse mortgage** A financial tool that enables a person age 62 or older to tap the equity in her home in the form of cash payments or a line of credit to meet expenses and needs.

**Roth IRA** A retirement plan made with after-tax contributions, which can be withdrawn at any time tax- and penalty-free. Earnings grow tax-free and can be withdrawn tax-free after 5 years and you have reached age 59½. Contribution and withdrawal limitations and restrictions apply.

**rule of 72** A quick way to calculate the length of time required for an investment to double in value; divide 72 by the percentage rate of return of the investment.

**Sandwich Generation** Those baby boomers who provide some kind of care for aging parents on the one hand and their children on the other.

**tax-favored health accounts** Savings options that with variations allow employees and individuals to pay for qualified medical (and in some cases dependant care) expenses with tax-advantaged money. These include health savings accounts, flexible spending accounts, medical savings accounts, and health reimbursement arrangements.

**testamentary trust** A trust that takes effect after death.

**traditional IRA** A tax-deferred retirement savings vehicle that allows an individual to contribute a certain amount of his income pretax (with income qualifications). No taxes are due on the earnings (or pretax contributions if applicable) until withdrawal.

**trust** Legal entity that contains assets for the benefit of someone else; may be living, which goes into effect while the individual is alive, or testamentary, in effect after her death; also can be revocable as in the grantor retaining full control, or irrevocable in which it becomes a separate legal entity and removed from the grantor's assets.

**trustee** The individual named in the trust to administer the trust; in a living trust can be the grantor or person who established the trust; successor trustee is named in trust to take over administration of trust if something happens to trustee.

**will** A legal document that specifies how an individual's assets and property will be disbursed after their death. Contains guardianship provision, too.